Anecdotal Shakespeare

A New Performance History

Paul Menzer

Bloomsbury Arden Shakespeare
An imprint of Bloomsbury Publishing Plc

B L O O M S B U R Y
LONDON • NEW DELHI • NEW YORK • SYDNEY

Bloomsbury Arden Shakespeare
An imprint of Bloomsbury Publishing Plc

Imprint previously known as Arden Shakespeare

50 Bedford Square
London
WC1B 3DP
UK

1385 Broadway
New York
NY 10018
USA

www.bloomsbury.com

First published 2015

British Library Cataloguing-in-Publication Data
A catalogue record for this book is available from the British Library.

ISBN: HB: 978-1-4725-7616-3
PB: 978-1-4725-7615-6
ePDF: 978-1-4725-7618-7
ePub: 978-1-4725-7617-0

Library of Congress Cataloging-in-Publication Data
A catalog record for this book is available from the Library of Congress.

Typeset by RefineCatch Limited, Bungay, Suffolk
Printed and bound in India

Anecdotal Shakespeare

RELATED TITLES

Shakespeare's Theatres and the Effects of Performance, edited by Farah Karim-Cooper and Tiffany Stern

Emotional Excess on the Shakespearean Stage, Bridget Escolme

Shakespeare on the Global Stage, edited by Paul Prescott and Erin Sullivan

A Year of Shakespeare: Re-living the World Shakespeare Festival, edited by Paul Edmondson, Paul Prescott and Erin Sullivan

Acting Companies and their Plays in Shakespeare's London, Siobhan Keenan

This book is dedicated to John Harrell and Thadd McQuade, just so long as they keep it to themselves.

It ain't Shakespeare, but it's laffs.

ADVERTISEMENT FOR GYPSY ROSE LEE'S *THE NAKED COMEDY*

CONTENTS

ACKNOWLEDGEMENTS

I talked this book before I wrote it and so am grateful to those institutions that gave me the chance to air it out. They include: the Arkansas Shakespeare Theatre; the Shakespeare Institute in Stratford-upon-Avon (twice); the Chesapeake Shakespeare Company in Maryland; the Oregon Shakespeare Festival; Victoria University, Wellington, New Zealand; the University of North Texas; Ohio Wesleyan University; the Arkansas Literary Festival; the University of Central Arkansas; the University of Maryland; Harvard University; Georgetown University; York University, UK; the University of Pennsylvania; Colorado College; Kings College, UK; and the Folger Shakespeare Library.

The Folger is listed last because they should come first. I enjoyed a long-term fellowship at the Folger in 2013/14 where I conducted the research that ballasts this book. The National Endowment for the Humanities made this possible. The Folger has been my home-away-from-home for the entirety of my academic life. I was barely out of my teens when I first worked there. That the Folger continues to suffer my return reveals that their patience rivals their resources. I am particularly grateful to the reading room staff, former colleagues like Carol Brobeck, and to my first boss and lasting role model Barbara Mowat. Many of those who read what follows already know what a special place the Folger is. Its collection is surpassed by those who maintain it.

Mary Baldwin College granted the sabbatical that made my stay at the Folger possible, and I'm grateful to my employer for their support as well as for employing me. I am further grateful to the Shakespeare and Performance programme, where I have the best job in the world because I work with friends. My colleagues Ralph Alan Cohen, Matt Davies, Julie Fox and

Doreen Bechtol not only picked up the workload while I was away but they make our daily work together rewarding and fun. Students of the S&P programme probably enjoyed my absence more than I did, but they are also a constant source of pleasure and provocation. Over the last couple of years, material from this book kept leaking out from around the edges while we worked on other things, and I'm grateful to them for their forbearance.

This is a book primarily about the way the theatre talks, and the theatre down the street – the Blackfriars Playhouse at the American Shakespeare Center – always gives me someone to talk to, and something to talk about. Thank you to Jim Warren and Ralph Alan Cohen for not coming up with a better answer to 'why not?' those many years ago. Theatre makers too many to mention have come and gone over the years. I have learned much from Jason Guy, Jeremy West, James Keegan, Miriam Donald, Daniel Burrows, J.P. Scheidler, Doreen Bechtol, Sarah Fallon, Vanessa Morocco, Matt Sincel, Benjamin Curns, Greg Phelps, Alli Glenzer, Dan Kennedy, Rene Thornton, Jr. and Jenny McNee. I save John Harrell and Thadd McQuade – this book's dedicatees – for last. They've taught me the most important things I know about performance, and I'll never forget that they stood up for me on 11 October 2014.

Jeremy Lopez also stood up for me in October 2014, and he heads the list of colleagues to whom I am indebted. Tweedledee to my Tweedledum, Jeremy reads everything I write, whether he reads it or not. I gladly acknowledge my debt to a long list of other friends, including Genevieve Love, Andrea Stevens, Sarah Werner, Zack Lesser, Andrew Hartley, Kirk Melnikoff, Holger Syme, Alice Dailey, Richard Preiss, Jim Marino, Matt Kozusko, Peter Kanelos, Farah Karim Cooper, Walton Muyumba, Alex Pettit, Jaqueline Vanhoutte, Robert Upchurch and the marvellous Tiffany Stern. You all have made my work much better and often my nights much longer. Mentors and models like Tom Berger, Russ McDonald, Roz Knutson, Barbara Mowat, Stephen Booth, Laurie Maguire, Gail Kern Paster and Katharine Maus have supported my work over and often, and you should not hold it against them. Finally, without knowing it, several other colleagues asked exactly the right question at precisely the right time, and in so doing pointed out doors that I hadn't ever noticed. They are Paul Prescott, Daniel Shore, Ewan Fernie and Diana Henderson.

My love of the theatre is due entirely to my parents, who took me to Interlachen at the age of four to see an outdoor performance of *William Tell*. Over forty years later, the images come back to me in high-definition flashes (as do other memories such as my father calmly covering my ears during Sondheim's *Company*). I owe Robert and Sara Lee Menzer for this and everything else. My hero Eric, his wife Kendall, Joan, Frances, and our boy eternal Reid – I'm grateful to you all.

Finally, I acknowledge – though 'brag' is more apt – that I had not even met Kerry Cooke when I began this book. Now I'm the happiest man who ever put pen to paper. If there's even a modicum of Kerry's effortless style in this book, it's because its composition coincided with the time that our lives came together. If there's any intelligence or grace in it, it's because it was written with her.

PREFACE: CURTAIN RAISER

Fifteen minutes after the first curtain fell, the number of words spoken *about* the play surpassed the number spoken *in* the play, and the stage has never caught up. Theatre was invented to give us something to talk about. This book is about that about.

That 'about' is a hold-all, however, and contains everything from reviews of a play's aesthetics to smutty speculations about an actor's home life. This book is about a particular 'about' that has always circled the theatre: the anecdote – the brief, capricious, ribald, trivial, pungent, piquant, witty, gossamer genre of little lies and half truths that plays spin out of themselves. And we know one when we hear one. It opens with 'one time' and ends in a punch line. In between, the anecdote makes its implausible way, wandering off the credible path but with enough hold on the facts to avoid turning into a bald-faced fable. It shares this errancy with lo-fi legends and minor-key myths. Urban legends, for instance, have been described as 'highly captivating and plausible, but mainly fictional, oral narratives that are widely told as true stories.'[1] Like urban legends, anecdotes are always just plausible enough. In the standard formula a theatre anecdote details a play, an actor, sometimes a location, but always withholds the date – 'One night, at *Hamlet*, Richard Burton . . .'. The 'one night' is the crucial move that lets us know we're about to hear an anecdote and not a theatre review. It also lets us know that it is not true. Or, to draw a distinction that prevails in this book, is probably not a fact though no less true for it.

The major difference between an anecdote and a myth is that most anecdotes are funny, though, to be sure, Zeus had his zingers. Tales about the theatre are usually trying to be funny at least. Or were found funny by someone at some point – 'one time' we might refrain. Laughter has a short shelf life – what is funny today will be cryptic tomorrow – but theatre anecdotes are at least usually formally comic. Joke shaped, if not always funny, to borrow a formula from one of this book's dedicatees. And what shapes a joke is narrative completion – jokes and anecdotes contain within themselves everything you need to use them. Jokes are called 'gags' because after a good punch line there's nothing left to say.

Which brings us to a strain of anecdotes that asks for tears not laughter, a sub-genre that performs last rites at an actor's final exit. In fact, the longest anecdote of this book is also the saddest. 'Booth's Trunk' in Chapter 4 finds Edwin Booth raking the ashes of John Wilkes's theatrical legacy. And theatre history is full of fitting exits. A nineteenth-century anecdotalist compiled a catalogue of exit lines:

> A yet more striking instance is that of the celebrated Moody. He was playing Claudio in *Measure for Measure*. When Isabella had commanded him to prepare for execution, and he had begun to plead, 'Ah, but to die, and go we know not where!' he fainted, and died before he could be carried from the stage. Edmund Kean may be said to have died in armor. He appeared for the last time as Othello, his son playing Iago. In the passage beginning, 'Oh, now forever farewell the tranquil mind! Farewell content!' his articulation gradually died away, and he whispered to his son, 'Speak to them, Charles; I am dying.' A few days after he passed away . . . Peg Woffington, nearly one hundred years before – May 3, 1757 – became paralyzed on uttering the words of an epilogue, 'I'd kiss as many of you as had beards to please me;' and she never recovered . . . An actor named Harley, well-known for his impersonations of Shakespearean clowns, played Launcelot Gobbo, and when he quoted the words, 'I have an exposition of sleep come over me,' he grew speechless. He never recovered . . . Barrette died while

> being taken home in his Polonius dress. He had played in a farce, and was dressed again, when he was struck down with apoplexy. The French actor Bretcourt died precisely the same way while playing the part of Timon . . . Charlotte Crampton['s] . . . last appearance was with John McCullough, in Louisville, she appearing as the Queen to his Hamlet. She complained of illness during the performance, but remained on the stage till the last scene, and finished her lines, which were: 'The drink, the drink! I am poisoned.' She then dies, as is the business of the play; but with her it was nearly real. She was taken to her hotel, and expired the next day.[2]

Such 'last exit' anecdotes craft theatrical ends for men and women who spent their lives on stage (even while forgetting that it was not Gobbo but Bottom who felt an 'exposition of sleep' coming on, which underscores the anecdote's ability to remember what's important while forgetting what isn't). A punch line and an exit line are not the same thing, of course, though no one ever said a punch line has to be funny. They only have to establish that there's nothing left to say. Sombre anecdotes that perform last rites might seem antithetical to comic ends, then, but even anecdotes occasionally have something more profound in mind. They are, as developed in the coming pages, the way that theatre makes a history for itself, and the only history that sounds the way that theatre sounds is an anecdotal one.

In the main, however, Shakespeare's anecdotes go for laughs. This is one main detour this book makes from recent work on anecdotes. During the last decades of the twentieth century, anecdotes played a major role in the critical practice of new historicism, not least its work on English Renaissance drama. I review the differences between this project and those in the book's brief coda, but while new historicism was a fairly sober affair the items treated here want us to laugh or at least raise a rueful smile at an actor's apt finale.

The 'new history of performance' that this book proposes politely diverges from new historicism, then, but it respectfully parts ways with theatre history as well, at least as currently practised. Most recent theatre history treats the past as a place, a map with many known locations but with many more to be charted. Anecdotal history, at least the kind essayed here, tries to track the abiding concerns of actors and audiences as they produce Shakespeare's plays over and over across the centuries. Through the stories that trail those plays, actors and audiences script their own complicity in history but also their own creative resistance to Shakespearean inevitability. *Anecdotal Shakespeare* is a history of events, not locations, because while anecdotes feint at punctuality – 'once' – they aspire to durability. This book is therefore primarily interested in anecdotes that recur, ones that turn the event into the eventual.

To locate these recurrent anecdotes, I read dozens of actors' memoirs (so that you don't have to). Still other anecdotes appear in 'collectiana', or in biographies of actors, or in compilations of theatre stories. Still others were told to me as I worked on this book and shared early versions of its argument. I was often approached at the end of a talk and asked if 'I'd heard the one about . . .'. I would always try to hear the query out, since the answer – 'yes' – was an impolite one and wasn't the answer to the question they were asking anyway. Still, it was surprising how few 'original' anecdotes emerged. They had simply read the same books I had. Anecdotes often come pre-cooked, prepped by the hands of master storytellers. Much of the material that ballasts this book is time worn, then, though no less durable. They fill memoirs, bios, and miscellaneous collections and therefore comprise Shakespeare's anecdotal canon.

But another great swath of the material here comes from the Folger Shakespeare Library and other research libraries. This material is a bit more raw, for the archives I scoured thousands of theatrical scrapbooks, which fall into various sorts. Many were created by particular theatres, such as London's Drury Lane, the Haymarket theatre, or Covent Garden. During the eighteenth and nineteenth centuries, these houses combed London's papers on a daily basis, clipping any mention of their theatre regardless how trivial. The material was culled and collected in scrapbook after scrapbook, which collectively cover decades and decades of theatrical labour. Read cover to cover, these collections represent an exhaustive (and exhausting) chronicle of the daily work of high-functioning theatres. One take-away from such reading is an awed respect for the sheer amount of labour, day after day, year after year, that repertory playhouses demanded of the professionals that made them run. Still other scrapbooks record amateur enthusiasms. Such books might follow a particular actor, from the famous – Garrick, Irving, the Booths, the Keans – to the less well known – Harry Sanders, Minna Gale. Or they might organize themselves around a play or a playhouse, such as the multiple scrapbooks that treat the three Stratfords (Ontario, Connecticut, England). Whether collected by professionals or amateurs, these scrapbooks produce the same awe for and at the sheer rich strangeness of the theatrical industry.

Another take-away from such research is that theatrical anecdotes are popular; and 'popular' in the technical sense. They are not just tradecraft, although they certainly are that, a sort of secret handshake that all actors seem to know. Actors are terrible at keeping secrets, though, since anecdotes have spread far beyond the green rooms and bar rooms where they are most often traded. They reach a lay audience through memoir, biography, newspapers, magazines, chat shows and collections, and so have something going for them that other forms of shoptalk don't. One of the things that anecdotes have going for them is that they often relate the lives of the actors who endlessly fascinate us. In this respect, they are a form of gossip, even celebrity. But even when they're not catering to the stars, anecdotes give us a glimpse backstage, a place of enduring mystery since nothing, it seems, more tantalizes the world than the sight of a closed curtain.

By raising the curtain anecdotes reveal what a play looks like from the actor's point of view. What happens at the end of *Othello*, for instance, is not that 'Othello', the moor of Venice, murders 'Desdemona', his Venetian wife, but that one actor gets his makeup on another or strenuously tries to keep it off (one subject of Chapter 2). Anecdotes often reveal the gaps between what actors are actually doing and what they want us to think they are doing. They are not theatre's blooper reel, then, they are the 'making of' features that sometimes come with films. However captivated we are with the events that take place on stage, they are only ever half as good as the events that take place off.

All of the above might equally be said of anecdotes about Shaw or Sheridan, and this book is about Shakespeare (although Noël Coward makes a cameo in Chapter 3). In fact, this book is not just exclusively interested in Shakespeare but almost embarrassingly so with his most canonical plays. It opens with *Hamlet* and closes on *Macbeth*, and never strays from the syllabus in between. This is a function of the book's interest in endurance. By spotlighting Shakespeare's longest-running anecdotes it ends up starring his most oft-performed plays. To build up a sort of canon of anecdotes – or an 'anti-canon' of them as the introduction argues – a play requires a robust stage history. The relationship between a robust stage history and rich body of anecdotes is reciprocal, of course. *Richard III* and its anecdotes deserve one another. But then anecdotes are shameless frontrunners. They seek the spotlight, suck up to stars, and only hang out with the hyper-canonical. There are no *Pericles* anecdotes in this book.

If there are no anecdotes about *Pericles*, there are also none about *Much Ado About Nothing*, and even a casual glimpse at the table of contents will reveal a generic exclusivity. Every chapter treats a tragedy or a tragic history, a design that was not intended – it wasn't even designed – but that followed the material. One cause of this myopia is that anecdotes, like tragedies, are star vehicles, and when an actor takes the wheel of *Hamlet*, the trunk is already full of fat ghosts and fake skulls (and one real one as the first chapter covers). Anecdotes are always along for the ride whether *Hamlet* conveys its star towards stardom, or makes a wreck of his career. Regardless of his destination, the next driver inherits the vehicle and a trunk-full of fictions.

Shakespeare's comedies just do not attract as many anecdotes, and not just because they don't attract as many stars. (Comedy's ensembles spread stardom so thin it evaporates, while the solo acts of tragedy concentrate it on the lead.) Though anecdotes are shameless star followers, they also have an aversion to tragedy, and so turn everything into a version of tragedy, which is to say a comedy. I do not mean that anecdotes avoid tragedy. Just the opposite. Anecdotes are determined to disrupt tragedy, to interrupt them at the least opportune moment – or the most opportune one – to countermand their ends. The most portentous assessment of these endless interruptions is that anecdotes put off the promised end. (Or, when they can't, play an actor off on an elegiac note.) Anecdotes are an eschatological gag, one that comedies, with their drive toward union and procreation, already get.

While I'm playing in this ponderous key, claiming that anecdotes resist the death drive, I'll call them the life force of theatre itself. As a programmatically ephemeral art form, theatre is always on the verge of disappearing (which it constantly laments and by so doing celebrates). As Tom Stoppard puts it near the end of *Rosencrantz and Guildenstern are Dead*, 'Now you see me, now you . . .'. For this reason, theatre is desperately eager to survive its own vanishing act. Anecdotes are a way of keeping its memory alive. Let me draw a distinction. Anecdotes are not particularly concerned with keeping Shakespeare alive. He's doing just fine. Theatrical anecdotes are interested in theatrical legacies – honouring them but also making them. Anecdotes, then, are not just a form of history, they are a form of prophecy. The 'once' that launches every anecdote receives an echo from the future. 'Once' calls out, and 'once' again replies.

In these terms, every actor aspires to become anecdotal. To become a legend is to play the lead in a time-worn anecdote – even or especially when it is not yours. That is probably so for actors whether they play principally in Shakespeare or not. But if the drive towards anecdotalism is general to theatrical practice, the anecdotes that follow Shakespeare's plays are not arbitrary. It is the main argument of this book, in fact, that anecdotes do for Shakespeare's plays what Shakespeare's plays will not do for themselves. While they provide a kind of prophetic history, then, Shakespeare's theatrical anecdotes also draft a form of vernacular criticism. They defibrillate dormant material in the plays, resuscitating buried or half-formed ideas that the plays abandon or cannot stage.

Following an introduction, in which I explain how I've done, where I've done, and why I've done what I've done, the core of this book treats the anecdotes that have most durably attended five of Shakespeare's plays. Each chapter focuses on a single play and explores clusters of anecdotes that have tested time. It does not work through them chronologically, though, since chronology is an argument about time that is not in this book's interest. Instead, this book essays what art historians call a 'non-chronological hang', in which, for instance, Cezanne's 'Bather' from 1885 hangs next to a 1993 photograph of a pale boy in red bathing trunks.[3] Similarly, here, anecdotes about Charles Kean hang with ones about Kenneth Branagh. These anecdotes are linked by ideas, not time (by tartan kilts, not bathing suits, in Kean's and Branagh's case). This is not to say that anecdotes are timeless, but that time and time again they pick out features of a play that they cannot leave alone. The book keeps time, then, but not the sort that counts to a clock. It observes what Greil Marcus calls 'pop time', which cannibalizes history and rewrites it according to its own warped logic.[4]

Each chapter is discreet, then, which is to say that you might skip the introduction and conclusion, although there are two or three good stories there. Read in sequence – or even out of it – certain dominant chords will sound again and again. Shakespeare's theatrical anecdotes constantly rehearse actors' preoccupations about stardom and anonymity, for instance (not least because anecdotes come preoccupied by other actors). Read from far enough away, the anecdotes can all look like the same one, one that worries over the actor's nightmare of his own anonymity. This approach – a junior-varsity structuralism – would miss important details, however, since at the granular level anecdotes pick on something the play left incomplete and do so in ways peculiar to the plays they treat. If a play attempts to hide something, anecdotes are sure to find it. For anecdotes notice the same stuff that we do from our side of the curtain – that Yorick's skull looks fake, that Othello's makeup is rubbing off, that Romeo and Juliet are a bit too old to be acting that way, and so on. Anecdotes talk about the same things we do in the bars and pubs after the curtain falls, after the closing line tells us to 'go hence and have more talk of these sad things'.[5] Perhaps, in the end, theatre is just an excuse for anecdotes – a funny way to talk some more about sad things. Maybe that's what theatre is, in the end, a place to render memories, as we sit there in the dark making up things to remember.

Introduction: Anecdotal Shakespeare

Stop me if you've heard this one before. Actually, don't, because you probably have. Back in the 1950s, two English actors named Robert Newton and Wilfrid Lawson were appearing in *Richard III* at the Lyric Theatre, Hammersmith. Their agents came to town one Saturday to take in a matinee, and the four men gathered for a pre-show lunch. By the time the matinee rolled around they'd put away a few bottles, and Newton and Lawson were fathoms deep. Robert Newton was playing Richard and so opened the show. He comes on stage – followed by nearly thirty yards of aquamarine tulle and a vapour trail of Chateauneuf-du-Pape – and begins: 'Now ish the winter of our ... dish-content ... made gloriossummer by ...'. Before he can slur another word, a woman cries from the house: 'You, sir, are pissed!' Robert Newton stares over the footlights, draws himself up to his full height, and says, thoughtfully, 'Madam, if you think I'm pissed, just wait 'till you see the Duke of Buckingham.'

I heard this story one afternoon from a Welsh actor who works with me. He'd heard it from his parents, both of whom worked in London's West End at the tail end of the Binkey Beaumont years. And I didn't stop him, though I'd heard it before. In my case from Peter O'Toole, who told it about Richard Harris. Both actors were regulars on the Johnny Carson show in the 1970s and '80s – along with Richard Burton and Oliver Reed with whom they formed a liquor-shop quartet. They would stumble out from behind Carson's curtain, looking as though they'd just swum to shore, and I grew up enraptured by their barnacled tales. Peter O'Toole was my favourite. Back then, his redundant name seemed like the funniest thing I had ever heard. Still does.

So my memory of 'you think I'm drunk' was about Richard Harris and Peter O'Toole not Robert Newton and Wilfred Lawson. I told my colleague so and wagered him a whiskey that I was right. And I was. For a quick bit of research turned up a version that Peter O'Toole tells that ends, 'You think I'm drunk, you should see Harris.' As well as one that Richard Harris tells that ends, 'You think I'm drunk, just wait till you see Burton.' And one that ends with O'Toole sprawled across the footlights saying, 'You should see the other fella.' Another that ends with Robert Newton saying, 'You think I'm drunk, you should see Lawson.' One from Lawrence Olivier's *On Acting* that closes with Edmund Kean saying, 'You should see the Duke of Buckingham.' Another nineteenth-century account features a 'Mr. Mumford', an English actor prone to, and sometimes by, drink. He is reported to have once replied to an audience member who accused him of drunkenness, 'If you think I'm drunk, wait till you see Bailie Nicoll Jarvie' – which has lost something in the intervening years. And finally, a possible prototype from 1748 when a man whom David Garrick employed to play the Bishop of Winchester in *Henry VIII* sent a pre-show note to Garrick one night with the following words: 'Sir, the Bishop of Winchester is getting drunk at the Bear, and swears, d—n his eyes, if he will play to-night.'

On the night that Peter O'Toole died, 15 December 2013, Stephen Fry stepped out on the stage of New York's Delacorte Theater after the curtain call of *Twelfth Night,* in which he'd just played Malvolio. He wanted to say a few words in O'Toole's honour. Mentioning that he had worked with him on a few projects, Fry eulogized the great actor with a series of anecdotes, including one that began, 'One time, when O'Toole was playing Richard III' and ended in a punch line that you can by now anticipate. Stephen Fry knew what he was doing in reheating an old chestnut. He didn't need to say what a great actor O'Toole had been. We've got *Laurence of Arabia* for that. But Fry wasn't making the case that O'Toole was a great actor, he was too busy making him a legend. And what makes actors legendary is not just what they do on stage or screen, but what they do when the curtain drops or the camera stops. Even an *ad hoc* eulogy will want to tell us, then, not what the great actor did on stage, but what he did just off it. Because film will not let us forget O'Toole, but the anecdote ensures that we remember him, and those are not the same thing. Forgetfulness is a cognitive act, remembrance a cultural one. Anecdotes are the places where theatre remembers itself.

A bit of Sunday research revealed, then, that my colleague and I were both right and therefore both wrong. Variants of the 'you should see' anecdote show up across at least 250 years and feature a dozen different actors. I will not be a bit surprised when a seventeenth-century jest book turns up with a version that ends, 'You think I'm drunk, just wait till you see Burbage.'

In terms of its veracity, I do not trust this anecdote as far as I can throw it, but just because it did not happen does not mean it is not true. When it comes to the Duke of Buckingham anecdote, I believe every word of it, except the words of it. For what is above all true about this anecdote is that it has become anecdotal, and anecdotes comprise a vital sub-genre of theatre history, a history largely free of facts but no less full of truth. But then history just isn't what it used to be, or, at least, history isn't *just* what it used to be. Theatrical anecdotes are every bit a part of theatre history as the remains of the Globe Theatre, and frequently much funnier. In the telling and retelling of theatrical anecdotes, we listen to the theatre build a museum to itself.

It is an odd museum, though, since it features artful fictions instead of artefacts. Moreover, it houses its collection in green rooms and bar rooms rather than a central repository. For that matter – as the opening anecdote demonstrates – the collection is under constant revision, dusted off by actors and authors whenever it might come in handy. It seems that from the moment the curtain first went up, theatre has been at home to anecdotes. They tessellate across theatre history, a fugitive chronicle of exploding wigs, loutish drinking, petty rivalries, and priceless put-downs.

Since he forms the central figure of the Western dramatic canon, it is unsurprising that Shakespeare's stage history is garlanded with anecdotes. They bloom in the penumbra of his surpassing presence. The following pages trace and treat just some of the anecdotes that have most durably attached themselves to his most popular plays. In so doing, the book tells a new performance history of those plays and their reception across the last four centuries.

The title of this book – *Anecdotal Shakespeare* – therefore conveys both its material and its method. It attempts to marry the 'how' of its approach to the 'what' of its inquiry. This book is, in other words, interested in the brand of history that theatre tells about itself, which is largely an anecdotal one. This book therefore talks about theatre the way that theatre talks about itself, with an emphasis on the piquant, the trivial, the punch line and the rim shot. By doing so, the book essays a history of Shakespearean performance out of step with current fashion. In the wake of the 'archival turn' in theatre history; the modish 'micro-histories' of salt, steel, guns and lots of other stuff, and the flourishing sub-genre of histories-of-the-world-in-one-thousand-objects; theatre historians have recently focused on archives and artefacts in an attempt to set the record straight, to – as W.B. Worthen describes the aim – 'Write it up, get it down, get it right.'[1] This ambition has exploded long-cherished myths of the Shakespearean stage (not least that there was a 'Shakespearean stage'): that companies toured only in times of plague; that a metropolitan bias existed in the minds of Shakespeare's contemporaries and not just in ours; that just two companies dominated London's theatre scene, and so on. We have a firmer grasp than ever before on the ways that theatre companies worked – their ways, their means; their protocols, practices, and politics; their affiliations, economics, and affairs; their resources and expenditures; and the times and places in which and at which they played. The map of early English playing has never been so detailed, and it grows more nuanced with each passing year.

Anecdotal Shakespeare is not at odds with such projects – in fact it's both complimentary and complementary – but the emphasis here is elsewhere. The initials 'n.d.' and the name 'anon.' appear, for instance, more often in the notes than the reader might expect to find in a book with 'history' in its subtitle. In fact, every anecdote, whenever recorded, should probably be followed by 'Anon., n.d.', for anecdotes evade the archive by avoiding the indexical means by which an archive might be searched: name, date, place, etc. (An archive that cannot be searched is not an archive; it is a curiosity shop.) Even a subject-arranged archive of anecdotes would read like a police report: '*Arrests*; *Defenestrations*; *Drunkenness*; *Exploding Ducks*', and so on. The anecdotal history of Shakespeare in performance is unindexical, because you can never quite put your finger on it.

Sourcing an anecdote to a particular time, place and person would probably violate the means by which anecdote becomes anecdotal, anyway, because covering its tracks as it travels is how an anecdote escapes its origins. To make a broader claim, to trace an anecdote to its origin violates the anecdote's ontology. In the introduction to *Anecdotes and Traditions, Illustrative of Early English History and Literature* (1839), Lord Bacon tells us that 'Cicero prettily calls [anecdotes] *Salinas*, salt pits . . . [T]hey serve, if you take out the kernel of them, and make them your own.'[2] Even when they're not salty, anecdotes can be liberally appropriated and just as liberally sprinkled. Anecdotes, like salt, both spice and preserve, and it will always seem beside the point to worry where they came from.

In fact, the most successful anecdotes have no beginning and no end, they just get printed now and then. Furthermore, many of the accounts contemplated over the coming pages are almost certainly not factual, and this project has no interest in verifying or exploding them. If dates are gold dust to historians, they are fool's gold for this book. Inaccuracy, even outright errancy, is the fuel on which anecdotes feed, and an anecdote is well on its way to achieving anecdotalism when it is told with a discrepancy – a slip of a name, place, or event as the opening tale of *Richard III* reveals. This book is interested not in whether an anecdote is accurate but in what work it performs – what meanings it nurtures not what facts it conveys. What might those anecdotes that prove most adhesive tell us about the plays to which they adhere? It is also worth asking what variety of historiography goes on when actors, directors, producers and reviewers compulsively repeat the same handful of anecdotes over and over and over again across the ages. It is worth asking because the history of theatre told *by* the theatre is an anecdotal one. It is a history told from within, not without, and it is almost wholly and exclusively not history in fact. The history of theatre – told by its makers – is an anecdotal one.

Tarlton's head

The anecdotes began when the first curtain fell. For as soon as there was theatre, there were theatre anecdotes. The earliest are the least imaginative. Often of the 'snuff' variety, they collapse the artifice into the actual. A second-century tale from Lucian of Samosata tells of an actor who played the madness of Ajax so well that he became mad in fact.[3] Various Caesars are variously attested to have cast condemned men in 'tragic' roles to guarantee the realism of their onstage deaths. The medieval period has its own tales of 'death by drama' – a fifteenth-century priest left hanging as Judas a trifle too long, devils who burst through the fourth wall, of flayings that peeled the actor's flesh while they raised the spectators' hair.[4]

This strain of anecdote – of actors caught in the theatrical crossfire – reaches forward to our own time and so embraces the English Renaissance. Francis Beaumont and John Fletcher discuss the plot for the *The Maid's Tragedy* in a pub, and are subsequently arrested when their talk of regicide is mistaken for the real thing.[5] A version from the 1830s outlines the broad contours: 'There is a story related of Beaumont and Fletcher, that while consulting over a bottle of wine in a tavern, about the catastrophe of a tragedy—one said, "You kill the king and I'll poison the queen." A waiter, who had been listening at the door, immediately took the alarm, and went for a constable to apprehend them.'[6] (The event is well known enough to have been parodied in the 1980s television series *Blackadder*.) This strain is struck in Thomas Heywood's wan defence of acting – *An Apology for Actors* (1612) – where he records an anecdote about a night in Cornwall when,

> certain Spaniards were landed ... unsuspected and undiscovered, with intent to take the town, spoil, and burn it, when suddenly, even upon their entrance, the players (ignorant as the townsmen of any such attempt) presenting a battle on stage with their drum and trumpets struck up a loud alarm: which the enemy hearing, and fearing they were discovered, amazedly retired.[7]

Heywood's anecdote relays the rewards, not the hazards, of imitation. Still, apparently the easiest thing to imagine happening during a play is that it is really happening (which it is, but you know what I mean), which only goes to show that imaginations have been failing since time immemorial.

Heywood's story notwithstanding, the English Renaissance left us disappointingly few theatrical anecdotes. A couple of desultory tales survive about performers who dried before Queen Elizabeth, who then magnanimously forgives the terrified actor for being understandably awed. Of Harry Goldingham, for instance, who was to represent 'Arion upon the Dolphins backe' before the Queen, 'but finding his voice to be very hoarse and unpleasant when he came to performe it, he teares of [*sic*] his Disguise, and sweares he was none of Arion not he, but eene honest Harry Goldingham; which blunt discoverie pleasd the Queene better, then if it had gone thorough in the right way'.[8] The real affront at such a moment, it seems, would have been to remember one's lines in the awful presence of her majesty. It's not generally recommended that you forget yourself in the Queen's company, but for an actor it is the sincerest form of flattery.

The most telling anecdotes concern clowns not queens, however. Though they be few, they place themselves in the threshold between the fictional and the factual, where anecdotes tend to eddy. And while the earliest anecdotes erase the line between the real and its resemblance, later anecdotes insist upon it. For instance, in 1592 Thomas Nashe in *Pierce Penilesse* described the reaction to Richard Tarlton's face:

> Tarlton when his head was onely seene,
> The Tire-house dore and Tapistrie betweene,
> Set all the multitude in such a laughter,
> They could not hold for scarse an houre after.[9]

In 1638 Henry Peacham dilates this doggerel into anecdotal form, telling us:

> A tale of a wise Justice. Amongst other cholericke wise Justices, he was one, that having a play presented before him and his Towneship by Tarlton and the rest of his fellowes, her Majesties servants, and they were now entring into their first merriment (as they call it), the people began exceedingly to laugh, when Tarlton first peept out his head. Whereat the Justice, not a little moved, and seeing with his beckes and nods hee could not make them cease, he went with his staffe, and beat them round about unmercifully on the bare pates, in that they, being but Farmers & poore countrey Hyndes, would presume to laugh at the Queenes men, and make no more account of her cloath in his presence.[10]

Tarlton was apparently a funny-looking guy, and these are just two versions of the tales of Tarlton's head. What they have in common is the moment of disclosure, when the clown is literally both onstage and off: 'Tarlton when his head was onely seene . . .'; and 'the people began exceedingly to laugh, when Tarlton first peept out his head'. Not onstage or off, but onstage *and* off, because the threshold between backstage and on, between the tapestry and the tiring-house, is the productive space of the theatrical anecdote. As Bakhtin and bouncers know, it's in the spaces in between where culture comes to play.[11]

Tales of Tarlton signal an important development in the anecdote's *mis en scene*, the tantalizing glimpse at what goes on behind the curtain. As a journalist for the *New York Sunday Mercury* pointed out in 1876, 'The stage of a theater, like the deck of a ship, covers a world hermetically shrouded from popular gaze . . . It is, therefore, perfectly natural that an insatiable curiosity pervades society to learn all that pertains to the unexplored regions vailed [sic] from the popular eye by the folds of the curtain and the glamour of the gas jets.'[12] The current Theatre Royal at Drury Lane offers visitors a backstage tour that will leave you ten pounds shy but none the wiser. It does, however, offer a glimpse below the stage, where all the action happens. It resembles nothing more than a Victorian submarine, with hydraulic pumps the size of mature oaks and an array of handles, levers, winches, wheels. Inches below the luminous surface of the enormous stage lurks a wheelhouse of industry and mystery.

Anecdotes try but can never satiate our curiosity about what's going on below the decks. If we accept the cod philology that defines 'obscene' as offstage, *ob scaena*, theatrical anecdotes are always obscene. For a common element to theatrical anecdotes is that they lift the hem of the theatrical fabric to give us a glimpse of what goes on beneath. Anecdotes perform a striptease that simultaneously promises and withholds access, like all really good smut.

I claimed above that the English Renaissance left a thin cache of anecdotes. What that really means is that only a few from the period made it into print. We have no access to tales that evaded transcription, of the ordinary talk that followed an afternoon at the playhouse. ('You think he's funny, just wait until you see Tarlton . . .') An anecdotal history has an element of the perverse, then, since it relies upon a means of transmission – print – that is not the medium to which anecdotes aspire (like playbooks, for that matter). After all, the etymology of 'anecdote' derives from *anekdota* – things unpublished. Therefore, a book on theatre anecdotes that relies on print is riven by contradiction. On the other hand, as Natalie S. Loveless points out, 'for something to exist as unpublished it must have the possibility of being published – made public'.[13] Furthermore, 'print' and 'publication' are not synonyms, which is to say that even the speaking of an anecdote is a means of publication, a way of putting it into circulation and making it public. To be fair, though, this project is interested in an oxymoron, the published anecdotes – those that became, to be etymologically fastidious, 'un-anecdotal' by finding print. Print is not a measure of an anecdote's 'success', though. It is just one means of its survival, the vehicle that transports it across the ages. Still, by remaining true to form, many early English theatre anecdotes must have remained unpublished – lost to time's amnesia.

At the same time, the anecdote has long since outgrown its etymology and spangles the ruffle of printed ephemera that surrounds the theatrical profession. Ironically, it would take the closing of the theatres to open the book on anecdotes. In works like Richard Flecknoe's *Short Discourse of the English Stage* (1664) and James Wright's *Historia Histrionica* (1699) we find the dawning of theatrical self-consciousness, a threnody steeped in nostalgia. 'Happy the country without a history', the old saying goes. In other words, it took the trauma of the civil war, the closing of the commercial playhouses, to create an elision that required explanation. In these terms, theatrical self-consciousness – even theatrical self-regard – arises from an awareness that it could all disappear. Oliver Cromwell may have a lot to answer for, but among the more unlikely consequences of his actions is the fact that theatre won't shut up about itself.

The birth of English theatrical self-consciousness – of British theatre history even – was born out of loss, an anxiety that if theatre goes quiet, theatre goes dark. In 'A Prologue to the King', in Thomas Jordan's *Royal Arbor* of 1663, we find the following passage: 'For doubting we should never play agen, / We have play'd all our women into men.' The prologue's riveting *non sequitur* explains the appearance of women on stage, but the opening clause, 'For doubting we should never play agen', conveys a plangent terror of disappearance. 'We are almost all of us, now, gone and forgotten' are the closing words of *Historica Histrionica* (1699), put into the mouth of Truewit, the 'Old Cavalier' who faintly remembers the Elizabethan Stage.[14] The English interregnum bequeathed to us a theatrical self-consciousness born out of terror.

If the 'first wave' of British theatre history seems preoccupied by theatre's losses, the second wave is determined to titillate it back to life. The century after Flecknoe and Wright saw the emergence of a 'green room' industry of theatrical chatter, part of what Malina Stefanovska identifies as the period's 'fetish for exchanging curios in the form of objects and stories. Printed anecdotes therefore, like the cabinets of curiosities of the period, often ended up organised in collections and were widely circulated.'[15] 'Tit-Bits', 'secrets' and 'gossip' percolated throughout the popular press. In 1766, the *Theatrical Register: Or, Weekly Rosciad* recommended the 'Secret History of the Green Rooms', which features the 'whimsical adventures of all the London Actors and Actresses . . . and the anecdotes occasionally met with are new and producing a very risible effect'.[16] Other representative publications offer 'GENUINE GOSSIP. / BY AN OLD ACTRESS' (1790);[17] 'green room witticisms' (1795);[18] 'Bon-mots, Anecdotes, Opinions' (1805);[19] and 'Recollections of The Mess-Table and The Stage' (1855).[20] In the 1860s, *The Sunday Times* ran a 'Gossip of the Green Room' column that followed more conventional theatrical reviews, penetrating accounts of what went on 'behind the curtain' after respectable reviews of what went on before it. Joel Fineman perceptively argued that 'the anecdote is what lets history happen', but the opposite must be true as well.[21] The anecdote is history's handmaid, in that it gave the theatre a sense of its own history. And by giving it a sense of where it had been, it gave it some hope it might be going some place.

Anecdotes are not unique to the theatre, of course. All professions have their own shop talk, banter, and fake lore. Theatre is virtually unique, however, in spawning a minor industry of collections, columns, anthologies, memoirs and chat-shows in which anecdotes take on a leading role. Academics have anecdotes too – most involve thick-headed students and ham-fisted administrators – but no one other than other academics wants to hear them. Why should they? Anecdotes do for academics what they do for every trade, signal membership, which means excluding others. By contrast, from the Restoration to the Johnny Carson show there has been a public appetite for the well-told backstage tale. Theatre anecdotes do more for actors than signal membership in a guild, though they certainly do that. They are a populist form of theatre history, sourced for public consumption, and they followed hard upon the birth of British theatre history, and have followed it ever since.

Guildenstern's bassoon

The plural of anecdote is not data, the old saying goes, and questions about the anecdote's historiographical usefulness have preoccupied historians – and literary critics – for years. The coda to this book – 'Archives and Anecdotes' – takes up the question of the ways that archives and anecdotes require and enable one another. In what follows here, however, I sketch a working model of how anecdotes operate in this book and lift the curtain on my methodology.

As just noted, anecdotes are not unique to the theatre, but the theatre is an arena of anecdotal profligacy and the reason is plain: No one lives more teleologically than actors, obligated by their occupations to live out the whole journey every

Tuesday through Sunday night, and twice on Saturdays. Various actors have various names for the dread that hangs over them every day until curtain: a cloud, a tiny fist, a black dog. Theatrical practice is, as a rule, highly repetitive, and in practice extremely conservative, which is why it has such a reputation for liberality. ('Our stage', a nineteenth-century correspondent put it, 'is steeped in the deepest Toryism, and a change . . . would certainly be energetically denounced . . . as "un-English".'[22]) Theatre has an institutional commitment to repetition, and we might conclude that it convenes all the resources necessary so that anything might happen and then takes every possible pain to ensure that nothing does. In these terms, actors live out literally prescriptive lives. Condemned to completion, actors are finished before they are started.

In these terms, the usual torque of the theatre anecdote is not that surprising: they are nearly all about breaking character or the fourth wall, disappointing the schedule, or going 'up' or 'off' the script. They are all about preventing the play from running its predictable course, reaching the anticipated, the necessary, the promised end. Actors' anecdotes are a desperate attempt to insert a wedge of unpredictability into the remorseless logic of a literally prescriptive existence. (Taken together they add up to a history of Shakespeare in one thousand objections.) Anecdotes offer alternatives to a job that's preoccupied with and by the end. Every anecdote is a bleat of protest, a resistance against the dramatic death wish. And if that sounds overly melodramatic, we're talking about actors. But to be fair, only one other occupation regularly ends its workday by drawing a curtain, and that's the undertaker.

To take one example, a bleat of protest interrupted John Philip Kemble one night when he was playing Hamlet, at least according to an anecdote from the early nineteenth century:

> KEMBLE was once playing Hamlet; a countryman, a novice, who acted Guildenstern, but who was a tolerable musician, on being repeatedly beseeched by Hamlet to 'play upon the pipe,' at length said: 'Well, if your Lordship insists

> on it, I shall do as well as I can;' and to the great confusion of KEMBLE and the great amusement of the audience, he played God save the King![23]

The recorder anecdote is a disruption *par excellence* (though not so great as the 'raw carcase of a sheep' that some 'ruffian from the left side gallery threw into the middle of the stage' while Macready was 'speaking of the pipe' in *Hamlet*[24]). But if Guildenstern actually did play 'God Save the King', the English crowd would have done as the Danish king did, rise, and in so doing replay the scene they just watched. Claudius rose, called for light, and put a stop to the play, as well as the trap about to be sprung. Claudius stops the play because he can see where the story is going, and he does not like the way it turns out. *The Mousetrap* is, to him at least, a history play that he isn't eager to see through to the end. Playing 'God Save the King' in a crowded playhouse is the surest way to prevent a play from reaching a prescribed end, as it prompts the audience to leave their seats before the play is through.

The recorder anecdote also sees where the play is going and does not like the way it turns out. After all, given its hyper-canonical status, *Hamlet* is also a history play. The anecdote first casts the audience as Claudius but, second, 'God Save the King' is the last song Hamlet wants to hear, and the least appropriate song one could possibly play in *Hamlet*. Read in these terms, the name 'recorder' is oddly apt for being so incongruous. A 'recorder' is a weird name for an instrument, after all, since it produces music, rather than records it. (But then, at least according to anecdotal evidence, it's almost impossible to play upon a producer.) The more pertinent point is that this anecdote – like most theatrical ones – is about the actor's reluctance to be merely a recorder, played upon by history or the script. If archives record history, anecdotes produce it.

I have just drawn a conclusion from this anecdote, which is more than one can say for the anecdote itself. For this anecdote ends but the play does not. This is typical of the anecdote, which is always eager to interrupt but utterly careless of consequence. Ending with a punch line or an upshot, anecdotes foreclose the question of 'what happened next', even though there is often a great deal of the play left unsaid. In fact, it sometimes seems as though plays were first written so people would have something to interrupt. Unlike coughs and mobile phones, however, anecdotes offer a welcome diversion, though they leave the play to draw its own conclusion. In this respect, Fernand Braudel's critique of the anecdote – which he calls 'capricious and delusional' – is pertinent since he opposes the anecdote to the history of important events, which are ones that 'bore consequences'. And he is right, in that an anecdotal history is eventful but inconsequential, though only, I would argue, in the literal sense. (He's right about the 'delusional' part as well, since at least in the theatre anecdotes break the illusion, leaving the audience to pick up the pieces.) There is no end to the anecdotes that accompany Shakespeare on the stage but there is also no end of them, though they be of no consequence. An anecdotal history of Shakespeare in performance is a history of interruptions without end.

And what those interruptions do is introduce difference into the numbing sameness of theatrical repetition, a tantrum thrown against the annihilating familiarity of Shakespeare in performance. Anecdotes attempt to make a difference because anecdotes are made *by* difference, are made out of the difference that human behaviour – wilful, petty, mendacious, meretricious, unreliable, inexplicable, unpredictable – can make upon the order of things. In these terms, anecdotes produce deviant history, not a history of deviants but a history of deviations because anecdotes relay departures. What makes the brief drama of the Kemble incident an anecdote rather than a theatre review is that it accounts for a deviation, since 99.99 per cent of the time Guildenstern does just what the script tells him.

At the very least, anecdotes remind us that plays aren't archives, they are themselves quasi-anecdotes, which Braudel calls, after all, 'the drama of the short time span', or what we might call 'theatre'. Anecdotes remind us that play scripts don't say 'this happened' but 'this might happen'. But then again, it might not. Something different, *other than*, might happen. *Hamlet* isn't an archive, it's an anecdote with a deadly punch line.

And yet, for all its desire to introduce 'other than', anecdotes routinely fail to do so by, perversely, succeeding. The Kemble anecdote appears not just 'once' but over and over again. It echoed in later newspaper accounts but began to morph as time went by. By 14 October 1871, it has dropped Kemble entirely: 'So prosaic a Marcellus is only to be matched by that literal Guildenstern who, when besought by Hamlet to "play upon this pipe," was so moved by the urgent manner of the tragedian, that he actually made the attempt, seizing the instrument, and evoking from it most eccentric sounds. But this is, perhaps, one of those stories of which the theatre is abundantly possessed, remarkable rather for their comicality than their truthfulness.'[25] Kemble is gone, but the tale is not forgotten, since the theatre is, as the correspondent put it, 'possessed' by anecdotes.

Finally, in 1881, after nearly a century of shape shifting, the story has come to accommodate a different actor with a different outcome:

> The last night of Jefferson's engagement he played Hamlet, for his own benefit; and Tom Blanchard, ever accommodating, agreed to double Guildenstern with the Grave-Digger. When Hamlet called for 'the recorders,' Blanchard, who delighted in a joke, instead of a flute brought on a bassoon used in the orchestra. Jefferson, after composing his countenance, which the sight of this instrument had considerably discomposed, went on with the scene: "H. Will you play upon this pipe? / G. My lord, I cannot. / H. I pray you. / G. Believe me, I cannot. / H. I do beseech you. / G. Well, my lord, since you are so very pressing, I will do my best." Tom, who was a good musician indeed, immediately struck up "Lady Coventry's Minuet," and went through the whole strain, which finished the scene; for Hamlet had not another word to say for himself.[26]

By this point in *Hamlet*'s history, Blanchard knows the recorder gag – knows his anecdotal history – and plays a change upon the story, self-consciously interrupting not just *Hamlet* but the anecdote, deviating from the script, which calls for 'God Save the King'. Blanchard is making history.

As with the 'you should see the Duke of Buckingham' story, the kernel of the story has been extracted, and the anecdote sprinkled upon another dish. We could read this repetition as evidence of durability and even see reoccurrence as a verifying feature of 'the drama of the short time span' as it attempts to join the *longue duree*. Yet as it creeps ever closer to archival, even canonical status, it simultaneously undermines itself by changing passengers along the way – Kemble for Jefferson – while shuffling its score – 'Lady Coventry's Minuet' for 'God Save the King'. (I stated above that 'God Save the King' would be the least appropriate song to play during *Hamlet*. I retract that opinion.) Its repetition over the course of nearly a century might seem like the anecdote's attempt to demonstrate its consequence by its endurance – we might imagine that the aspiration of every anecdote is to grow up and join the archive – but that is to miss the anecdote's point: this anecdote pretends to be a drama of the short time span, an event that happened, it tells us, just 'once'. In other words, what makes this an event is its singularity, that it only happened once, rather than every night, since if it happened every night, it wouldn't be an anecdote, it would be a play.

At the same time, if the anecdote does not exactly aspire to join the archive, it does aspire to repetition (or 'iterability', in Derrida's terms). It happened 'once' it tells us, and it tells us so over and over and over again. The anecdote is built for repetition, after all. The efficient 'one time' or 'one night' enables its adaptability to changing circumstance, providing a ready template to accommodate difference. Its characteristic gesture – 'I heard' or 'I heard from a friend' or a 'friend of a friend' – guarantees easy adoption. Hearsay is another formal tag of the anecdote, the distinguishing characteristic that is also the vehicle of its own transmission. The paradox is plain:

the most successful anecdotes violate their insistence on singularity by entering into an economy of repetition. The most successful anecdotes become their own opposites, victims of their own success.

Anecdotes insist, then, on being punctual, but they aspire to become durable. For all their pretence to disruption, anecdotes ultimately capitulate to repetition, if they are successful. These interrupting counter-acts become, then, the very thing they purport to counter. They turn difference into sameness since the theatre eventually turns everything back into a script, even its incidental accidents. And thus ephemerality gets written into history. Here are all the things that might go wrong, they say. And here are all the ways we might comically mitigate errancy. The anecdote provides an encyclopaedia of accidents and ends up reassuring us that, in the theatre, even the interruptions are staged. However diverting, the theatre anecdote at its most successful forms another element in theatre's attempt to control for difference ('different every night' my foot). Though they pretend to account for accidents, anecdotes are about control, which is what differentiates them from a police report. They are then only pseudo-anarchic, fair-weather deviants. Anecdotes convert error into laughter, now into ever after, and difference into sameness. In this way, anecdotes end up administrating difference and mastering contingency.

This may seem another version of the fatal end that the new historicism ascribed to the anecdote. Whatever creative resistance the anecdote offered to history, it ultimately capitulates to history's end. In the case of the theatre, however, the anecdote's 'creative resistance' is, weirdly, a resistance not to history but to creativity itself – to the prescriptions of a creative script not the dead hand of history. It may seem odd on the part of the anecdote to resist the dictates of a dramatic script, but the anecdote does not disable the theatre any more than anecdotes disable history. It enables it. To quote Fineman again – though this time with a difference – the anecdote is what lets theatre happen.

Shylock's son

I have outlined above some general ideas about theatre anecdotes – the kind of history they produce, the sort of work they do – but this book is concerned specifically with anecdotal Shakespeare, the peculiar histories of the anecdotes that cling to Shakespeare like burrs to your knee highs. And if my general notion about the remorseless teleology of theatrical practice is correct, then it must be trebly so for Shakespeare, whose plays are exhaustingly familiar. In fact Shakespeare's 400-year performance history is full of little stories like the one I opened with – gossipy, trivial, and ever but loosely allegiant to fact. These anecdotes are a vital index to the ways that Shakespeare's plays generate meaning across varied times and in varied places – they form a vast and diffuse Shakespeare apocrypha. Furthermore, particular plays accrete particular anecdotes – stories of a real skull in *Hamlet*, superstitions about the name *Macbeth* – and therefore express something particular about the plays to which they adhere. Anecdotes constitute then not just a vital component of a play's performance history but a form of vernacular criticism by the personnel most intimately involved in their production.

Take, for example, the following episode from an amusing book by Peter Bowles, best known for his role as a Czechoslovakian supermarket magnate in *To The Manor Born*. It is called *Behind the Curtain: The Job of Acting* and clocks in at a tidy 99 pages, which works out roughly to one typo per page (the subtitle – 'the job of acting' – expresses one common theme of the modern actor's memoir, the deglamorization of the profession – actors are not the effete toffs we take them for but working-class stiffs who just want to 'get on with it', their brawny hands covered with grease paint and cocaine). Bowles reports in his book that,

> there used to be a tradition that the last line of a play was never said in rehearsal as it was considered bad luck. The only time I can remember it happening in a play I was in,

> was in a production of *Romeo and Juliet*. The last lines of that play of course, are famously 'For never was a story of more woe / Than this of Juliet and her Romeo.' They are spoken by Prince Escalus, the part I was playing. I never said the lines until the first night. That is, I didn't say them on the first night either. I said, 'For never was a story of more woe / Than this of Romeo and, er, his Juliet.' I think I'll bring the curtain down on what happened next.[27]

The archives will tell you that Peter Bowles played Abraham in a production of *Romeo and Juliet* at the Winter Garden Theatre in 1956, and his own bio will tell you that he made his London debut at the Old Vic as a spear carrier in the same play. The point of this brief verification exercise is that there is no archival evidence that Peter Bowles ever played Prince Escalus other than, of course, this anecdote, which also shows up in a zestier form in his autobiography, which has the unimprovable title *Ask Me If I'm Happy*. But what on earth is the point of fact-checking an anecdote? It's like proof-reading an actor's memoir. Anecdotes are not built to convey facts, they're designed to deliver truth, which are not the same thing. And just one truth this anecdote reports on is that the 400-year history of *Romeo and Juliet* has been troubled by the play's awkward ultimate inversion of its title's elegantly metrical couple. Indeed, not long after Shakespeare's play appeared, we find John Marston in the *Scourge of Villainy* (1598) writing,

> Naught but pure Iuliat and Romeo
> Say, who acts best? Drufus or Roscio?

Just over twenty years later, in a prefatory poem to the first folio, Leonard Digges writes that it is '(Impossible) with some new strain t' out-do / Passions of Juliet and her Romeo'. Then, in 1640, Richard Goodridge writes in a prefatory poem to James Ferrand's *Erotomania*, 'Were thy story of as much direfull woe, / As that, of Iuliet and Hieronymo.' (Yes, the poem couples Juliet to 'Hieronymo'. It is impossible to know if this is a compositorial solecism or a purposeful, ersatz homophone in which Goodridge joins Juliet to Hieronymo in 'direfull woe' and leaves Romeo out altogether.)

For that matter, I have heard a version of Peter Bowles' anecdote before, very close to home. John Harrell is a veteran actor at the American Shakespeare Center's Blackfriars Playhouse in Staunton, Virginia, and he told me a story to similar effect when he was playing Paris. He recalls, 'All year I'd been encouraging Josh Innerst [the Escalus] to screw up that last line, assuring him immortality in the memory of the ASC. He finally said, "Look, I've played this part before. I'm already immortal at another theatre." He said that the stage manager was so stunned by his error that she forgot to call the blackout cue that was supposed to follow the couplet, so the lights stayed up on his shame, and on the helpless giggling of the dead Tybalt and Romeo.' (Let me point out before you do that Harrell's anecdote might be factual, but it is certainly inaccurate, since it would be an odd production that left Tybalt dead upon the stage from Acts 3–5. As noted, discrepancy and error play an instrumental role in the anecdote's morphology.) As the 'you should see the Duke of Buckingham' incident also reveals, original anecdotes are always second hand – they provide ready templates to administrate difference with an off-hand easiness to those who suffer, or enjoy, it.

You get the point. The inverted eponym 'Juliet and Romeo' recapitulates a problem Shakespeare encountered with his closing line, which is that Romeo is much easier to rhyme on than Juliet. 'Romeo' will couple with nearly anything – Rosaline, Juliet, Mercutio in a number of anecdotes – but Juliet's more particular: she'll rhyme with Romeo or nothing. In other words, it is fairly easy to see the way the 'Juliet and Romeo' gaffe participates in a reception history of *Romeo and Juliet*, and to then turn that reception into a form of demotic criticism that works to invert, subvert, at least to trouble the symmetrical central billing that the play insists upon. Indeed, this book reads the theatre anecdotes that attach to Shakespeare's plays as such a kind of criticism – anecdotes act out something furtive and submerged in the plays that they accompany. They are playful in that respect, both a form of extra-curricular play but still full of the play from which they blossom. In the coming chapters, I trace and treat the anecdotes that have most durably attended *Richard III*, *Hamlet*, *Romeo and Juliet*, *Macbeth* and *Othello* across the years.

There is, still, the question of affordances to consider. *Hamlet* calls for skull anecdotes because *Hamlet* calls for skulls. It would be surprising, though excellent, to discover skull anecdotes attached to *A Midsummer Night's Dream*. Hamlet also calls for his tables, however, and I have not discovered any anecdotes about his commonplace book, though there's a joke available here about a dense property master who takes Hamlet literally (the chapter on *Macbeth* recounts a version of just this joke). The skull in *Hamlet* allows theatre history to puzzle over something the play suggests but suppresses, a question of anonymity and ignominy, which I take on in Chapter 1. To pursue these plays through the anecdotes they produce is an attempt to illuminate their incongruities – to see Shakespeare's plays as smiles without cats, to listen for chords that never resolve, to attend to the jokes that won't deliver a punch line. By this method, we can hear *Hamlet*'s 'Who's there?' as the opening to history's longest knock-knock joke. ('You are', is the answer, as Chapter 1 suggests.) In sum, when a play has an itch, there will be always be an anecdote on hand to scratch it.

Anecdotes constitute then not just a part of a play's performance history but a form of criticism that usually critiques a play's incompleteness. Let me say what I think I mean by that. In his poem 'To Hart Crane', Philip Larkin wrote, '[T]he poem in my pocket is like a hole, since art and incompleteness are the same.'[28] Like the best of Larkin, the observation is both banal and transcendent. When you consider that art might represent everything that is the case and all that is not – what was, what is, what may be – of course all art is incomplete. But then, 'incomplete' and 'incompleteness' do not mean the same thing, which is why we have the two different words. The former suggests a state of being, the latter a state of becoming. If Larkin is right, and art and 'incompleteness' are analogous, then every act of representation contains within it a latency, a thought-line left unthought (or thought unthinkable). Shakespeare's plays may seem to surfeit, but they are, in Larkin's terms, charged with incompleteness – an incompleteness that is nevertheless able to contain and convey meaning, like a pocket that holds but always leaks loose change.

Shakespeare's plays are particularly liable to the charge of incompleteness since they contain within the impulse of their own being an urge towards becoming plays they chose not to become. This is true not just of Shakespeare but much of the drama of the English Renaissance, of which inchoate becoming is a constitutive feature. These plays tend to 'preserve traces of what they might otherwise have been, or what they might otherwise like to be', as Jeremy Lopez writes.[29] This is so, I think, not just at the strata of plot, where we so often find shadows of undeveloped action, but at the level of causality, since Shakespeare usually excises the causes and stages the effects. Simon Palfrey diagnoses this latency when he writes, 'Shakespeare has an extraordinary . . . nonchalance about results which belies the intensity of his creative processes . . . regularly embedding scenes and speculations which . . . permit only furtive, half-swallowed recognition. Often these things cannot be acted, any more than they can be acted upon, on-stage or off-stage.'[30] Shakespearean anecdotes frequently attempt to act out or upon these furtive speculations, to resolve the unresolvable, to complete the incomplete.

To offer a brief example, in James Stoddart's *Recollections of a Player* from 1902 he recalls:

> On another occasion she [Charlotte Cushman] played Rosalind in 'As You Like It,' and Mr. Alexander's company never being over-numerous . . . the property-man went on

> [as Jaques Dubois]. The gentleman . . . related to me the trouble he had to get hold of the words. 'The first time I did it,' said he, 'I kept on repeating the words, "I am the second son of old Sir Roland," for I couldn't for the life of me think of the rest of my speech, and at last, being completely dumfounded, I exclaimed, "Oh, why the devil did Sir Roland ever have a second son!" And I think the audience heard it.'[31]

If so, they probably agreed. A Drury Lane critic observed of the play on 1 October 1771: 'New characters appear from time to time in continual succession.'[32] ('Can You Take It?' the play is called by an actor I know.) The improbability of the eleventh-hour appearance of yet another son worries this anecdote into existence. For theatre anecdotes – particularly those that accompany Shakespeare across the centuries – form a supplement we might call, broadly, 'theatrical chatter', in two senses: first, 'chatter' as the tradition of gossip, jokes and anecdotes that leak out from around the edges of theatrical performance but also 'chatter' in the sense that carpenters use the term. 'Chatter' refers to the rough edges left on a piece of wood once it has been through the plainer, those frayed edges not intended to be part of the finished product but which are the by-product of its making. Chatter apparently forms most thickly around knots or whorls in the wood, around flaws in the timber that disturb but do not break it. Anecdotes are chafed into existence by what Palfrey calls the 'furtive' speculations embedded in plays. Anecdotes organize the chatter, tidy the shavings into meaningful form.

As with the *Romeo and Juliet* example above, then, the *As You Like It* anecdote emerges from a frustration with the play. These anecdotes merely express rather than correct their frustration, however. In that respect, they can look like mere abbreviations of the plays from which they spring. Other anecdotes have larger ambitions. Consider the case of Charles Macklin, accounted by the late eighteenth century to be 'the Jew that Shakespeare drew' out of respect for his performance but also, less flatteringly, for what a newspaper reviewer called his 'Israelitish visage'.[33] An anecdote of Macklin from *Stage Gossip or Theatrical Tit-Bits Ancient and Modern* gives an account of the play from Macklin's perspective, and provides a fifth act for Shylock that the play withholds.

> The two front rows of the pit, as usual, were full of critics. 'I eyed them,' said Macklin, 'I eyed them, sir, through a slit in the curtain, and was glad to see them there, as I wished, in such a cause, to be tried by a special jury. . . . I knew where I should have the pull, which was in the third act, and accordingly at this period I threw out all my fire, and as the contrasted passions of joy for the merchant's losses and grief for the elopement of Jessica opened a fine field for an actor's powers, I had the good fortune to please beyond my most sanguine expectations. The whole house was in an uproar of applause, and I was obliged to pause between the speeches to give it vent, so as to be heard. The trial scene wound up the fulness of my reputation. Here I was well listened to, and here I made such a silent yet forcible impression on my audience that I retired from this great attempt most perfectly satisfied. On my return to the greenroom, after the play was over, it was crowded with nobility and critics, who all complimented me in the warmest and most unbounded manner. No money, no title, could purchase what I felt. By G—, sir, though I was not worth £50 in the world at the time, yet, let me tell you, I was Charles the Great for that night.[34]

The trial, the jury, the 'sanguine expectations', Macklin's profession that he was 'satisfied', his desire for an outcome beyond price. . . . The anecdote reads like a synopsis of the play, but with an alternate ending. (It was Shylock's lack of 'sanguine expectations', after all, that doomed his attempt to collect on his bond.) The play produces the anecdote, which is both of the play but also beyond it – a recognition of an *a priori* essence and the addition of a *post hoc* supplement. Or, as Terry Eagleton wrote in a rather different context, 'The supplement is here constitutive rather than superfluous, or, if you prefer, constitutive in its very superfluity.'[35] The Jew that Shakespeare drew ends the play not an outcast but an insider, one who joins the aristocracy as 'Charles the Great'.

And who sends his son to Eton, at least figuratively speaking, for the anecdote is not unique. It appears again in the early nineteenth century, where it again provides the vehicle in which an actor finally arrives. An oft-told anecdote of Edmund Kean records his memorable debut as Shylock at Drury Lane in 1813. At the time, Kean was impoverished, with a young wife and child at home. Surpassing all expectation, he made a hit of the play. '"Now, Mary," he said to his wife upon returning home, "you shall ride in your own carriage, and Charles shall go to Eton".'[36] The fact that Charles Kean *did* go to Eton turns the anecdote into a prophecy. As with Macklin, Edmund Kean's Shylock enjoys a fifth act the play deprives him, an offstage anecdote that scripts his successful bid to join the establishment. Kean surpasses even Macklin in leaving a legacy to his son, a bequest the play denies to Shylock. This anecdote – unlike the *R&J* and *AYLI* ones – is not content merely to worry over a flaw in a play; its ambition is to fix it.

If the plays of William Shakespeare, with his extravagant disregard for unity and completeness, embed traces of what they might otherwise wish to be, anecdotes animate these traces and express these desires, attempting to fill in holes left by and in the plays, clustering most densely around their whorls. The anecdotes fail. To fill in one hole you have to dig another. Hence the compulsive retelling of particular anecdotes – they dig into the history of Shakespearean performance, filling in holes, but leaving pitfalls behind. In anecdotes, we read a desire upon the part of actors to open up a space in which something might happen within the foreclosed history of Shakespeare on the stage. The Shakespearean anecdote emerges from the friction between the all-too-complete life of the player and the incomplete artistry of the playwright. The anecdote is the chatter that friction creates.

Richard's will

Don't stop me, because you've definitely heard this one before.

> Upon a time when Burbage played Richard the Third there was a citizen grew so far in liking with him, that before she went from the play she appointed him to come that night unto her by the name of Richard the Third. Shakespeare, overhearing their conclusion, went before, was entertained and at his game ere Burbage came. Then, message being brought that Richard the Third was at the door, Shakespeare caused return to be made that William the Conqueror was before Richard the Third.[37]

If ever there was an anecdote reverse-engineered from its punch line, surely this is it, from John Manningham's diary in 1602. To give just a short example of this anecdote's evolution and endurance, here's another about Richard Harris and Peter O'Toole. In this version, Richard Harris and Peter O'Toole were

> competing for the affections of the same woman and after a night of drinking went their separate ways, only to bump into each other twenty minutes later outside the girl's block of flats. The game was up and so a deal was struck. O'Toole would try to smooth talk his way into her bedroom using the intercom, while Harris would climb the drain pipe up to the sixth floor and try to attract her attention that way. First come, first served, as it were. 'I nearly killed myself with my mountaineering efforts,' Harris later recalled, 'but eventually reached her balcony and peered in. Peter had literally that moment walked into the room to claim his prize. As they headed to the bedroom, he looked back and saw my disheveled figure and winked. I nearly fell down just from laughing.'[38]

Peter the Great comes before Richard, etc. At first blush these Richard anecdotes seem to be about the sexual charm of a celebrity actor and therefore to extenuate Richard Gloucester's unlikely appeal. After all, it has long been a critical canard that Richard is the 'consummate actor', quite possibly because that is what we desire from Richard – and from actors – all along, consummation. But if these anecdotes end in consummation they never do so for Richard, be it Richard Burbage, Richard Harris, or Richard Gloucester. Richard remains on the threshold, at the window, on the outside, looking in. And that is because, like the play that engenders them, these anecdotes are not stories of heterosexual success but ones about homosocial rivalry, triangulated through the body of an anonymous woman, and which, as in so many of Shakespeare's plays, always leaves the odd man out.

What nags these Richard anecdotes into life is rivalry, and in particular the barely suppressed rivalry between writer and player – one that possibly underwrites every theatrical anecdote. Who comes first? Author or actor?

One last tale for now, then – one that turns into a sequel to the William-the-Conqueror gag. Antony Sher relates in his diary about playing *Richard III* that Terry Hands warned him about 'sustaining a crippled position all evening'. He urged him to alternate legs from night to night and said, 'It's a little known historical fact, but apparently after the original production Burbage said to Shakespeare, "If you ever do that to me again, mate, I'll kill you."'[39]

The line gives us Burbage's unrecorded comeback to Shakespeare's William-the-Conqueror punch line. It is an idle threat, of course, because Shakespeare will do it to Burbage again, and again, and again. After all, the point of the Manningham anecdote is that William the Conqueror will *always* come before Richard the Third, because that's the way that history happens, and history won't have it any other way. History doesn't just repeat itself, history is an endlessly recursive process that turns the event into the eventual.

Driven by a desire to open up a hole in history, actor anecdotes constitute the life force – even the live – against the dead hand of history. Anecdotes are drafts of dramas the authors didn't quite write, or didn't know that they were writing, a counter-canon of fugitive history and demotic criticism. Ultimately, these anecdotes attempt to poke holes in theatre history, to offer an out from its relentless foreclosure. The following pages open up some holes in history too; holes through which Desdemona might escape in the likeness of a boy, through which Juliet elopes with Romeo – or Mercutio. And a history in which, with even a modicum of careful estate planning, we might all one day get to play Yorick, as the next chapter relates.

1

Hamlet:

Skulls are good to think with

When David Tennant played Hamlet at the Royal Shakespeare Company in 2008, there was a brief kerfuffle over the revelation that he'd been using a real skull in the Yorick scene, that of a Polish pianist named Andre Tchaikovsky who bequeathed his skull to the RSC in 1982. Other actors, like Mark Rylance, had rehearsed with the skull before, but Tennant was the first to use a real live skull – or a real dead one – before a paying public. Once the news broke, the real skull was replaced with a fake one when the show transferred to London, although the director, Gregory Doran, muddied the question by later revealing that he never made the switch. He was just trying to hush the chatter. In *The Guardian*, Jonathan Bate called the incident a 'silly sideshow to a great theatrical event'. Given the anecdote's tenacious grip on our attentions, this bit of theatrical chatter is more than just a sideshow. It's the main event.

The first thing to be said about the incident is that there's a long history of actors using real skulls in *Hamlet* or, more to the point, a long history of theatrical anecdotes about actors claiming to use real skulls in performance – even when they aren't, a point to which this chapter grows. As early as 1755, the theatre scribbler Paul Hiffernan complained about the regular use of 'real Skulls and bones in the Gravedigging Scene of Hamlet, to which a wooden Substitution might be easily made'.[1] The second thing to be said is that such stories are always about *Hamlet*, which is probably no surprise. No one ever bequeaths a skull so that it might be used in *The Revenger's Tragedy*. It is always *Hamlet* that makes us lose our heads.

This is due to the fact that the pose of Hamlet, skull in hand, had become as early as 1606 a talisman for theatrical eschatology.[2] In all the iconic poses Hamlet stares into the 'eyes' of the skull, searching for signs of life. And yet there's no one there. Yorick no more has eyes in the front of his head than he does in the back of it. Hamlet might as well stare at the bottom, back, or top of the skull, or – what's the same – at the theatre's exit signs. Who is Hamlet looking at, then? Himself? Is the skull a mirror or a lens? Perhaps the preposition is wrong here. Who is Hamlet looking *for*? He is looking for us. Hamlet stares at the skull and we stare after him – into the desert of the real in which the only oasis is artifice.

The tableau taunts us with the uncomfortable truth that all skulls look alike. You can never ever really know just whose skull you're holding. The only thing you may be sure of is just whose skull it isn't, which is your own. The scene confronts us with a terrible truth: you couldn't pick your own skull out of a line up. We imagine that we are actors, but in the end, we all turn into props.

If we judge by the chatter that the scene has produced, the gravedigger scene might be the knottiest that Shakespeare ever wrote. Over the past four centuries, a thick fringe of anecdotes, jokes, and images have gathered at its edges. In this instance, it is not a flaw in the design of the play that has produced so many anecdotes. It is a flaw in the design of life, which grants us the capacity to apprehend our mortality but not the ability to do anything about it. 'Alas poor Yorick' sounds like a lament, but it's a prophecy.

These worries *always* hover around *Hamlet*, however, whether the skull is real or fake. Anecdotes about the skull's 'real' identity therefore rehearse a more specific concern, what Hamlet calls a 'necessary question of the play', the unresolvable one of how to tell the difference between the real and its resemblance – of 'seems' versus 'is'. The question of the skull's identity therefore poses an epistemological *and* a theatrical question, but I repeat myself.

Skull anecdotes locate with particular precision Hamlet's sincerity problem, which the play never fully resolves. After all, Hamlet's special problem is theatre's special problem, which is that in the theatre 'real' knowledge always eludes us, coming either too early or far too late to do us any good. We have to be told that a prop is real to know that it is real because the *distinction* between the real and its resemblance eludes representation. I am told by one who has handled both Tchaikovsky's skull and its replica that the real skull is much heavier than its simulation. I'm sure he's right, but on the stage a skull is always and only exactly as heavy as it looks. This is a more general phenomenon about theatrical knowledge, which is that you have to already know something to really know something in the theatre.

One man thought he knew something about Yorick's skull, and so sent a letter of complaint to Forbes-Robertson following a production of *Hamlet* in the late nineteenth-century. In his retirement, Forbes-Robertson recalls:

> A particularly close observer wrote the other day, complaining that the skull of Yorick used in the graveyard scene of 'Hamlet' was emphatically and incontrovertibly that of a woman, and protesting against its use. Out of curiosity I had this skull examined by an authority, and was assured it was that of a man, but one of an exceedingly low order of intellect, in fact, likely a criminal or a decadent of pronounced character. This was gathered from the small and sloping forehead, and the high bones underneath what had once been eyebrows. The skull had been broken in two places during life.[3]

The man might more credibly have objected that the actor who played Hamlet was emphatically not a medieval Danish prince. Perhaps the correspondent responds to the play's morbid forensics, Hamlet's fascination with worms, guts and bungholes. (This play so often turns the audience into Hamlet.) Or perhaps something about Yorick's skull frustrates the physics of theatrical presentation, since it shimmers simultaneously with life and death, with reality and all of its opposites, bringing more pressure to bear than the thin membrane between the thing and its semblance can readily withstand. But throughout the play's long performance history the skull used for Yorick – which is obviously not the same as 'Yorick's skull' – has often 'pronounced' its 'character' by giving a name to the actor that once inhabited the hollow crown.

Of course, in the case of David Tennant's *Hamlet*, we did know whose skull it was – Tchaikovsky's. How did we know? Somebody told us. Hamlet also knew whose skull it was. How? Because somebody told him. 'I knew him Horatio', says Hamlet, contemplating Yorick's skull. But he didn't, not at first, not until the gravedigger translated the 'it' of the object into the 'him' of the subject. Whose skull is it? David Tennant's? Hamlet's? The gravedigger's? Tchaikovsky's? Yorick's? It's whoever's you tell us it is. To be precise, it isn't Tchaikovsky's any longer. It's a prop, so strictly speaking it's the RSC's property.

In other words, if an audience doesn't know it's a real skull before they see *Hamlet* they're not going to know it's a real skull when they see *Hamlet*. To know the skull, we have to have been told so, either by a gravedigger or by the morning paper. We might then consider the way these anecdotes express and extend one of the play's unresolved concerns, since the case of Tchaikovsky and his skull rearticulates Hamlet's real problem, which is a problem with the real. Hamlet ultimately realizes that 'seems' is the best that he can do. Only God and the property man get to know 'is'. Yorick's skull consolidates these questions, since Yorick is, in a very real way, a property man.

There's a street-corner magician in the town I live in, and he plays to groups of adoring children, me included. He has a pat answer for the question kids will put to him after he's pulled a rabbit from his hat or a coin from their ear. 'Is that *real*?' the wide-eyed kid will ask, wanting to know – with Larkin – if it's a sham or a sign. The magician replies: 'This is as real as it gets kid.'

Yorick's skulls

As the gravedigger scene consolidates these real questions, it also complicates them. 'This same skull, sir, is Yorick's skull' (5.1.178-79). 'Same'? As what? What is the Gravedigger comparing the skull to other than itself? He seems not to compare it to the other skulls on stage since it isn't any different, unless of course it is real and the others are props. How many skulls does it take to identify Yorick's? Identification requires resemblance, since skulls are not particular. The three early texts of *Hamlet* actually multiply – and ambiguate – the number of skulls on stage. As so often, recourse to textual determination only muddles the question. The practice of using a real skull might therefore be an intervention to solve a textual crux while doubling down on the play's central riddle. These are not separate matters. Textual cruxes are always riddled with identity crises.

Fixing a face on the skull, or a name on the actor playing Yorick, tries to resolve the question of anonymity but always resolves into indeterminacy, as one skull always somehow turns into two. Indeterminacy turns into paradox, since you only ever get one skull. Ultimately, the anonymity of *Hamlet*'s skulls worry these anecdotes into existence, anecdotes that seek to address the play's unresolved problem of how to tell one skull from another. Not to mention the related problem that you need two skulls for one to be the same. Not this skull, *this* skull.

This book usually resists anecdotes about Shakespeare himself and sticks to his plays instead. In the present context, however, it's worth mentioning that Shakespeare had his skull dug up as well – at least according to a Victorian anecdote – despite the best efforts of his effigy, who has his grave under constant surveillance. This tale includes the requisite confusion. The skull may or may not have been Shakespeare's but, if it was, according to at least one disappointed grave robber, it was 'smaller than I expected' since it did not look like his effigy. The body snatcher is disappointed to learn that Shakespeare doesn't look like the original, which in this case is a copy. The failure of a poet to measure up to his effigy is just one more reason why it's best to let them lie.

Apparently the tomb-raiders started to dig up the wrong grave at first, because 'they were illiterate and could not read the name on the tombstone'. At this point, the anecdote almost eats itself, since the only reason you'd want to open Shakespeare's tomb is because of what's written there. Incidentally, you may find a group of illiterate grave robbers digging in the wrong place for Shakespeare's head to be a highly suggestive image, but I don't.

Why would anyone want to handle Shakespeare's skull? Would it tell us anything new? That depends a great deal on whether you're a Shakespearean or an epidemiologist. One would search for signs of life, the other the cause of death. In either case, there is nothing much weirder than digging up a writer's skull and expecting him to say something original. Ultimately, the story of Shakespeare's stolen head resolves into ambiguity. The skull was stolen – of that the anecdote is sure – but it is not clear whether it was ever returned. If we were to open Shakespeare's tomb, we might roll back the stones to find he isn't there. But then since Shakespeare, anecdotally at least, was born on the day he died, every day is Easter in the Shakespeare industry.

Back to *Hamlet*, where in one respect the focus on the relic used for Yorick's skull simply rehearses Hamlet's (and *Hamlet*'s) preoccupation with questions of knowing. But skull *anecdotes* – as apart from the *practice* of using a real skull in *Hamlet* – do something a bit different. As outlined in the introduction, actors live remorselessly end-stopped lives. It's curtains, every day. No scene in the Shakespearean canon – in perhaps the Western dramatic canon – stages this problem in a more crudely reductive and beautifully effective way. Hamlet wanders into the graveyard, only to find that he's already there. For there are graveyards full of Hamlets. Indeed, just a few moments after his one-sided conversation with Yorick, the actor rehearses his own death, leaping into the graveyard *precisely* after his most full-throated assertion of self-identity: 'It is I, Hamlet the Dane.' Hamlet, and the actor, is never more fully himself than when at the edge of an open grave.

Anecdotes often interrupt *Hamlet* at precisely this moment since the play has brought the actor to the brink of disaster – 'disaster' in theatrical terms meaning anonymity. In some respect, these anecdotes protest the unfair casting practices of death, which is currently converting graveyards full of actors into nobodies. Or, for that matter, the unfair casting practice of Shakespeare, who insisted upon giving a skull a name, of troubling the hard-and-fast distinction between a character and a prop. The gravedigger scene in *Hamlet* is a version of the actor's nightmare: anonymity. Worse, utter ignominy. Compared to *that* fate, forgetting one's lines is a daydream.

Rather than quarrel with the logic of death, skull anecdotes promote Yorick to the cast list, where he never appears, and not because he isn't a 'character'. After all, he has a pretty fleshed-out back story for a skull, more so than, say, Osric. Yorick does not appear in your programme, however, not because he is not a character but because he is not an actor. Cast lists require two columns, parallel but separate – one for characters, one for actors. The accounting for character we get in our programmes is always a form of double-entry bookkeeping. One character is the product two entities (actor and role). It takes two people to make a person on the stage.

Anecdotes insist, therefore, on giving the skull a name. Not 'Yorick', or not *just* 'Yorick', but the name of the actor who deadpans the part:

There was a low comedian, familiarly called Dick Hoskins, who . . . played the grave-digger one night, at the Rochdale theatre, in Lancashire, to the Hamlet of a Mr C—. This gentleman's tragedy was, in Dick's eye, much more intensely comic than his own broadest strokes of farce . . . When, therefore, Hamlet approached the grave to hold his conversation with Dick in it, the latter began his antics, and extemporized all sorts of absurd interpolations in the text which he spoke in his own broad Lancashire dialect . . . The theatre was built on the site of an old Dissenting chapel which had formerly stood there, in which a preacher named Banks had held forth, and in the small graveyard attached to which, the doctor (for he was popularly dubbed Dr Banks) had been buried twenty years before, and his name was familiar yet. So, after answering Hamlet's question, 'How long will a man lie in the earth ere he rot?' Dick proceeded in due course to illustrate his answer by Yorick's skull; and taking it up he said in the words of the text: 'Here's a skull, now, hath lain you i' the earth three and twenty years. Whose do you think it was?' 'Nay, I know not,' replied Hamlet. 'This same skull sir,' said Dick, pursuing the text thus far, and then making a sudden and most unlooked-for alteration, 'This was Dr Banks' skull.' Of course the house was in an uproar of laughter and confusion. The victimized tragedian stamped and fumed about the stage, as well he might, exclaiming 'Yorick's, sir; Yorick's!' 'No,' said Dick, cooly, when the tumult had subsided, taking up another skull and resuming the text, 'this is Yorick's skull, the King's jester; but,' going off again – ' 't'other's Dr Banks', as I told you!' This was too much; this was the last straw on the tragedian's back! He jumped into the grave, seized the low comedian by the throat, and a most fearful contest, never before – or since I hope – introduced into the play ensued, in which Dick held his own bravely, and succeeded, at length, in overwhelming, in a double sense, the worsted tragedian, whom he held down in the grave with one hand while he flourished Dr Banks' skull in triumph over his head. The

> curtain was dropped amidst roars and shrieks of laughter, in which King, Queen and Courtiers – who, in the vain hope of arresting the row, had been sent on with Ophelia's empty coffin – were compelled to join, forming a tableau which finished the play for that night.[4]

As so often with the anecdote, it converts tragedy into comedy by interrupting the play before it can reach the promised end, ringing down the curtain with laughter. The comedian jumps the tragedian, burying him with laughter as he brandishes the skull of Dr Banks in triumph. Perhaps this is the clown's revenge for Hamlet's earlier attempt to muffle him. In this anecdote, Yorick's skull is still present, but it has company, as Hamlet and the Gravedigger share the stage with another actor, an amateur this time, which presents the star player with a crippling option: on one hand, ignominy, on the other, amateur drama. The anecdote of Dr Banks rehearses the uncanny sense in this scene that someone else is always there, along with Hamlet, Horatio and a couple of bickering clowns. The two skulls allowed Dick to outnumber Hamlet. He overwhelms 'in a double sense' because he has two skulls and Hamlet only one. Banks is bested only by the economy of Mr Widdicobe, whose Gravedigger is celebrated in an 1877 obituary. Of special note was his 'skeleton-like head', which 'was a powerful "property" to him in this part'.[5] Mr Widdicobe is therefore surely the only actor in history to double the Gravedigger and Yorick. The scene often produces strange assertions of identity into the teeth of anonymity. Yorick reminds us that just because anonymity is toothless does not mean it won't bite back.

If children and animals give an actor pause, skulls, it turns out, are no treat either. Even a dog can play dead. According to David Howells, curator of the RSC archives, before David Tennant had used Tchaikovsky's skull, Mark Rylance had rehearsed with it but decided against using it because 'he couldn't get past the person implied by the skull and into the character implied by the play'. Ultimately, it turns out, skulls are terrible actors. They can't even play skulls.

Skull caps

A skull without a name is just a prop, and Hamlet's performance history is charged with attempts to cast an actor in the part. In the 1880s, Junius Brutus Booth acquired a skull with a name, as an account from *Harper's Weekly* reports:

> A romantic interest attaches to the skull used by [Edwin] Booth in the graveyard scene in Hamlet. During one of his father's visits to Louisville, years before, the horse-thief Lovett, then lying in jail, was pointed out to him. The elder Booth, being at all times a man of ready sympathy, and hearing that Lovett had no means of obtaining counsel, employed a lawyer for his defence . . . Lovett, out of gratitude, bequeathed his skull to Junius Booth to be used in Hamlet . . . After Lovett's death this skull was sent to the elder Booth. Edwin used it for some time, but finding that the grave-diggers injured it, he substituted for it a property skull.[6]

As so often, the story of Booth's skull circulated in variant forms, with details fading in and out. A version from 1866 upgrades – or down-casts – Lovett from horse thief to 'a murderer', who 'bequeathed his skull to Mr. Booth, the great artist, with the desire he should make use of it as Yorick's skull in personating Hamlet. So thoroughly had this singular idea seized on his imagination, that he continued excited until he obtained a solemn promise his wish should be complied with.'[7]

Yet another version from 1886 agrees the malefactor was a horse thief, agrees he was from Kentucky, but changes his name and clarifies the line of inheritance:

> The skull which Edwin Booth uses in 'Hamlet' was willed to the tragedian's father by one Fontaine, a Kentucky horse-thief, whom the eccentric actor once knew, and between whom and Booth's father a curious intimacy existed. The elder Booth never used the skull, as he left Louisville before

> Fontaine died, but it was given to the present star [Edwin] by Dr. Morris, of that city, into whose hands it came.[8]

Once again, a doctor lurks at the frame of the anecdote, providing a clinical credibility to the unlikely tale, but fittingly the anecdotes cannot decide on what to name the skull.

The shifting details canonize the anecdote while reducing its credibility – establishing its truth by discrediting the facts – though all agree that 'Lovett's skull is now carefully preserved on a bracket in the corner of the apartment at The Players which Mr. Booth reserved for himself, and occupied during the last years of his life.' 'The Players' is the Players Club, founded by Edwin Booth in 1888, and which still stands in New York City, across from Gramercy Park, and is crowded with theatrical memorabilia, relics really, including Lovett's skull, which according to *Harper's* was retired from production after limited use. As with those about David Tennant's *Hamlet*, the story circles the notion that the real skull was used but was then replaced. The presence of the live skull continues to shimmer over the dead one, however, hanging a halo of realism upon the temples of the fake.

Speaking of temples of the fake, when the Players first opened the newspapers and magazines of the day gave it major coverage, and many of these accounts include the detail of Lovett's (or Fontaine's, or what is now 'Booth's') skull. James Clarence Harvey, in a daily paper, noted: 'The sightless eyes of the skull over which he used to say: "Alas! Poor Yorick!" gaze vacantly upon the environment of his last moments.'[9] The slippery pronouns of this sentence are symptomatic of the problem that skulls pose. The 'environment' of the horse thief's last moments was presumably a gibbet in Louisville, but the writer has transferred subjectivity from the famous 'he' of Edwin Booth to the anonymous 'which' of the skull. More to the point, this *wasn't* the skull over which Booth usually said, 'Alas, Poor Yorick.' It was the horse thief's, which wasn't the skull Booth used, since it couldn't take the pressure, and whose identity is eclipsed by Booth's celebrity. With the theatre, what's real is relative, or what we think is real is whatever you tell us is real.

In that same account, we learn that the Players also displays the blond wig of Charles Fechter, the nineteenth-century Anglo-French actor. Casting the audience as the objecting Laertes, an 1869 newspaper predicted that, 'Mr Fetcher has done one thing, however, that shall carry his name to posterity – he has dared to seize the British prejudice by the throat, and play *Hamlet* in a flaxen wig.'[10] In the account of the Players quoted above, we learn that 'the blond wig which M Fechter chose to wear as *Hamlet* [is] perhaps the most chattered about of all theatrical wigs; that it is, in reality, red and not at all blond is not surprising to those who have mused on the unrealities of life, as *Hamlet* himself was wont to do'. Theatre has a hilarious history of hairpieces, and Fechter, in this report, bears the laurel toupee.

It is a matter of mere inches from the anonymous skulls to the wigs they used to wear, and this account perfectly represents the theatrical distinction between fact and truth, where the unreality is more real than the real, so that what is in actuality a red wig is called a 'blond wig' in an account that comments on the oddity that the 'blond wig' is really red. (Weird, as Hamlet himself was wont to muse.) To review, then, the Players Club displays a blond wig that's red and Booth's skull that isn't the skull over which he used to say, 'I knew him, Horatio.' The red wig plays a blond wig, and a real skull of Lovett the fake skull of Booth. These relics simultaneously celebrate the thing itself – theatre in all its gnarly materiality – while signalling the thing they aspire to be – blond and famous, not red-haired and anonymous.

If ignominy is the player's ultimate fear – and if the graveyard scene brings the actor to the brink – Edwin Booth found the perfect solution. Faced with the challenge of anonymous skulls, Booth 'directed that one of the skulls thrown up by the first grave-digger shall have a tattered and mouldy fool's-cap adhering to it, so that it may attract attention, and be singled out from the others, as "Yorick's skull, the king's jester"'.[11] This is one way of solving a skull's anonymity. It further points up the oddity that, here, Hamlet's famed scepticism fails him. What if the gravedigger's wrong? And why, of all people, would we take a gravedigger on faith? To 'single' out a skull, it has to wear a hat, the point of which is to personalize the skull among anonymous others, so that Hamlet and the gravedigger can tell which is which, or whose is whose. But then, again, the point of the hat is to turn a which into a whom, a problem upon which Shakespeare wrote a long but influential essay called *Hamlet*.

By casting an actor as Yorick – whether it be Lovett the horse thief or Tchaikovsky the pianist – these anecdotes always turn one skull into two. This is Yorick's skull but it's also Lovett's or Tchaikovsky's. Once the news broke about Tennant's real live skull the mystery increased rather than disappeared. The effort to ascribe identity to the skull only compounds the mystery it sets out to solve. One skull or two? The anecdotal urge to give a name to Yorick adeptly reads one of the play's critical knots. Yorick's skull conveys all manner of the uncanny – as its critical heritage suggests – but the anecdotal 'reading' of this scene suggests that the only thing freakier than a graveyard full of skulls is a graveyard with just one.

These anecdotes create a character for Yorick, then, by dilating the singularity of Yorick's skull into the bifold aura of Tchaikovsky or Lovett, which brands the temples of an anonymous prop with the identity of its original actor. What allows Yorick to ripple with life – if only for a moment – is the overlay of a fictional persona on the presence of a particular person, which suggests in the end we're all skulls in disguise. Yorick becomes Yorick when Yorick becomes Lovett, when one skull turns into two, as they inevitably do. To become a *dramatis personae*, Yorick needs more than just a back story, he needs an agent.

Like father, like son

Edwin Booth's father left him his own skull. A head that was his property though it belonged to someone else. His, but not his . . . It would be easy to go on at length like this, irritating you with irresolution, since heads confuse the distinction between pronouns and property, between titles and title characters, between one head and another.

There are certain locations in English Renaissance drama that are impossible to discuss without lapsing into trivial puns. Christopher Marlowe's *Edward II* is one, where it is impossible to talk about the end of *Edward II* without talking about the end of Edward II. *Hamlet* is another, where it is difficult to talk about Hamlet's skull without talking about *Hamlet*'s skull. Attempts to analyse such locations turn into comic routines that trivialize them. At such moments, Shakespeare and Marlowe bait criticism, producing it by baffling it. The history of *Hamlet* is riddled with skulls.

Puns might seem impertinent, but in their ambition to express two things at once they effectively condense the interpretive project. Art piles up paradox for analysis to unpack. And plays are good at paradox and puns, good at offering a perspective of 'is and is not' that remains entirely 'natural' as *Twelfth Night* tells us. Puns are baked into plays at the core of their creation. For *Hamlet*, the skull puns produce – among many other things – questions of property, which inevitably raise questions of inheritance. There are stranger things to leave a son than a head – an entire country, for one, or a toe for another, as we'll see below – but what belongs to fathers and sons, what inherent properties they share and which ones they inherit, is very much on *Hamlet*'s mind. Old Hamlet died intestate, though he might have assumed that his son would take his place as, inevitably, head of state. Less certain of succession, Tchaikovsky, Lovett, and other aspiring Yoricks engaged in more artful estate planning, as the case of John Reed demonstrates. John Reed was, in the middle of the nineteenth century, the 'gas-lighter' at the Walnut Street Theatre in Philadelphia, which, from its opening in 1809, has been the longest continuously operating theatre in America. A periodical in 1884 outlines Reed's bid for posthumous stardom by getting ahead of himself:

> John Reed was a gas-lighter of the Walnut Street Theatre, at Philadelphia, and filled this post for forty-four years with a

> punctuality and fidelity rarely equaled; there is not on record a single representation at which he was not present. John Reed was somewhat of a character, and appears to have had his mute ambitions. As he never aspired, however, to appear on the stage in his lifetime, he imagined an ingenious device for assuming a role in one of Shakespeare's plays after his decease; it was not the ghost of Polonius, nor yet the handkerchief of Desdemona – no; it was the skull in Hamlet; and to this end he wrote a clause in his will, thus: 'My head to be separated from my body immediately after my death; the latter to be buried in a grave; the former, duly macerated and prepared, to be brought to the theatre where I have served all my life, and to be employed to represent the skull of Yorick – and to this end I bequeath my head to the properties.'[12]

It takes a certain degree of detachment to plan to have your head removed. By doing so, Reed extended his run at the Walnut – forty-four years during which there was no 'representation at which he was not present' – beyond death, appearing for years in productions of *Hamlet*. He was 'somewhat of a character' during his life and continued his occupation into the great hereafter. The skull is now in the possession of the Horace Howard Furness Memorial Library at the University of Pennsylvania. It is brought to the desk of the interested reader in a hat box with a neatly typed label: 'Furness. A/Bo200.1 A. Yorrick's [sic] skull.' It may seem odd that John Reed's skull lives in a rare-book collection, but it makes for a good read. Its dome has been signed by a half-a-dozen nineteenth-century luminaries who played Hamlet to its Yorick at the Walnut Street Theatre.[13] The names of the actors appear in a neat column, a genealogy of nineteenth-century histrionic stardom. The first name – if the order of inscription moved from brow to crown – is 'Kean', below which 'Booth', 'Forrest', and other names appear, justified left if the skull had a hard return, which this one definitely has.

Reed's attempt to ascribe his head a character – and subsequent efforts to inscribe it with characters – reproduces the dilemma it sets out to solve, since, once again, the singularity of the skull dilates into plurality. (Booth's skull in the Players also bears a signature, though it is signed by the man who played the gravedigger in 1890, Owen Fawcett.[14]) It is hard not to feel for Reed in this scenario, since his plans for posterity have been overwritten by the stars. Despite the gas lighter's carefully laid plan to give a name to Yorick, Hamlet insists on top billing. Ultimately, the Walnut Street skull serves as a talisman of the contest between actors and anonymity – a contest between the question, 'Who's there?' and the ambitious assertion, 'It is I.' Fortunately, Reed did not live to learn the hard lesson that Yorick is not even in the running. It may be Yorick's skull, but it's Hamlet's property.

The assertion of identity always invites questions of resemblance, however: 'this same skull . . .'. Self-sameness is predicated upon difference, which the play ultimately frustrates. The play is called *Hamlet* but has two Hamlets. I suggested above that Hamlet is never more himself than at the side of a grave, where he asserts that he's 'Hamlet, the Dane'. At the same time, and in the same terms, he asserts that he's Hamlet the Dane by implying he's not the other one. I am Hamlet the Dane, not that other Hamlet the Dane. You see the problem here? Charles Kean did, and he found a solution that did not occur to Hamlet. Next to his name on John Reed's skull, well off in the left 'margin', almost as an afterthought, is the single initial 'C'. 'Charles' Kean, not Edmund Kean. 'C.' Kean reminds us of the parthenogenetic fantasies of patronymic names, and the burden upon famous sons of the names they're burdened with. One name turns into two. One 'Booth' could be two Booths, one 'Kean' could be two, one Hamlet, the other one. As so often in Renaissance dramatics, an attempt by a fortunate son to assert his identity turns into a succession crisis.

In 1866, the *Weekly Register* asked, 'When . . . Charles Kean retires, who will take his place and fill the great void?' Theatrical relics – not least Yorick's skull – often provide the materials through which such crises can be managed. As

Elizabeth Williamson describes it, theatrical relics, like Catholic ones, gather their power from 'proximity to the actor's body' and confer 'additional meanings as they moved from hand to hand'. Muriel Bradbrook once fantasized 'a moment from *Hamlet*'s first performance where, at Ophelia's graveside, Armin and Richard Burbage stand, each with a hand on Tarleton's skull – the present leading players remembering, and touching upon, their heritage'.[15] Once again Tarleton's head negotiates liminal relations. More recently, a publicity image from the 1992 BBC radio *Hamlet* shows Kenneth Branagh as Hamlet holding a skull, with Derek Jacobi (Claudius) and John Gielgud (Ghost) looking over each of his shoulders. The older actors confirm Branagh as the next great English Hamlet. The skull consecrates the tradition and the smooth succession from reign to reign. The skull is theatre's signature sacrament – and the Player's Club one main reliquary. The theology it serves is of the exemplary individual, its liturgy requiring a pledge upon the pate of Yorick's skull.

There's a fine line between consecration and desecration, and by pledging itself upon the bones of its own, theatre often crosses it. The stage has a hard time keeping a straight face when it looks too closely at its self, as Gielgud, Jacobi and Branagh probably did as soon as the photo shoot was done. The theatre's unofficial theology of the exemplary individual – 'stardom', in other words – is often undercut by the casual, even dismaying comic treatment of its own relics. The curious case of Frederick Cooke brings together the skeins of anecdotes surrounding Yorick's skull that this chapter has thus far followed. With Cooke, remembering gave way to dismembering and the theatre gives in to its irresistible urge to desecrate whatever it makes sacred, to turn a ceremony of remembrance into a goon show.

An actor as known for his capacity at the bar as on the boards, Cooke concluded his erratic career in New York City in 1812 where, after discharging 'a quantity of black grumous blood', he 'calmly expired'.[16] Then he took a turn for the worse. He was buried in the strangers' vault of St Paul's Church on Fulton

Street, lower Manhattan, but he did not remain a stranger for long. Ten years later, Edmund Kean removed the body to the public graveyard and erected a handsome monument to Cooke, though not before taking a memento of his own. In an article entitled 'Stage Properties' from 1878, Dutton Cook reports that, 'Kean possessed himself of one of the toe-bones; "it was a little black relic, and might have passed for a tobacco-stopper." Some other devotee stole the head.'[17] Others report that Kean stole a finger, and Booth somehow ended up with a tooth. Summarizing Cooke's dispersal, Dutton Cook could not resist adding, so that I don't have to, 'One man in his time plays many parts.'

(The toe formed a footnote to Frederick Cooke's posthumous career. Kean repatriated it back to London to leave to his son, though Charles was deprived Cooke's toe since, according to anecdote, Edmund's wife threw it out the window. Perhaps she objected to being made, along with Edmund's friends and associates, to go 'down upon their knees and reverently kiss the precious relic'.)

Cooke's head fared little better, though it came into the hands of a doctor not an actor. The anecdotes can't agree on the doctor's name – anecdotes are terrible with them – but more or less do agree on the histrionic fate of Cooke's head:

> Depredations having been committed, some years since, upon the Golgotha of the Park Theatre (New York), the 'properties man' was in great distress one evening. Kemble was to play *Hamlet*, and their only remaining skull was the well-known pyrotechnic automaton appertaining to the incantation scene of 'Der Freyschutz,' and with which there was danger of ignition. In his dilemma he flew to Dr Bartolo's, and begged the loan of a skull for one night only. From his cabinet of curiosities the Doctor produced a *cranium* which served for the 'grave scenes,' and was returned on the day following. Had any present known whose voice had once spoken within those fleshless bones, whose eyes had once flashed from those empty sockets – there would have been a sensation throughout the house. The skull thus unwittingly

> held up to an unconscious audience, was the *bona fide* caput of a *Yorick* Charles Kemble had known – *It was the skull of George Frederic Cooke!* Was not this an impressive *memento mori* of histrionic fame?[18]

Leaving aside – alas – the 'pyrotechnic automaton' from *Der Freischütz*, the anecdote compounds the puzzle of Yorick's skull. The audience did not know it was Cooke who played Yorick, and Hamlet was none the wiser, though the Dane in question, Charles Kemble, *had* known this same skull, though not, of course, as the anecdote suggests as 'a *Yorick*', since for all his theatrical ambitions, Yorick is one part that Cooke never aspired to play. Kemble had shared the stage with Cooke before, though Cooke had never gone so quietly into a supporting role. An earlier anecdote records a meeting between them, during which Cooke and Kemble allotted parts to one another. Not heads and toes, but stars and shadows.

> When Cooke and Kemble met to arrange what characters they should perform together, George Frederick was determined to be as courtlie-like as his more polished rival. *Iago*, and *Othello*, *Iachimo*, and *Posthumus*, were easily agreed upon, being equal parts; the conversation then proceeded : –
>
> Kemble: I will, with pleasure, play *Richmond* to your *Richard*, Mr. Cooke; will you, in return, play *Pizatto* to my *Rolla*?
> Cooke: With great pleasure, I assure you, Mr. Kemble.
> Kemble: If I do *Bassanio* to your *Shylock*, you will do *Macduff* to my *Macbeth*?
> Cooke: Most undoubtedly, my dear sir.
> Kemble: I will act *Welborn* to your *Overreach*, if you will perform *Horatio* to my *Hamlet*?
> Cooke: What! *Horatio*! I'll see Covent Garden in h—'s flames first! George Frederick Cooke play *Horatio* to your *Hamlet*! – Yours![19]

Cooke never did play Horatio to Kemble – at least not according to the archives – though a legend surrounding his introduction to the stage suggests that's where he got his start. An obituary reports that Cooke originally trained as a printer, and 'had he not been induced to play *Horatio* in Hamlet, when the approbation that he received, so intoxicated his young brain, that he forsook the important art of typographic composition, to learn the art of acting, and recite the composition of others'.[20] Perhaps recollecting his juvenile past, Cooke decided that Horatio just wasn't his type. Nevertheless, the skull anecdote finds Cooke quietly capitulating to his quondam rival. On this night, at least, not only did Kemble own Hamlet, but Cooke was his property as well.

Cooke's fate is a sad one. A modern placard at his graveside remembers the actor's life by honouring his head's posthumous career. It informs the visitor that Cooke was 'acclaimed as one of the greatest actors of his day, Cooke played Richard III to an audience of 2,000 in New York. After his death, legends abounded that his skull was stolen from his coffin and secretly used in theater productions of *Hamlet*.' It is a curious kind of honour, giving as much weight to Cooke's unintended stage career as to his intended one. But the placard is accurate, since legends did abound after Cooke's death. All dilate upon the attention his skull attracted. These morbid forensics – be they Hamlet's or a crew of amateur phrenologists – are licensed, of course, by the fact that the skull is in no position to argue:

> Poor George Frederick, who so often lost his head during life, was destined to lose it even in the grave. His friend and counselor, Doctor Francis, ruthlessly purloined it and he lies headless in St. Paul's churchyard. There is a smug complacency in the doctor's description of an event of later date . . . He wrote: 'A theatrical benefit had been announced at the Park and HAMLET the play. A subordinate at the theater at a late hour hurried to my office for a skull. I was compelled to loan the head of my old friend, George

> Frederick Cooke. 'Alas, poor Yorick!' It was returned in the morning, on the ensuing evening at a meeting of the Cooper club, the circumstance becoming known to several of the members and a desire being expressed to investigate phrenologically the head of the great tragedian, the article was again released from its privacy when Daniel Webster, Henry Wheaton and any others who enriched the meeting that night applied the principles of craniological science to the interesting specimen before them!'[21]

Yorick's skulls often solicit amateur phrenologists, like Hamlet himself. We might recall Forbes-Robertson's correspondent, or the provincial manager who once apologized to Edwin Booth about the skull he provided for Yorick by complaining of a headache: '"I'm a little sore about the skull, Mr Booth," he added, "dead sore. Doc Axtelle promised me a skull he had in his office, but he had to return it yesterday to its first husband, who is now leading a better life and wants all of his wives buried together. But I've got a phrenological head, with faculties all over it." '[22] The manager promises Booth a head with infinite faculties, so that even when Hamlet gapes in wonder at Yorick's mute map, he will at least be able to read it. The idea is even unwittingly articulated by Frederick Cooke's monument: 'Three kingdoms claim his birth / both hemispheres pronounce his worth.' Just what the hemispheres of Cooke's head pronounced is revealed at the end of yet another anecdotal account of the same incident:

> The head was pronounced capacious, the function of animality amply developed; the height of the forehead ordinary; the space between the orbits of unusual breadth, giving proofs of strong perceptive powers; the transverse basilar portion of the skull of corresponding width. Such was the phrenology of Cooke. This scientific exploration added to the variety and gratification of that memorable evening. Cooper felt as a coadjutor of Albinus, and Cooke enacted a great part that night.[23]

In the case of Cooke, attempts at veneration give way to quack forensics. In the theatre world, the hollowed crowns of hallowed grounds seem always to produce this collision of high minds with low brows. Is there anything more profound than the image of Hamlet contemplating Yorick's skull? Is there anything funnier? The accounts all articulate the same desire, however, which is to make the skull answer for itself. After all, it had 'a tongue in it once' (5.1.74). 'Who's there?' these anecdotes all ask of the skull. 'You are,' the skull barely bothers to say.

Ghost walkers

A website called, chillingly, 'findagrave.com' (as though it takes the internet to do so) reports that George Frederick was 'hailed on both sides of the Atlantic as the greatest tragedian of his era, he was dramatic even in death. The British star's skull was allegedly used in Edwin Booth's production of Hamlet, and his headless ghost is said to haunt this Manhattan churchyard . . .'. If a skull without a name is just a prop, a name without a body is a ghost. And if Yorick's skull offers actors the choice between the real and the fake, between tragedy and farce, the ghost scenes stage something that is not there. Anecdotes about *Hamlet*'s ghost (and, yes, Hamlet's ghost) therefore articulate not a pun but a paradox, a thing that is nothing. The theatre often shies when it has to embody the disembodied, and *Hamlet*'s graveyards are predictably full of anecdotes.

The most plausible representation of a Ghost would be one that does not appear, a solution the theatre has occasionally arrived at when confronted with *Hamlet*'s spectral challenge. On 4 October 1777, the *London Times* ran an almost certainly facetious letter to the managers of Drury Lane Theatre protesting the playing of *Hamlet*'s gravest scenes:

> GENTLEMEN, I Much approve your discarding from the Play of HAMLET that hasty, vulgar, and illiberal Scene of

> the Grave Diggers, fit only to make the Wretches in the Galleries laugh. I protest I was ready to puke when I saw the Men handle the Skulls! Let the Ghost and the Skulls go to the Devil together, they are not fit to come before a polite Audience.[24]

One solution to the skull is to bury it, as apparently David Garrick did in this instance, though the decision came back to haunt him. Just six years later, on 22 September 1783, *The Gazetteer and New Daily Advertiser* covered the repair of Drury Lane and reported the discovery of 'A human scull in the earth under the stage . . . An old scene shifter unravelled the mystery, by declaring it was no other than Yorick's scull used in Hamlet, and that he remembered it being lost many years since in Mr Garrick's time.'[25] The 'old scene shifter' has a spectral sound – like a Ghost in the cellarage who trips over Yorick's skull. It raises the question of where Hamlet is buried. Not that Hamlet, *that* Hamlet. For a play full of graves, Old Hamlet wants one. But then his body is not fit for burial, since an actor is still using it. Yet even when the scene is cut, the skull is always just beneath the stage. That's why it's called a 'remain'.

Across the ages, Yorick's skull and Hamlet's ghost have embarrassed the performance history of *Hamlet*. As the correspondent suggests, there is a tradition of cutting these scenes and, inevitably, a tradition that protests their excision. According to a later critic in 1902: 'The fashion of leaving the stage ghost to the imagination of the spectator, whether on or off the stage, is growing,' but '"Hamlet" without the spectre of the murdered king is not conceivable.'[26] Turning a ghost into one is something of a redundancy, and according to this account – and to continue a theme – a *Hamlet* with just one Hamlet is not *Hamlet*.

However sarcastic, the correspondent to the *London Times* locates the technical challenges of casting the ghost and Yorick. Both scenes challenge the theatre to represent the dead. But if Yorick's skull is all too plausibly dead – is all too plausibly *not acting* – Hamlet's ghost inverts the problem. The actor playing the ghost is too plausibly alive. The scene has therefore produced a cluster of stories that focus on the Ghost's intrusive body. A nineteenth-century correspondent summarizes the tradition, telling us that, 'Amusing anecdotes are told of the part of the Ghost in *Hamlet* being played by a Mr Stuart, of Liverpool, with his arm in a sling; of another performer who neglected to remove his spectacles before going upon the stage; . . . and more recently of an actor in New York, with loud creaking boots.'[27] And, of course, an anecdote connected with Charles Kean in which the ghost was too drunk to walk. A bespectacled spectre is a comic vision, as is one with an injured arm, as is one staggered with drink. The creaking boots of the New York ghost might seem less of a problem, since Hamlet claims that ghosts squeak and gibber. But a lead-footed ghost echoes the anecdote's most frequent complaint. To offer one more paradox, it is often the ghost's weight that diminishes his gravity.

> The anecdote we are about to relate of a *fat Ghost* is not less amusing. Mr Banks, for many years co-lessee of the Manchester Theatre, was a remarkably large, fat man . . . Mr Banks always played the Ghost in *Hamlet*: once on a time, while acting the part on the stage of the Manchester Theatre, his great bulk gave rise to a most laughable incident. The Ghost, it will be remembered by our theatrical readers, used to vanish from some of the scenes, through a trap-door on the stage. Well, on one occasion, Mr Banks had taken his station on the spot. The bolt was withdrawn, and slowly descended the Ghost, truncheon in hand. The legs disappeared in due course; but whether owing to the increase of his own bulk, or to some alteration in the size of the aperture, the moment the huge, round body touched the edge of the stage, the process of sinking suddenly ceased. The Ghost stuck fast in the middle. No contrivance, no squeezing, no exertion on the part of Mr Banks could force his Falstaffian body down through the trap-hole. The

auditory were convulsed with laughter; even the ghost himself joined in the laughter, and quietly submitted to be lifted out of the hole by the stage attendants.[28]

Here is a ghost fat with life. Like Falstaff, his body is, as in Hal's nasty eulogy, too wide for the grave. And here, too, is the Ghost of Old Hamlet who doesn't go down easy. To be fair, he is – to quote the eighteenth-century complaint – trying to 'go to the Devil' but stubbornly fails. Caught in between, the actor punctures the membrane between offstage and on and becomes a spectre of laughter. As suggested in the introduction, anecdotes often loiter in the alleys between onstage and off. Ghosts also make their home in the in-between, and so ghosts and anecdotes run into one another there. Efforts to leave the stage always leave themselves open to anecdotes. Most stages have at least one trap, and they usually end up catching anecdotes.

The weight of actors – both men and women – has long been a point of cruel emphasis. A dog-eared joke advises the actor playing Lear that a crucial point is, as Michael Hordern learned when he sought the advice of John Gielgud, 'to "get a small Cordelia" '.[29] The 'pound of flesh' in *Merchant* has frequently provided an irresistible *mot* with which to tweak a portly Shylock. There is even a minor precinct of anecdotes that reports on actors taking seriously Gertrude's comment that Hamlet is 'fat and scant of breath'. But a huge body of anecdotes has swelled around *Hamlet*'s ghost over the years. History is full of ghosts judged to have, as a reviewer of a Drury Lane performance put in 1813, 'nothing ethereal in it, but was a mass of most gross and palpable mortality'.[30] In a story of Larry O'Rourke's Hamlet debut at the Cork Theatre we learn, wearily, of 'the beefy, provincial ghost, with a sepulchral voice, and the usual difficulty of disappearing as a ghost ought'.[31] A piece of doggerel from 1889 criticizes the ghost on a number of fronts, but signals him out for being, cleverly, 'A shade too obese for my choice.'[32] The history of *Hamlet* is not just riddled with skulls, it is fat with phantoms.

In some respects, a corpulent ghost fulfils Hamlet's notion that a 'fat King' and a 'lean beggar' enjoy similar afterlives. But anecdotes administrate difference, and here the difference is between the body of the actor and of a disembodied character. Anecdotes come to the rescue when theatre produces accidents, and as often as not, staging the improbable produces the implausible. It is always both a spiritual and technical challenge to embody the disembodied, and when the solutions court disaster, anecdotes are on hand to provide triage.

One implausibility, for instance, is that the Ghost appears in armour, which raises impertinent questions about why a ghost needs armour in the first place. A ghost with armour is like a fish with a snorkel. Nevertheless, in a number of instances the ghost's armour becomes distracting and sometimes nearly fatal. In 1781 we learn 'that the *glimpses of the moon*, had such a visible effect, on the *compleat steel* of Denmark's Ghostly King, so to tinge the edging of the armour with a perfect *yellow* hue. – To speak more plain . . . instead of the appearance of steel armour, the coat of mail evidently looked like black leather with gingerbread binding.'[33] There's such a fine line between a 'visible effect' and a risible one, and the ghost of Hamlet haunts that perilous terrain. There are worse things, of course, than wearing armour laced with gingerbread, including being baked alive.

> When Garrick performed in Goodman's-fields, the stage was what might be called a rapid descent to the pit, and was very difficult to walk on. As fate would have it, it was the practice of all the ghosts to appear in real armour. The dress for this most august personage had, one night, in honour of Garrick's Hamlet, been borrowed from the Tower, and was somewhat stiff. The moment the King of Denmark that 'used to was' made his appearance at the stage door, unable to keep his balance, he rolled down to the lamps, where he lay exposed to fires somewhat too lasting, until a wag in the pit drew the attention of the other performers to the pitiable object by crying out, 'The *ghost* will be burned!'[34]

It was the fate of Old Hamlet to burn out his days in pitiless fire, but verisimilitude needs to end at the edge of the stage.

Both the cause and the effect of these haunting anecdotes is that for much of *Hamlet*'s performance history the part of the supernatural was left to a supernumerary, always an occasion for theatrical hilarity. An anecdote from *Everybody's Magazine* tells of

> a barnstorming company in the West in the old days that made a try at Shakespeare. Considerable complaint was heard relative to the efforts of the man who essayed to do the Ghost in 'Hamlet.' One day a dramatic man on a local paper said to the leading man: 'That fellow who plays the Ghost does not suggest the supernatural.' 'I should say not,' assented the leading man with alacrity, 'but he does suggest the natural super.'[35]

The pun on 'super' points to the superfluity of old Hamlet's part. He is a leftover, a fleeting memory of the old regime. And since he's something extra, he's best left to the extras.

The routine ineptitude of these super-failures is the frequent butt of theatrical jokes, as professionalism collides with naiveté. One evident solution to an implausible ghost is simply to kill off the actor – they're just extras after all. 'A player performing the Ghost in "Hamlet" very badly, was hissed; after bearing it a good while he put the audience in good humour by stepping forward and saying, "Ladies and gentlemen, I am extremely sorry that my humble endeavors to please are unsuccessful; but if you are not satisfied, I must give up the ghost." '[36] Like Shakespeare's 'William the Conqueror' joke, this one sounds reverse engineered from the punch line, but it echoes across theatre history. Since a ghost is a name without a body, the best bet is always to cast a nobody.

Like the fat Ghost of Old Hamlet, you can't keep a good joke down. 'A supernumerary in a western theatre, having been inducted into the ghost part of "Hamlet," "for this night only," performed the part so badly that he was hissed off. The manager came forward, bowed gracefully, put his hand on his heart, announced that "Smith had agreed to give up the ghost," bowed again, retired, and all was peace once more.'[37] And just once more:

> A country company were exhibiting *Hamlet*, when a person was allotted to perform the *Ghost*, who, though destitute of stage requisites, possessed great humour. After his first scene with Hamlet was terminated, the cry was so violent against him from all parts of the house, that he turned to the audience, and made the following laconic address: "Why, ladies and gentlemen, what can you expect, for, from my *own account*, I am a *damned ghost*, and suffer *penal fires*." The outrage still continuing, he made his second appeal. "Ladies and gentlemen, since it is your pleasure that I should not *exist*, I must of necessity *give up the Ghost!*" '[38]

The suffering super mordantly expresses the player's dilemma: the part demands of an actor that he disappear into the role. As with the skull, what produces ghost stories in *Hamlet* is the unrealistic demands the play makes on the players.

It is far less clear from *Hamlet*'s history just what might make a realistic ghost, which is of course one cause for all the anecdotes. In 1916, the *Courier-Journal* – which apparently knows something that we don't – celebrated a ghost for his realism, praising 'W.L. Thorne, . . . whose ghost in "Hamlet" was realistic, because of a well-modulated voice'.[39] Barton Booth took the precaution of covering his feet in felt, which 'made no noise in walking on the stage,' William Cooke recalled, 'which strongly corresponded with the ideas we have of an incorporeal being'.[40] The *Pall Mall Gazette* defines it, vaguely, as 'ghostliness' while doing a bit of anecdotal historicizing itself. Discussing Edwin Booth's *Hamlet* in 1880, the critic muses that it is not easy

> to fix the limits of stage realism; but limits there are. As Hamlet himself says, 'We do but poison in jest.' In this

respect, indeed, our remote predecessors went further than we are likely to go. It was among the Romans of the time of the empire that stage realism was carried to a point which permitted of the incineration of an actor who presented the death of Hercules . . . [Nevertheless] the Ghost of Mr. Ryder was wanting in the all-essential quality of ghostliness.[41]

The standard of realism is impossibly tautological: ghosts should be ghostly. We know one when we see one, although we've never seen one. The writer admits that there are limits to realism, but what is considered beyond the pale when staging something that does not exist?

According to anecdotal history, the Ghost leads *Hamlet* in two different directions – towards the hilarious, or towards the terrifying – for the most successful ghosts disrupt the play by becoming, if anything, *too* realistic. Thomas Betterton was famously effective at responding to his father's ghost by nearly becoming one himself, according to the author of the 'Lick at the Laureat', an invective against Colley Cibber, published in the year 1730:

I have lately been told by a gentleman, who has seen Betterton perform *Hamlet*, that he observed his countenance, which was naturally ruddy and sanguine, in the scene of the third act where his father's ghost appears, through the violent and sudden emotion of amazement and horror, turn instantly, on the sight of his father's spirit, as pale as his neckcloth; then his whole body seemed to be affected with a tremor inexpressible; so that, had his father's ghost actually risen before him, he could not have been seized with more real agonies. And this was so strongly felt by the audience, that the blood seemed to shudder in their veins likewise; and they, in some measure, partook of the astonishment and horror with which they saw this excellent actor affected.[42]

What renders the Ghost so impressive here is that he nearly exsanguinates his son – not to mention the audience. A further wrinkle on the anecdote appears in a later version, which adds a telling detail: 'The first time [Barton] Booth attempted the Ghost, when Betterton acted Hamlet, that actor's look at him struck him with such horror, that he became disconcerted to such a degree, that he could not speak his part.'[43] Here the Ghost is struck dumb by the reaction he elicits, and he and his son nearly change places (a successful succession that would obviate the play). Old Hamlet should be the only actor in the play completely immune to stage fright, but the realization of what he has become – what he will become – registers in the wan complexion of his 'son'.

One take-away from this tale is that Thomas Betterton was such a good actor that he could ably play the ghost even when he was playing Hamlet, which might serve to remind us that the role is always doubled. Furthermore, as Joseph Roach has argued, Betterton was always playing a ghost, most obviously that of Shakespeare since Betterton became the 'living incarnation of Shakespearean tradition' – supported by the venerable anecdote that Shakespeare had himself played the Ghost and to which legend connected Betterton through histrionic descent.[44] Descended of Shakespeare, Betterton performed for half a century through the reigns of four monarchs, trailing Shakespeare's memory like a train behind his 'ill figure'. Even at the heights of his histrionic power, Betterton was a ghost of his former self.

In other words, Thomas Betterton acted like he was already dead, and his fame produced another anecdote in which he disguises himself in anonymity, which we wore like a shroud on stage. There's a story of him in the provinces, passing himself off as an amateur to a company of visiting players. He proposed to the manager that he play the Ghost in *Hamlet*. The offer was received and Betterton ham-fists it through rehearsal. The word goes out to an expectant audience that 'the amateur was a sorry stick . . . and most of them were prepared for an exhibition of awkwardness when the "borrowed majesty of Denmark" received his cue'. On the night in question, Betterton appears in all his terror and in all his talent: '"Mark me," said the spectre, in deep, sepulchral tones, and fixing a dreadful eye upon the astonished manager, "mark me." "I do," said Hamlet, in tremulous tones, looking as if really distilling to jelly with the act of fear. "By Heaven I do, and I shall never forget you." '[45] Betterton confirms the memory of his own performance by reminding other usurpers to 'mark' him. In so doing, he solves the problem of how to produce the realistic ghost of Old Hamlet, which is that young Hamlet needs to play him.

Far more recently, Daniel Day-Lewis's celebrated Hamlet one night thought that 'his father's apparition had actually risen before him', though it is not clear if Day-Lewis is just staying in character when he says so. The stage manager's report reads:

> Thursday 5 September 'On the Ghost's exit in Act 1, Scene 5, Mr Day-Lewis left the stage and told me that he could not continue the performance. An announcement was made and the audience invited to take an extra interval. The announcement only specified technical problems. After 32 minutes the performance resumed with Mr Northam as Hamlet. Mr Bedford played Osric and Mr Nicholas a Switzer. Mr Northam coped brilliantly (not an exaggeration) and received an outstanding reception from the audience.[46]

Day-Lewis could literally not go on, and he never did, retiring from the production after that night. Day-Lewis more recently recanted. In 2012 he clarified, 'I don't remember seeing any ghosts of my father on that dreadful night!' It is not entirely clear what he saw that night, or what he did not, or even if he's simply forgotten to remember, since he hasn't played Hamlet since.[47]

Hamlet without a ghost is, perhaps, inconceivable, but a *Hamlet* with too many, as one final ghost story from the Haymarket Theatre suggests, raises the spectre of raising too many spectres, which circles back to the problem of multiple skulls. Ultimately, the anecdotes argue, there are far more dead kings than live ones, more dead jesters than Yorick, and the dead will always outnumber the living. Moreover, they're gaining on us. At the same time, the following anecdote brilliantly solves the dilemma of a realistic ghost. The most realistic ghost, as a Mr. Hughes unwittingly suggests in the anecdote that follows, is one that doesn't show.

> A GHOST STORY. – At the Haymarket Theatre on Thursday the play was *Hamlet*. The audience assembled to witness the tragedy in respectable numbers and due solemnity. The hour of seven arrived – and the curtain was ready to rise; but the ghost, Mr Hughes, was by no means like the curtain. The call-boy called but the obstinate spirit refused to obey. No wonder; the boy was on the stage, and the 'poor Ghost' was solacing himself with the comforts of domestic peace ... There is historical authority for playing *Hamlet* with the part of Hamlet omitted, but *Hamlet* without the Ghost was never heard of. Every man who had ever played a Ghost was sent for. Mr Wallack arrived first, resolved to address himself boldly to the difficulty, and set about dressing himself in complete steel, with the full intent to *read* the part. Some one who was less courageous suggested that as the Ghost appeared 'in the dead waste and middle of the night,' he could not see to read. So a candle was resolved upon, and the Ghost had by these means been duly laid – but for the messages to the ghostly regions now beginning to produce their effects. Hansom cabs crowded to the stage door, each depositing its ghostly contents. There was a very deluge of Ghosts of all sizes – thick, fat, short, and tall, among whom was Mr Stuart, and finally came the delinquent himself, Mr. Hughes, whose absence had caused this impromptu entertainment. The tragedy was at last played with great applause, Mr and Mrs Kean and Miss L. Addison being called on to receive marks of hearty and well-merited approbation. But the wicked Ghost had gone to his place, and 'would not come, though they did call for him;' he had had enough of it, and retired to the 'Shades.'[48]

The superfluous extras of *Hamlet*'s history return to their familiar haunts. The anecdote articulates the labour surplus of theatrical work – just as there are always more dead than living, there are always more actors out of work than on the stage. As Marx acknowledged, in a different context and in different terms, unemployment is like a living death. Simon Callow calls unemployment the 'primeval slime from which the actors emerge and to which, inevitably, they return', which produces an 'ontological anxiety' about being out of work. The dole is death for an actor, and even playing dead is still a way to make a living.[49]

Though most anecdotes insist on their own punctuality – 'one time'; 'one night'; 'at the Haymarket Theatre on Thursday' – Mr Hughes' failure to be punctual opens a seam in singularity through which all the extras pour. If an actor's work – in fact his or her stardom – is predicated upon erasing the memory of other actors, these anecdotes – from Betterton's 'mark me' to the reminder to Hughes that extra ghosts are gathering at the door – work to surround 'this night' with all the others and 'this actor' with an army of unemployed extras. For every Ghost who chooses to walk out, there are a thousand who'll walk on.

Hamlet offers one final entry into its morbid triptych, the corpse of Ophelia, which poses a final challenge to a play fascinated with decomposition – as well as Fetcher's flaxen wig, it turns out.

> The well-ordered 'property' boy at Booth's Theater was seriously disconcerted on the first night of 'Hamlet' upon discovering that Miss DeBar, who was cast for 'Ophelia,' had determined to dress with a flaxen wig, an innovation wholly unexpected and possibly precipitated in compliment to Mr Fetcher, who assisted at the performance as Mr Booth's guest. 'Here's a precious go!' said Michael Themistocles, 'there's "Ophelia" gone and dressed herself up a blonde while we've been more'n a month faking up her dummy with black hair, and an awful waterfall.' (The 'dummy' served in the grave yard scene, be it

> understood). – 'But it can't be helped now. It's too late. If anybody in front wants to know how it was the dummy's hair turned, we'll have to tell 'em that "*Ophelia's dyed* according to Shakspere, and so she has!"'[50]

The terrible pun echoes a play full of them. Perhaps that's fitting, since *Hamlet* is an extended pun about a star who can't act.

Ophelia's grave is Hamlet's trap and recalls us to the threshold that all the skulls, ghosts and dummies have to pass through. The stage manager who had to inform the audience about Day-Lewis's disappearance might have reported that he fell for the trap, but instead he called it a 'technical' problem. He meant it as a euphemism, but he was telling the truth. One of the reasons that theatre can't shut its trap about these scenes is that, technically speaking, the play will not let it.

> The principal trap in almost all theatres is known as the grave trap. This is one of the conventionalism of the English stage, and is a testimony also to the enduring influence of Shakespeare. It is well understood that at some time or another the play of 'Hamlet' will be performed in every theatre, and *Ophelia's* grave must therefore be dug in every stage – hence the grave trap. It may be that it is not always placed in the right position to suit the ideas of each new representative of the Royal Dane, and it has happened that it has been found too short for the reception of poor *Ophelia's* coffin; but it is never omitted in the construction of a stage.[51]

Shakespeare's enduring influence left a hole in every English stage, one that every aspiring actor ultimately has to pass through, or fall into (after jumping through the hoop that Max Beerbohm called *Hamlet*, one through which every eminent actor must eventually hop). Sometimes the trap is too short, and sometimes the Ghost is too fat, and so a grave trap becomes a booby one. In some respects, *Hamlet* is just asking for anecdotes.

Hamlet is full of unquiet graves – Hamlet's lover, Hamlet's father, Hamlet's clown, Hamlet's. Anecdotes gather at the tomb of the unknown actor to audition their embarrassment. (The graveyard is the only theatre in the world where there are more parts than actors.) They come together to administrate embarrassment, to diffuse the stage's shame about the way it dummies death – its wooden skulls, its tubby ghosts, its mannequin corpses. As a body, *Hamlet*'s anecdotes dilate the distance between exemplarity and anonymity, which Yorick's skull celebrates. The anecdotes stage in the space between fame and ignominy a complementary comedy. But the anecdotes have also a more serious intent. They gather not just to mock death or allay the shame of mock-death but to protest. And what they seem intent on protesting is the real meaning of *Hamlet*. The real meaning of *Hamlet* is that it ends.

2

Othello: The smudge

In the late nineteenth century, a popular actor named Louis James played Othello in New York. One night while he stood over the sleeping Desdemona, he deliberately transferred some of his makeup to her face, inscribing a moustache and a small beard upon her as she 'slept'. Here I quote directly from the anecdote as later transcribed in 1920: 'It was unnoticed by the audience, but later, as other actors came upon the scene and saw the face of Desdemona lying on the pillow wreathed in golden hair but disfigured by apparent hirsute tufts over her mouth and chin, they were convulsed with laughter and the effect of a great tragic scene was destroyed.' By bearding and blacking his sleeping Desdemona, James converted a deadpan tragedy into a black-faced farce and telegraphed the anecdotal history of *Othello* in performance across the last 400 years.

The James gag is not an isolated anecdote, and not because an 'isolated anecdote' would be an oxymoron. Othello actors have been coming off onstage for ages. For instance, while Louis James intentionally blacked-up his Desdemona, Stephen Kemble could not help himself. When he embraced Desdemona at Covent Garden in 1783, he left an impression: '[S]o fond was he of Miss SATCHELL, the gentle *Desdemona*, that in embracing her he *would* have a kiss; the collision left one side of her face quite black, much to the entertainment of the audience.'[1] Audiences are usually more gleeful than resentful when the mask slips – even when the mask is made of skin – but Kemble's collision with Miss Satchell's face raises the immediate question of just what's so funny about a black-faced Desdemona and why history keeps insisting upon blackening her name.

A century after Kemble, Edwin Booth proved more circumspect, a shrewd move when you find yourself isoscelesed between Henry Irving and Ellen Terry. In 1881 the two men alternated as Othello and Iago to Terry's Desdemona. (*Othello*'s many anecdotes about alternating actors is a subject this chapter will get to; the ping-pong of 'alternation' and 'alteration' encapsulates *Othello*'s performance history.) Terry reports in her memoir, *The Story of my Life*,

> At rehearsals he [Booth] was very gentle and apathetic. Accustomed to playing Othello with stock companies, he had few suggestions to make about the stage-management . . . 'I shall never make you black,' he said one morning. 'When I take your hand I shall have a corner of my drapery in my hand. That will protect you.' I am bound to say I thought of Mr Booth's 'protection' with some yearning the next week when I played Desdemona to Henry's Othello. Before he had done with me I was nearly as black as he.[2]

Confirming Othello's worst fears, Terry yearns for a white man while she's in his arms, but, as this chapter argues, the erotic comedy of *Othello*'s history is marked by collisions between the made up and the real.

Anecdotes about the smudge have proven so popular that they have their own theme song. A comic ballad from the 1820s tells the story from Irving's end, about what it is like for Othello to see his face reflected in Desdemona's. Called 'When I Performed Othello', the song works through a series of misadventures (including the actor forgetting to black his hands) and in one verse reports that, 'The Actors, ever rife for fun, Plann'd me to make their Button, / They 'stead of burnt cork, told me that My face I should put soot on, / When Desdemona I embrac'd, Oh dear! How she did bellow For I daub'd her cheeks all over soot, When I perform'd Othello.'[3] The broadside that tells you where to buy the lyrics includes a cartoon of a black-faced actor embracing a struggling Desdemona, her nose, cheeks and forehead smudged with soot. Simultaneously comic and anxious, these anecdotes and this song reassure us that the tragedy of *Othello* is a comedy, only just below the surface. And however dirty the collisions make us feel, it'll come out all white in the end.

These stories – and there are many more – nervously narrate the perils of proximity. The courtly concern of Edwin Booth notwithstanding, the source of his worry is transparent: 'I shall never make you black . . . the drapery . . . That will protect you.' One fold of theatrical fabric – the drapery – protects Desdemona against another element of theatrical representation – the makeup – a material allegory for the play's thematic torsion. As with *Hamlet*'s real-live skulls, it is easy to see the way these anecdotes re-articulate, even abbreviate the play from which they emerge. It is easy, that is, to read this anecdote as an adumbration of the play's anxiety about racial identity and sexual exchange. The worry over Othello's makeup – and the desire to keep it off Desdemona – diverts and sluices the play's thematic obsession with the darkness of Othello and the fairness of Desdemona, exercising and exorcizing the theatre industry's anxiety about these matters. Questions about *Othello*'s make up are never purely cosmetic.

In fact there's a durable critical heritage that worries over how black Othello should be – an at least 250-year-long smear campaign against blacked-up actors (a theatrical side-show to the main event, which is the seemingly endless campaign against black men and women). A brief survey can start at Drury Lane in 1775, where a critic advised 'this young Gentleman, not to black his face so unmercifully in future, for last night it resembled the bottom of an old boiler'.[4] When Quick went to see Garrick, he blackened Garrick's name as well, asking, 'Why does not he bring the tea-kettle and lamp?'[5] These weird inversions of the old saw – calling the black a kettle – crescendo in a barb at one of Garrick's rivals, Spranger Barry, who made his visage 'as black as a tea kettle'.[6] If the actor wasn't too dark, he was often criticized for being too pale, as a critic complained of Mr Young in 1812, who 'colours the countenance of *Othello* so, that we might take him for Tippoo Saib, or a Mahratta Chieftain: but SHAKESPEARE instructs us, that he was a Black'.[7] Shakespeare's all-cap instructions notwithstanding, it's historically proven hard to determine just what colours make up a black.

The question of how black Othello should be nags *Othello*'s more recent history as well. In the 1960s, the *New York Times* complained that Laurence Olivier's Othello 'looks like Rastus or an end man in an American minstrel show. You almost wait for him to whip a banjo out from his flowing, white garments or start banging a tambourine.'[8] Even after black men took over the role for good, criticism could inadvertently maintain the tradition. When Omar Sangare played Othello at the Vanderbilt Museum in 2002, he was said to have been 'born to play Othello'.[9] The reviewer was not referring to his Polish heritage.

Even when critics do not explicitly address the actor's makeup, assessments often take on this complexion. A critique of Spranger Barry hints at the cause of these complaints. Because he made his Othello 'black as jet', Barry's 'workings and subtlety of passion was absorbed in an unnecessary and false darkness of tint'.[10] In this case, Barry was too black to act – a kind of invisible ham. (This is not just a terrible pun, but an hosanna to the history of ham fat, which early actors used to grease their faces, from which the terms derives for an obvious actor, though in Barry's case, too much makeup made him a mystery.) In other words, criticism of Othello's makeup shifts perceptibly into critiques of his performance. Of Mr Cambray's Othello at Covent Garden in 1787, a critic decided, 'The concluding scene was, upon the whole, well coloured',[11] but that in another production, although Mr and Mrs Pope were adequate in the leads, the play would have gained, 'were the hypocrisy of *Iago* rendered less obvious in the colouring'.[12] In 1790, 'The subtilty [sic] and hypocrisy of *Iago* was but faintly depicted by Mr MURRAY . . . but the consummate villainy of this character has been painted in a bolder, a more imposing stile by Mr MURRAY'S predecessors in the part.'[13] In 1798, an Othello at Covent Garden is praised for his 'rich colouring', while, in 1801, 'The villainy of *Iago* is depicted by COOKE in just and glowing colours.'[14] In 1811, the play itself is judged to be 'less tinctured with violations of probability' than Shakespeare's other plays,[15] an opinion seconded in 1887 when the play is called 'rich in coloring'.[16] It's like a compulsion.

Desdemona might seem exempt from these tinctured terms, but early in the twentieth century Cecilia Loftus was criticized for a Desdemona that was '[g]entle and sweet', but 'colorless'.[17] Kate Terry Gielgud repeated this cliché when she asked of an *Othello* at the Lyric Theatre in 1902, 'Is it again that the Desdemona is so wholly colourless as to make Othello's violence quite unpardonably crude?'[18] In Desdemona's defence, keeping her 'wholly colourless' is one point of the play, a point a venerable tradition has repeatedly, even compulsively emphasized.

One hundred and fifty years later, the venerable had become vulnerable. The 1964 National Theatre *Othello* at the Old Vic featured Laurence Olivier in black face, which prompted the reviewer cited above to lambast its minstrel memory. The production was filmed and released in America in 1965. If you watch the film today, you will note that by the end Olivier has begun to rub off on his Desdemona, Maggie Smith, as strikingly pale as Olivier is startlingly dark. There is a well-known photograph of Olivier with Smith in his arms – the infamous 'dirty still' – in which Olivier's makeup has left a smudge on Smith. When critics discussed the Olivier and Smith affair, they invariably describe the effect in the terms I just purposefully used: 'Othello has begun to rub off on Desdemona', the transfer of makeup blurring into sexual *frottage*. Though discreet, the daub upon Smith's forehead triggers the underlying panic, the famous 'one drop of black blood' anecdotally alchemized into a smudge of Max Factor.[19]

The experience of the black South African theatre artist John Kani aptly glosses this affair. Kani recalls playing Othello in 1987 in Cape Town, when he was detained and questioned by the police. In what must have been a bizarre interview, the police interrogated him about an act of textual interpretation: They asked him why he was kissing Desdemona on the lips when the script called only for a brief embrace. In a later interview, Kani recalls that, 'When Lord Olivier did this play with Maggie Smith, his black makeup kept rubbing off on her, so they couldn't exploit the love relationship.' A problem, he recalls, 'that I didn't have'. Kani suggests that in this case the technology of racial representation – the makeup – kept the bodies of Othello and Desdemona (of Olivier and Smith) from 'exploiting the love relationship', an instance where theatrical representation polices the same boundaries that Brabantio and the South African authorities were concerned to protect. As Kani suggests, the question of the makeup and its transfer onto the skin of Desdemona becomes tangled up in questions of the play's racial erotics. Kani's black skin 'solves' one problem of the play, but that does not make it go away. When Paul Robeson played Othello in 1943, Margaret Webster, its director, wrote in the programme: 'The white robes of the disputed Moor have been stained with every shade of grease-paint from burnt cork to cafe-au-lait.'[20] Even when Othello is played by a black man, the cosmetic question remains. At least for the South African police, however, even – or especially – when Othello is played by a black man, his relationship with Desdemona is dirty still.

Today, of course, Othello is not performed in blackface. We might think of Olivier's 1964 performance as a landmark and an end-point. Symbolically at least, his performance represents the last gasp of a nearly 400-year tradition of white men playing Othello in blackface. We might imagine that this tradition died a natural death, assisted by an emancipated sensitivity to the political perils of blackface. And yet. A certain critical tradition ascribes the change to the technical problems of makeup. Summarizing reactions to Olivier's film, a scholar writes, 'Olivier's Othello on the London stage in 1964 was coal black, and when some of his make up came off in touching the snow white Desdemona . . . critics questioned whether any white actor should ever take the role again.'[21] The notion here is that it was the transfer of the makeup alone that prompted critics to question the casting of a white man as Othello. The implication seems to be that if Olivier's makeup had been more adherent, had Maggie Smith's 'snow white' skin remained undisfigured by Othello's 'coal black' makeup, then a white man in blackface was perfectly fine. The necessary conclusion of this line of thinking is that the *real* reason that black men should play Othello is that they are permanently made up.

From *Othello*'s earliest illustrations to twentieth-century production stills, Othello's and Desdemona's collision has appealed to both graphic and anecdotal artists for the compositional austerity of dark and light. In an historical coincidence, colour photography became the norm around the time that blackface disappeared, though as Catherine Belsey points out, 'in the matter of cultural history there are very few coincidences'.[22] It is tempting to conclude from this convergence that the realistic representation of race onstage is not a triumph of realism, or of emancipated sensitivity, but one of mere technology. It seems that long after colour photography emerged and blackface performance receded, we continue to dream of *Othello* in terms of black and white.

Pillow talk

As suggested above, it is easy to read anecdotes about the 'smudge' as paraphrases of the play. And they are. But anecdotes do not just recite plays, they express something the play cannot. After all, the anecdotes above are largely redundant, capitulations to – and recapitulations of – the play's racial anxiety. That doesn't rule such readings out of court, but if anecdotes speak an event into the teeth of the eventual, we can turn to still others that riff on the play's remorseless drive to what Somerset Maugham calls the 'comprehensive conclusion': death. Anecdotes do not resign themselves to *Othello*'s foreclosed inevitability. They produce a comic 'this might happen' against the annihilating 'this must happen' of tragedy. Leave it to an anecdote to wring some laughter at the scene of a crime.

In fact, questions of makeup hover over *Othello*'s crime scenes, for however amorous things get between Othello and Desdemona, nowhere does the text more explicitly invite the actor to touch her than when he must kill her. (Kani does not mention whether the authorities questioned that.) Othello opens his final scene worried about the problem of how to kill Desdemona without scarring her skin. Othello's concern is about blood, but the actor's is just as pressing – how to keep his makeup off of Desdemona. Stopping her breath while saving her skin is therefore both a narrative worry and a technical one – a fusion that often breeds anecdotes.

Enter the pillow, which has become for *Othello* what Yorick's skull is to *Hamlet*, a central icon of the play that – along with the handkerchief – provides a simple, legible glyph that registers the play's complex entirety. Indeed, on the stage, it has become conventional to turn Desdemona's murder into a fatal pillow fight. Unlike Yorick's skull, however, the pillow is uncalled for. For however conventional today, the pillow was not always present. Indeed, it's hard to say exactly where it came from. The earliest stage directions suggest that Othello 'smothers' (F1 TLN 3342) or 'stifles' (Q1 TLN 3340) Desdemona. Othello stops Desdemona's breath, something he might do with his bare hands. Nevertheless, Othello has been pillowing Desdemona for centuries. Nicholas Rowe's 1709 illustration of *Othello* 5.2, for instance, shows a waist-coated Betterton pointing a pillow at Desdemona in a threatening manner. The image was rendered nearly a century after

Othello's initial production, and we cannot know whether it shows an historical, a contemporary, or a hypothetical staging.[23] At the least, it captures what has become a theatrical convention, one that solves the actor's perennial dilemma of what to do with his hands (while keeping them off Desdemona). Whatever its origins, the pillow cushions the cultural unease of watching Othello put his hand over Desdemona's mouth, of turning her black (though verisimilitude suggests that that is precisely what suffocation does). Bolstered by convention, Othello decorously lowers a pillow over Desdemona's face. Good night Desdemona, says fastidious convention, let her be hid. Most importantly, when the survivors lift the pillow, she'll be white still.

Anecdotes are seldom as tasteful. Driven by their own tacky mania, anecdotes often provide the punch lines that plays are too shy to deliver. *Othello* famously has something to hide, the spectre of its romantic couple coupling romantically in bed. And if a play has something to hide, an anecdote will always find it. A story that ricocheted through the pages of the early nineteenth century tells of a night when the infamous Lady Elizabeth Berkeley went to see *Othello*. The story exists in several versions, but all of them detail what it might look like when Othello and Desdemona finally slip between the sheets, providing a punch line to the play's running joke about their interrupted *coitus*:

> [T]he Margravine of Anspach had a seat in the neighbourhood of Newbury, and occasionally honoured Mr Thornton's Company with a bespeak. The play selected on this occasion was *Othello*, and Mr Thornton was of course the *Moor of Venice*. The heroine being strangled, the Margravine rose to retire – Mr Thornton . . . with a pair of wax candles, was in duty bound to bow her Highness to her carriage. A change of dress was out of the question: with candles elevated above his head, his sable visage, and his moorish apparel, he walked before his venerable visitor, bowing profoundly, and capering backward . . . when lo! a

> blast from envious Boreas rushed through the entry, and his wax-tapers were no longer *lights* . . . and nothing but her own bright orbs could possibly have guided the Lady to her carriage through the palpable obscure. Mr Thornton then very quietly retreated home, and, weary of his command at Cyprus, crept into bed, totally forgetful of the part he had performed, and consequently unaware that lampblack and pomatum (for the Moor in those days was a palpable Ethiopian) have but an indifferent sympathy with white sheets and coverlids. The astonishment of Mrs Thornton, when the peep of Aurora betrayed her sable bed-fellow with sheets and pillow-cases chequered like the keys of a piano, may be more easily imagined than expressed.[24]

There are three or possibly four jokes in here, depending how puerile your sense of humour is, not least one about what happens to a star when he twinkles off the stage. (You can walk her Highness to her carriage but you'll wake up with your wife.) There is in this anecdote, after all, just a glimmer of a chance that Thornton will wind up in Lady Berkeley's bed, lit only by her luminous orbs. Circling this anecdote like a carrion question is the nagging one of why it – or Othello for that matter – needs to put out the lights in the first place. Is it that it takes light to distinguish difference? Between an aristocrat and an actor, between a husband and a wife, between black and white? Anecdotes often discover the jokes that plays try to smuggle past us. Here, the gag is apparently the fact that everyone is black in the dark.

But not in the morning, as Aurora reveals. This anecdote gives us Act 6 of *Othello*, re-imagined as domestic farce. Unlike the play from which the anecdote issues, it wants to show what the play tries to hide. 'Happiness to their sheets!' cries Iago, but one man's happiness is another woman's nightmare. Even this anecdote can't bring itself to tell us what exactly Mrs Othello thinks on the morning-after-the-night-before. We are left to imagine what the eloquent sheets express. Let them be hid, or laundered at the least. Perhaps, in the end, the surest way to convert the romance of Othello and Desdemona from tragedy to farce is to turn their happy sheets into our dirty laundry.

Desdemona's beard

To be fair to Louis James, he did not exactly 'rub off' on his Desdemona. She was being played by his wife, after all – a detail I forgot to mention. James had a different exchange in mind. He rendered his wife black and *male*, which probably prompted a pillow fight of its own for James and his wife a bit later that night. Let's return to the anecdote: '[W]hen other actors came upon the scene and saw the face of Desdemona lying on the pillow wreathed in golden hair but disfigured by apparent hirsute tufts over her mouth and chin, they were convulsed with laughter and the effect of a great tragic scene was destroyed.' James 'dis-figures' Desdemona, disguising the tragic body of the white Desdemona as a comic body of a black man. In doing so, James destroys the 'great tragic scene' and scripts a different outcome, one right out of Shakespearean comedy in which a woman escapes suffocating male attention in the likeness of a boy. Like Celia in *As You Like It* – who smirches her face in umber as part of her male disguise – this anecdote offers Desdemona a comic out from her tragic end. In these anecdotes, Desdemona becomes Othello in more ways than just one.

Anecdotes often make a comedy of catastrophe and play the comic sidekick to thuggish tragedy. *Othello* anecdotes are not just a form of racial worry, then, but a comic antidote to it. Close and distant readers alike, from Susan Snyder to Michael Bristol to Stephen Orgel to Harry Berger, Jr, to, more recently, Jonathan Hope and Michael Witmore, have recognized the comic contours of *Othello*, which lurk like a hidden reef just below the surface. (Sometimes even the state intervenes. An anecdote reports that, 'Herr Schroder, a performer of great ability and an ardent lover of Shakespeare, in 1776 brought *Othello* in German on the stage at Hamburg. It was not a success, however; the close of the tragedy was much objected to, that the Hamburg senate commanded the *denouement* to be altered, and ordered that *Othello* should end happily.'[25]) If the comic potential of *Othello* is apparent to critics (and Hamburg senators) at local and global scales of language, structure, and plot, we can read these anecdotes as the actor's attempt – with the ink of his own face – to script a comic outcome he finds drafted in *Othello*. Louis James' *Othello* is a *fabliau* of alteration and escape. By changing Desdemona's gender, he changes *Othello*'s genre.

The anecdote doesn't alter *Othello* forever. It just provides some passing laughter. But if the anecdote is only a passing comedy, it's also a comedy *of* passing. For the anecdotes honour theatre's two-faced history, where men passed for women, where whites passed for blacks, and where actors pass for people. Desdemona's beard betokens theatre's ersatz history, its crazed fascination with the significant gap between reality and its resemblance – and the various technologies like beards and makeup that affect to close it. As so often, anecdotes arise to administrate – if not celebrate – difference. Anecdotal history insists, therefore, on treating Othello and Desdemona as a couple of big differences.

If Othello's makeup lets the theatre organize its racial anxieties, Desdemona's body lets it gather its thoughts about transvestism. Blacked up or dragged out, Desdemona is where Shakespeare's performance history giggles over the memory of the boy beneath the dress, where theatre memorializes its transvestite stage. For whether or not Desdemona was *in fact* the first part professionally played by a woman upon the English stage – and she probably was not – she is always the first actress in the anecdotal version of performance history.[26] Two hundred years after integration, in 1875, Charles Dickens recalled that

> a memorable representation of Othello took place at the Vere-street Theatre, Clare Market. As historians of the stage have related, there then appeared, for the first time upon the

> English stage, an English actress. A certain Mr Thomas Jordan provided for the occasion 'a prologue, to introduce the first woman that came to act on the stage in the tragedy called the Moor of Venice.' Desdemona was the part she played. The actress, it would seem, was Mrs Hughes. There can be little doubt that Emilia was also personated by a woman; but, in regard to that matter, history is altogether silent.[27]

History doesn't want to talk about Emilia. Desdemona is where the action is because Desdemona is where the actor was. The prologue Dickens refers to introduced Desdemona but reminds us that she's always been a man, albeit a defective one:

> The Woman playes to day, mistake me not . . .
> In this reforming age
> We have intents to civilize the Stage.
> Our women are defective, and so siz'd
> You'd think they were some of the Guard disguiz'd;
> For (to speak truth) men act, that are between
> Forty and Fifty, Wenches of fifteen;
> With bone so large, and nerve so incomplyant,
> When you call *Desdemona*, enter Giant[28]

As with the suggestion that black men should play Othello because they are permanently made up, here the stage's sexual integration is due not to a triumph of equal opportunity but to another technical failure. The men have grown too old and big to body Desdemona. It's not that women *should* play Desdemona, it's that men should not because they are so evidently men. Men make defective women, but then so do women, as Desdemona's anecdotal fortunes relate.

The concern that the boy beneath the dress has grown into a man produced one of the most famous anecdotes of Shakespeare's performance history, one centred on the body of the 'last' male actress when he played the 'first' woman actor. If ever there was an anecdote with hair on it, it is the 'shaving' story about Edward Kynaston, the Restoration actor whom theatre history celebrates as the last man mincing. In its broadest form, Kynaston's cue has come, but he's busy offstage shaving. Kynaston plays a number of different women in the anecdote's many versions – Desdemona, Juliet, Gertrude, Evadne in *The Maid's Tragedy* – but the punch line is always the same: The maid's tragedy is that she's a man. Percy Fitzgerald reports, for instance, that, 'It is known Kynaston played Juliet to Betterton's Romeo. . . . It is said that on one occasion Charles II enquiring the cause of a long "wait" was told by the manager that they . . . were waiting for the Queen to be shaved!'[29] (As so often, the story gets a detail badly wrong, or baldly so, since Juliet is no queen. Fitzgerald interpolates two versions into one, since an anecdote exists in which the play is *Hamlet* and Kynaston Gertrude.) A more pertinent version was told by Henry Irving to a reporter from the *Toronto World* in 1895. Irving substitutes Desdemona for Juliet while pedantically claiming his rights to the tale:

> There is a good story of Kineston [sic] conducting a rehearsal of 'Othello.' Desdemona was missing and the manager called for her. 'Please, sir,' said a suer. 'Desdemona's away shaving.' Have you heard that story?

The reporter replies:

> Yes, I think I read it in Fitzgerald's 'Theatrical Anecdotes.'

Irving:

> Oh! He got the story from me. It is an old one of mine.[30]

The exchange conveys the hurly-burly of hearsay and print by which anecdotes traverse time. Perhaps Fitzgerald got it from Irving, but Irving got it from someone else since the anecdote appeared in *The Morning Herald* in 1791. Anecdotes are always second-hand, especially when they are original: '*Kynaston* was once the cause of considerable interruption in a play, at which King Charles was present. His Majesty became impatient, and demanded the reason of the delay – One of the actors very innocently told him, that *Desdemona* had not been *shaved* in time.'[31]

The plays change names, but the punch line stays the same. It also remains plangent. As with Jordan's reference to men of fifty playing wenches of fifteen, the joke mourns the boy actors lost in the interregnum. It memorializes the boy that Henry Jackson saw at Oxford in 1610, who 'moved us especially in her death when, as she lay on her bed, her face itself implored the pity of the audience.'[32] Jackson famously uses the feminine pronoun, not seeing – or choosing not to see, or seeing perceptively – the boy beneath the body. Ironically, once women took to the stage, anecdotes seem determined to remind us that the boy is still there, that Desdemona is always male, especially when she's played by a woman.

If Desdemona is the theatre's first actress, however, she is also its first victim. Anecdotes hint that the conditions are one and the same. On one hand, Jordan's complaint that 'our women are defective' sounds like a wistful memory of the good old days when men were men and so were the women. Jordan's defective 'women' are the big-bodied men too large for Desdemona. At the same time, his present tense voices an antagonism toward women actors, who are defective women because they are not men. (After all, the alternative to males of forty or fifty used to be boys of fourteen or fifteen. Now, alas, boys will be boys, men will be men, and women women, diminishing the differences in which anecdotes delight.) When anecdotes grudgingly allow women to play Desdemona, therefore, it is often for one night only. Of his Stratford *Othello*, Frank Benson recalls, 'A lady wishing to book seats for a second performance came back to the box-office to apologize for her stupidity: "Because, of course, as Desdemona died on Monday night there can be no performance given by her on Tuesday".'[33] A martyr to misogyny, Desdemona sacrifices herself for the sake of a woman stupid enough to want to make a habit of the theatre.

Unsurprisingly, tales of Desdemona bristle with snuff, as anecdotes bare their teeth at the demise of the all-male stage. In a grisly account from 1824, the lunatic patriarch of the Booth clan, Junius Brutus, shows up for work in a bloody mood:

> About 11 o'clock on Saturday he was in the entrance of the Theatre, conversing with Mr Woodhull, when suddenly, but with an air of calmness, he said to Mr Woodhull, 'I must cut somebody's throat today, & whom shall I take?' . . . Miss Johnson, in *Desdemona*, certainly ran a risk of being murdered by the jealous Moor in good earnest, and may felicitate herself upon her escape.[34]

We're not told how Johnson escaped Booth's blade, but roughing-up Desdemona is part of *Othello*'s lore. Another time, 'while playing Othello, he [Booth] bore down so heavily with the pillow on the Desdemona, that she was in danger of her life, and was only rescued from suffocation by the other actors, who rushed upon the stage to save her'.[35] The unfunny alternative to the decorous pillow is captured by a critic in 1905, who recalled that Salvini's Othello 'dragged Desdemona about by the hair in the mad frenzy of a jealous animal'.[36] Madge Kendal remembers in her 1890 memoirs that Ira Aldridge, the 'African Roscius', used to 'take Desdemona out of bed by her hair and drag her around the stage before he smothered her'.[37] These two instances obviously alienate the Italian Salvini and the black American Aldridge from the decorous behaviour of native English actors (use a pillow, for heaven's sake), but the supine Desdemona is the anecdote's silent victim. From drag to dragged, Desdemona is the site where anecdotes take out theatre history's resentment at the introduction of women to the stage.

Anecdotes will admit women to the stage, therefore, just so long as they play dead. Desdemona makes her appearance, for instance, in the venerable annals of 'last exit' anecdotes, where actors expire after giving their last breath to Shakespeare.

Edmund Kean famously collapsed after issuing Othello's 'farewell' and was borne off the stage on the back of Charles his son, who began the night playing Iago to his father's Othello and ended it giving Aeneas to his Anchises. Less celebrated is Mrs Pope of Drury Lane, who was 'seized with an apoplectic fit, when performing in the character of *Desdemona*. The second attack of this disorder proved fatal', the result, according to the surgeon, 'of her professional exertions'.[38] Pope stayed perfectly 'in the character of *Desdemona*' by dying. Cause of death: acting.

Other anecdotes beautify Desdemona's death, celebrating the way that death becomes her. Samuel Pepys conflates two female beauties when he records a visit to see *Othello*, during which 'a very pretty lady that sat by me, called out, to see Desdemona smothered'.[39] One pretty lady wants the other one dead, inverting the play's triangulated male envy, recorded to be later savoured by the theatre's leading connoisseur of erotic memorabilia (Pepys's theatrical memories are all first-hand accounts). By not being a man, Desdemona's body leaves something to be desired, and what the theatre desires is her death. Channelling Othello, a critic in 1888 reacted to Minna Gale's Desdemona in repose, concluding that, 'if one looked as pretty after one was smothered as did this special *Desdemona*, it might prove that, if marriage was a failure, death certainly was a success'.[40] Like Jackson's recollection of 1610, the review is a form of necrophilia. Nothing becomes Desdemona – or an actress it seems – like when she plays dead.

These various anecdotes suggest that the only good actress is a dead one, and emerge from a play that suggests the same about a wife. At the same time, these anecdotes refract the strange ambiguity of what it means to 'pass'. We speak of the deceased as having 'passed' on just as we speak of black men who 'pass' as white or a female who 'passes' as male. The liminality of these strange passings marry in the body of a Desdemona who is black and dead not quick and white. Anecdotes ultimately exchange one kind of passing for another, then. Blackened or bearded, dragged in or snuffed out, Desdemona's body consolidates the anger of the all-male, all-white stage at having to integrate the Player's Club. Sometimes anecdotes fill in a hole left in a play, but in doing so they dig another, which, for Desdemona, turns out to be her grave. One way to doom Desdemona is to black-and-beard her face and accuse her of a sex crime. She's marked for death since makeup, in the words of Simon Callow, 'is a dying art'.[41]

Othello and Desdemona are, then, the first couple of theatre history, its primary proxies of prosthetic difference. The anecdotes are there to remind us of the central dynamic behind every performance of *Othello*, that blackness is a cover up. Even when black actors play Othello, the anecdotes insist that the face is white beneath. And even when women play Desdemona, she's always on the verge of sprouting a beard. *Othello* is, among many other things, a pageant about theatrical integration, a subject of profound anecdotal ambivalence. Taken together, anecdotes about Othello's smudge and Desdemona's beard remind us that Othello was originally a white man, but then so was Desdemona – a nudge and a wink to the boys in the back that, in the words of the old song, I've got you under my skin.

Another man

By bearding Desdemona, anecdotes introduce yet another man to *Othello*, increasing the geometrical complexity of a play latticed with desire. Like so many of Shakespeare's comedies, *Othello* produces a romantic problem of supply and demand – too many men, too few women. Cassio passed between Othello and Desdemona when they wooed, a shadow of a plot to which we all know the outcome – including Iago the diabolical dramaturge. Roderigo, Iago and an unspecified number of curled darlings also long for Desdemona. Whomever Desdemona affects, there is always another man waiting in the wings. Or under the bed, according to James Stoddart, who remembers the time that '[Edward] Sothern played the *Moor*, and was imperfect in the words; in the last scene he had a prompter concealed under *Desdemona*'s bed.'[42] (There's another joke here, of course; the cartoon caption, 'Prompter? I hardly know her!') But the anecdote fleshes out Othello's fantasy of catching Desdemona red-handed. Worse, he has the script. Once again, an anecdote gives us what the play frets about.

There is, figuratively speaking, always another man under Desdemona's bed. It's not Desdemona he wants. She's just a Macguffin for what all actors crave: to be the leading man. This may seem like a settled matter today, but as Edward Pechter points out, 'Iago's domination of *Othello* has gone on for so long that it might seem like an empirically defined fact of the play's matter rather than an interpretatively derived artifact of its meaning.'[43] In other words, Othello is not alone in wondering who is Desdemona's leading man. Over the ages, anecdotes have paltered over which is the better role. When Frederick Cooke and John Philip Kemble got together to dole out parts between themselves, and quarrelled over Hamlet, '*Iago*, and *Othello* . . . were easily agreed upon, being equal parts.'[44] Kemble and Cooke rarely agreed, and this point of consensus is the rarer still, since history hasn't come to the same conclusion. Even when Desdemona does not explicitly appear in stories of rival actors, she is there disguised as stardom.

Richard Burton, for one, had no doubt which was the better part when he alternated Othello and Iago at the Old Vic in the 1960s.

> One Saturday lunchtime Burton was invited to attend a charity cricket match organized by the Lord's Taverners. Amongst the group was a young actor, Ian Carmichael. . . . 'We had all downed a considerable number of pints,' recalls Carmichael. 'And my turn had come round once more. "Same again?" I enquired of all concerned. I then said to Burton, "Shall I skip you this time?" Burton stared back at me. "Why

> the hell not!" "You've got a matinee, haven't you?" I asked. "Yes," said Burton, "but it's only Iago this afternoon."'[45]

Burton's pint made his point. It's 'only Iago', whom Burton could play on his head, or off it. Burton's might have been a minority opinion, however, since another anecdote relates the woes of a 'prominent British Othello of this century' (the twentieth), who found himself consistently cashiered by his Iago. He ran into trouble when he

> took an acting company into the provinces – a good company, with a particularly talented Iago to give the show balance. At the first stop, Iago drew all the rave reviews. The Moor promptly disengaged himself of this evil man, and for his next booking took a rather less competent Iago. This substitute also proved a villain and drew the best notices, and again the injured Moor rid himself of his crafty Ancient. For the next stop, he protected himself by giving the Iago role to an untried stage hand. This time, when the reviews came out, all the critics' good words were still for the villain. The distinguished actor capitulated. He engaged the best Othello he could find, and took the part of Iago for himself, and basked in glowing notices for the rest of the tour.[46]

If you can't beat them, fire them. Olivier had more success at the National in 1964, when he insisted a low-charisma actor, Frank Finlay, be cast opposite him as Iago. On one hand, the anecdotes simply calibrate the play: Iago makes Othello jealous. But the anecdote spins another narrative out of the play's triangulations. For despite what the story says, this prominent Othello did not want a balancing act, he wanted a one-man show. Desdemona holds the spotlight for which Iago and Othello compete, a cynosure for fame, as another anecdote about an old campaigner reveals:

> [O]ne night [Edmund Kean] played 'Othello' with more than his usual intensity. An admirer who met him in the

> street the next day was loud in his congratulations: 'I really thought you would have choked Iago, Mr. Kean – you seemed so tremendously in earnest.' 'In earnest!' said the tragedian. 'I should think so! Hang the fellow, he was trying to keep me out of the focus.'[47]

The problem with a triangle is that it's difficult to balance. It has no single focus, and so the point can never be finally resolved as to whom Desdemona most favours. Sometimes it's easiest just to call it a tie, as another story about Kean suggests. Beginning, as so often, in and with high spirits, the anecdote resolves into imprecision about who will be the last man standing:

> One evening [F.T. Bass and Edmund Kean] had been dining together and the bottle had been passed too freely. They got through the play, however, without their condition being discovered by the audience until they came to the scene in the third act in which Othello seizes Iago by the throat and delivers the speech beginning, 'Villain, be sure thou prove,' etc. Kean, who on this occasion was the Othello, as he spoke, grasped Iago so fiercely that, being somewhat unsteady on his legs, he fell, dragging his companion down with him. This accident confused them both, and, when they regained their feet, Kean, instead of waiting for Bass to continue the dialogue, himself uttered the exclamation, 'Is it come to this?' which properly belongs to Iago. Bass, who was 'letter perfect' in either part, took the cue, and went on with that of Othello. For a moment or two the audience were not a little puzzled by the interchange of characters; but as soon as the real facts of the case dawned on them, they appreciated to the full the absurdity of the situation, and the remainder of the scene – usually listened to in breathless silence – was greeted with frequent peals of laughter. Both actors were alike surprised and disgusted at the merriment they caused. Kean in particular was in a towering rage. Anger in some measure sobered him. Still he

> had no suspicion of the blunder he had been guilty of, and when he quitted the stage he made his way hastily to the greenroom. As he entered the apartment, however, the reflection of his bronzed visage and Moorish garments in a small mirror over the mantelpiece caught his eye, and, turning to his fellow-actor, he abruptly exclaimed, 'By heavens! Bass, I'm Othello!' 'Of course you are!' was the response. 'Then why the deuce did you assume my character?' was the angry query. 'Because you on the first instance took mine, and being as drunk as you were, I simply followed your lead.' Kean was about to make a furious rejoinder to this retort when suddenly, the humorous side of the incident striking him, the heavy frown which had gathered on his brow relaxed, and, bursting into a hearty fit of laughter, he said, 'Well after all, I believe it was as much my fault as yours. But I fancy we shall find the people in front in no very appreciative humour during the remainder of the evening.'[48]

The story could have chosen any one of Shakespeare's buddy tragedies – *Julius Caesar*, *Hamlet*, *Macbeth* – but the fact that the anecdote chose to tickle *Othello* reveals the quantum characteristic of its complementary leads, who wish to pass as one another. Whatever role one actor has he always wants the other. In addition to the inverted spectacle of a black Iago and a white Othello – a negative of the play – the anecdote makes it clear that the point of a triangle is that it has three points, and so every cat is also a mouse.

Across *Othello*'s history, anecdotes blossom around the rim of a triangle that runs through another man. When she was in Irving's arms, Ellen Terry longed for Booth. So, probably, did Irving. Even when she's bodily absent from these tales, Desdemona is the vehicle that actors use to drive each other crazy. In the end these stories give the actor's answer to the question that has bedevilled centuries of *Othello* criticism. Iago's 'motiveless malignity' is all too palpably clear. He wants to play Othello.

The impossible fix

Sometimes anecdotes blossom, at other times they blister. *Othello*'s been rubbing us the wrong way for over 400 years. Maybe it's the friction between theatre's means and *Othello*'s end, rubbed up by the embarrassment of blackface makeup. Maybe anecdotes form the blush that black face tries to hide. For if anecdotes clarify difference they just as often tend to embarrassment. This happens in the theatre when there's a significant gap between the thing that something is and the thing it tries to be. Shakespeare's performance history is full of such things: Hamlet's ghost, Richard's hump, Falstaff's fat, Othello's face. Anecdotes are on hand when things go wrong, and a lot can go wrong in the space between things, including the space between the first and second skin. This chapter opened with stories about makeup that comes too easily off, but another rash of anecdotes record the anxiety (or fantasy, there's such a fine line . . .) about the other problem. And if the laughter is anxious when the makeup comes off, it's downright nervous when it won't.

In his efforts to fix his uncertain makeup, Frank Benson recalls in his memoir that he would use 'permanganate of potash, with the result that I remained of dusky hue for weeks on end'.[49] Benson commits to keeping his makeup on (and off his Desdemona) and thereby commits to Othello for an extended run, which presumably kept him from playing other parts unless he chose to white up his blackened face (keep that up for long enough and you'll forget yourself). Blackfaced Othellos find themselves in an impossible fix: keeping Desdemona white means keeping themselves black. Exposing themselves either to embarrassment or the sting of racial hatred, white actors of Othello are damned if they do, and damned if they don't.

Spranger Barry learned this lesson in an anecdotal version of Marcel Marceau's nightmare about the mask that won't come off. In yet another hairy story, a barber visits the theatre to deliver a wig and forlornly wanders the wings, where he runs into an exercised moor:

> The barber made his appearance at the wing in the midst of Othello's address, and protruded his body so far as to become visible to half the house. The sudden glare of lights and human faces at first astounded, and then transported him and there being no one in the way to remove him, he soon excited the risibility of the pit by his gestures and grimaces. The Moor was not of a more fiery temperament than Barry, who attributed this intrusion to design, particularly when flashing his face fully upon the fellow, and interlarding his oration with side speeches, they, instead of effecting his removal, served only to stupefy and root him more firmly to the spot . . . To these several pointed addresses the barber yielded no other response than 'Go to the devil!' which was loud enough, however, to be heard in the first row of the pit. Barry now concluded this to be a scheme on the part of Garrick, to ruffle and insult him; and when he quitted the stage, rushed on the unconscious criminal with all the fury of a hungry hyaena, grasped him by the throat, shook him most unmercifully, and would no doubt have proceeded to determine how far the barber's head resembled one of his own blocks, when the actors interposed, and set the man at liberty. Growling, and shaking himself like a tousled cur, he looked at Barry an instant with a smile of ineffable contempt, and then exclaimed, 'Never mind, Master Sambo, – never mind – I'll do your business for you, depend on it!' – 'Do my business, you villain!' shouted Barry, 'what do you mean?' – 'Why, you black rascal!' said the barber (evidently mistaking Othello for a *bona fide* Moor), 'I'll speak to Mr. Fawcett, and have you discharged!'[50]

Barry's immersion in *Othello*'s leading role exposes him to its paradox – to pass as a *bona fide* Moor is to risk being treated like one. Subject to a fusillade of racial taunts – 'devil', 'Sambo', 'black rascal' – Barry encounters yet another peril of Othello. In this case, erasing the significant gap between the thing you are and the thing you're pretending to be can have serious consequences. He learns in a moment a lesson the play takes five acts to drive home. It does not matter how big a star you are, once you insult someone who's white all they can see is black. This anecdote beats the rush and teaches Barry that the Moor is treated equably until he behaves 'like a Moor', after which he's treated like a Moor. In his role as Othello, Barry was often praised; in his role as a Moor he is damned.

Barry had run into this problem before, of being so black you could not see him act, as the critic quoted earlier complained. As the blackface separates Barry from himself, we hear a whisper of a shadow of an echo in these anecdotes of the actor's primal scene, in which he gets to watch himself perform. These passing anecdotes indulge themselves in another fantasy then – the chance to watch yourself act. To bring in, for a moment, a ubiquitous non-Shakespearean anecdote as a gloss, one afternoon,

> Wilfrid Lawson took Richard Burton around to a local pub just before a matinee performance of a play in which Lawson was appearing. Since he wasn't required on stage during the early part of the first act, Lawson settled into the stalls with Burton to watch the opening scenes like any other audience member. Finally, Lawson tapped Burton on the shoulder and said, 'You'll like this bit. This is where I come on.'[51]

The anecdote dead-ends here, of course, the ultimate example of the anecdote's carelessness of consequence. Lawson can't go on, and so neither can the anecdote (or the play of course), but it concisely captures the limits of self-awareness while flirting with the fantasy of watching oneself play. In 1909, according to *Harper's Weekly*, Edwin Booth was mistaken for a Moor and got what he called the most 'candid tribute he ever received'. As usual, it's the bar room where theatre becomes anecdotal, and where Booth discovers that praise for a Moor is always faint, and therefore always damned:

> We opened our engagement in Atlanta, Ga., with 'Othello,' said Mr Booth, 'and I played Othello. After the performance my friend, Mr Malone, and I went to the Kimball House for some refreshment. The long bar was so crowded that we had to go around the corner of it before we could find a vacant space. While we were waiting to be served we couldn't help hearing the conversation of two fine looking old boys, splendid old fellows with soft hats, flowing mustaches, and chin tufts, black string ties and all the other paraphernalia. 'I didn't see you at the theatre this evening, Cunnel,' said one. 'No,' replied the other. 'I didn't buy seats till this mawnin', and the best we could get were six rows back in the balcony. I presume, suh, you were in the orchestra.' 'Yes, Cunnel, I was in the orchestra,' said the first man. 'Madame and the girls were with me. We all agreed that we nevuh attended a mo' thrillin' play. The company was good, too; excellent company. And you know, Cunnel, in my opinion that d—d nigguh did about as well as any of 'em!'[52]

In the final line, *Harper's* leaves out what we would leave in but forthrightly prints what we would expurgate. The punch line delivered to the 'Cunnel' thus captures the shifting history of what offends a polite readership. Booth calls it a 'candid tribute', however, not just because he passed for that which he only played but also because the praise was not meant for his ears. After all, he was there disguised as himself. But these anecdotes articulate a fantasy that blackface releases, since it doubles the chances of an actor getting to face off with his uncanny other.

Edmund Kean came the closest to finding out just what happens when an Othello wears his mask off stage, of being taken all too seriously. And if Booth got the chance to overhear a candid tribute, Kean nearly got to read about his own funeral. In the 1820s, Edmund Kean conducted a notorious affair with the wife of a London citizen, 'Alderman Cox', whose subsequent lawsuit titillated the public. It turned out, for instance, that 'Kean gave Mrs Cox the name of "Little Breeches" . . . by reason of his having presented her with a sailor's uniform, in which she often arrayed herself when she accompanied her paramour in an amourous [sic] excursion. The "breeches," it is said, sat particularly elegant on the limber frame of Mrs. Cox.'[53] The games people play. Kean's libidinous reputation had preceded him on the stage before. One critic of his Othello sniffed, 'We pitied poor Mrs West [Desdemona] from our hearts. Whenever Kean touched her (and it is a degradation to undergo his touch), his wolfish friends applauded loudly.'[54] Kean survived that review, but was nearly not so lucky when he visited Boston. A biographer describes the city's reaction to Kean's 'infamous' behaviour in London:

> 'Oh, damn his soul!' screamed the audience, who rushed on the stage and into the dressing-rooms seeking Kean for what purpose they themselves presumably did not know. Mayor Quiney was called to quell the riot, and in the mean time, without pausing to wash off the makeup of Othello, which he was to have played that awful night, Kean fled to New York. There, next day, he read in the *National Advocate* of his disgrace, coupled to such epithets as 'coward' and 'double-faced beggar.'[55]

The story synopsizes a familiar American narrative. Damned by the audience, Kean beats a blackfaced retreat. There's more than a suggestion in the newspaper's account that if they catch him the audience will lynch him for the crime of seducing a white woman. Split in two, Kean's white face reads what his black face did, and came face-to-face with an end that Othello's self-slaughter forestalls. Had Othello *not* made off with himself, he would have faced the wrath of a Venetian audience who would have damned more than his soul.

A number of *Othello* anecdotes pivot around the reaction of an audience to Othello's handling of Desdemona – the verb 'paw' shows up with depressing regularity – so it is surprising to discover the popularity of the play in the ante-bellum American South. In fact, the play was performed on all

Southern stages up to the Civil War, running a close fourth behind *Richard III*, *Macbeth* and *Hamlet*. For example, Charleston, South Carolina, saw sixty-three *Othello*'s from the earliest in 1809 through to one late in 1860. It was performed in Memphis twenty times between 1837 and 1858; forty-one times in Mobile, Alabama from 1832 until 1860; twenty-two times from 1846 through 1860 in Louisville, Kentucky; and in New Orleans it averaged more than one and a half performances annually through 1860 – no idea why one would want to produce just half an *Othello*, but then I'm not a statistician. It might seem odd that this play – of all plays – would gain such traction in the ante-bellum South, but then one is tempted to adapt a line from the play itself and conclude that the Southern audience was in love with what it feared to look on.

For all its popularity, *Othello* often brings out the mob in us. It is not, however, in the major cities of the American South that anecdotes about violent audiences most often sprout. Instead, the play features prominently in tales of the American West, particularly rough-and-rowdy towns where an audience can be relied upon to be both armed and credulous. Edwin Forrest, for instance, 'had an eventful time, playing Shakespereian [*sic*] tragedy – *Richard*, *Othello* – low comedy, negro dandies'.[56] I don't *think* that '*Richard, Othello* – low comedy, negro dandies' is meant to be an apposition, but Western American audiences usually reacted more violently to Iago's mischief than to Othello's mien. For instance, if Edmund Booth was flattered when one man mistook his Othello for the real thing, his Iago received a similar review in a mining camp in California:

> Mr Edwin Booth says that the most genuine compliment he ever received was on the occasion of his playing Iago for the first time at Grass Valley, then a new mining camp. The audience, which had not seen a play for years, was so much incensed at his apparent villainy that they pulled out their 'shooters' in the middle of the third act and began blazing away at the stage. Othello had the tip of his nose shot off at

> the first volley, and Mr Booth only escaped by rolling over and over up the stage and disappearing through a trap-door. A speech from the manager somewhat calmed the house; but even then Mr Booth thought it best to pass the night in the theatre, as a number of the most elevated spectators were making strenuous efforts to turn out and lynch 'the infernal sneaking cuss,' as they called him.[57]

Booth claims to have been complimented by both the incidents recounted here, but whether he was playing Othello or Iago he also discovered the perils of trying to pass for the night in a theatre. Other stories find audience members promising to 'pistol' Iago for his 'infamous' behaviour 'just as soon as he leaves the stage', demonstrating the equilibrium of scepticism that Stanley Cavell finds the play requires. Here, the fact that the audience 'had not seen a play in years' accounts for their difficulty in distinguishing between villainy that is real and that which is only apparent. Once again, however, the anecdote delivers what the play will not – wild justice for Iago's villainy, which the play promises to provide but only after the curtain's closed. The threat of a lynch mob returns us to Edmund Kean, and recalls to us the fact that *Othello* is a play that requires but punishes credulity. The inconsequential nature of the anecdotes assures us, however, that neither Kean nor Booth were actually hung, leaving us strung out between the suspension of disbelief and our disbelief in suspension.

That Edmund Kean preferred Mrs Cox in a breeches role turns the whole episode into one of the stories that's just too good to be true, which is just the way that theatre likes its double-faced history. Sometimes when things are too good to be true, it's because they aren't. While that proposition does not faze this book's project, it allows us to see, here, how an arch anecdote evolves out of and away from the play it hedges – and about the way that a seventeenth-century English play produces a nineteenth-century American adaptation. A black man who hops a train before he's run out of town on a rail by a mob outraged at his sexual adventures has more to do with us than with *Othello*. But the collision of Kean's offstage antics with his onstage role produces a tale that polices the limits of *Othello*'s appeal as well as its many uses. Escorted through history by attendant anecdotes, *Othello* presents a racial pageant while pretending to talk about makeup.

Sometimes that makeup slips, and sometimes it sears. Henry Irving recalls

> an incident which throws an interesting sidelight on the way in which the actors made up in those days, for it would be impossible in these days, when the materials for making-up have been so improved. The Iago was very hoarse, so he mixed a lot of red pepper with some whisky for a gargle. He had used most of it when the Othello, who dressed in the same room, entered to prepare for the performance. Seeing the red stuff in the tumbler, he thought it was the mixture of Armenian Bole which he was in the habit of using to darken his face. He took some of it, mixed it with grease, and applied it to his face. It acted like a mustard-plaster, and even when it was removed and the ordinary makeup substituted, the irritation . . . was terrible; but the actor had to endure it all the evening.[58]

In this story, the makeup retails a blistered history of *Othello* in performance. We imagine that our makeup has improved, but *Othello* can still get under our skin.

One moor

As noted above, when Frank Benson played Othello in Stratford-upon-Avon, he ran into the usual makeup mix-up: 'Sometimes,' Benson recalls, 'they complained that Desdemona was black at the end of the play and that Othello was white.'[59] Benson reveals what the others don't, that as Desdemona grows increasingly black, Othello grows decreasingly so. Othello the blackamoor becomes half-a-moor, but then so does Desdemona.

We recall that Kemble left 'one side' of Miss Satchell's face 'quite black', which, presumably, left one side of his own quite white, turning them both into double-faced beggars that were just asking for laughter. Ellen Terry leaves it unsaid as well, but if she was as black as Irving, he was as white as she. With every ardent act Othello becomes white, and with every osculation Desdemona becomes black. *Othello*'s racial economy turns out to be zero-sum. There can only be one moor.

Unlike the early modern idea of washing the Ethiope white, expressed in forms like Ben Jonson's *Masque of Blackness* (1605), where blackness simply evaporates under the benign radiance of the king, in theatrical practice, either Desdemona or Othello is black, or both, but not neither. There is a definite quantity of blackness in the play that must be distributed across the bodies of Othello and Desdemona. In these anecdotes, the blackness has to go *somewhere*, hence the obsession with restricting it to its proper body, to preventing it from spreading, particularly to the body of the white woman playing Desdemona. This strain of anecdote reveals the relentless racial arithmetic of *Othello* – one plus one equals one. After all, Othello is not *a* moor of Venice, he is *the* moor of Venice – as far as the play knows, the only living moor in the world (even Shylock gets Tubal – even Aaron makes one moor). Othello is not a member of a racial category, he is a racial category, a category of one or, in other words, not a category at all: in other words, a freak.

The collision between white skin and black face shadows a fear of the 'monstrous' birth such exotic collisions produce. In the introduction, I suggested that anecdotes express unexpressed elements in Shakespeare's plays, ones the play cannot or will not or does not pursue. No play labours harder than *Othello* to evoke but suppress what might come of its central couple, and of their coupling. The product of Othello and Desdemona's always deferred union is forecast in the mulatto issue of these anecdotes – of a biracial Othello and Desdemona becoming one another and therefore creating some creolized other. Collisions between the made-up and the real produce a form of wishful thinking but simultaneously contain it. *Othello*'s onstage collisions perform their own limits: however black Desdemona becomes, however white Othello, they will never add up to more than one.

I don't wish to belabour the wishful thinking that produces *Othello*'s many masques of blackness. But just one more, and then an end. Edmund Kean's Boston audience rushed the stage in outrage, ready to do they knew not what, but one night Charles Macready felt a rush of love. If anxiety is a longing for what we fear, *Othello*'s anecdotes are always anxious parables about loving Othello too well.

> On the last night of Macready's engagement at Paris, he performed Othello, and when he was called before the curtain a vast number of his French audience leaped on the stage and overwhelmed him with embraces. This *epanchement du coeur*, as they would have called it, brought its inconveniences, and many faces showed the effects of their contact with that of the Moor.[60]

From Macready's side of the frontier – in front of the curtain but still on stage – he might have wondered whether the audience came to love him or to lynch him. Your French would have to be pretty good to know that this rush of blood came from the heart.

The story flirts with the idea of racial dilution through the vector of cosmetic diffusion, but within the ludicrous arithmetic of racial divisions – 1/2, 1/4, 1/8, etc. – the anecdote will never add up to more than one. Unlike the *Masque of Blackness*, in which black assimilates itself into a white nothingness, Macready's mask of blackness won't simply evaporate. In an inversion of Jonson's masque, Macready washes the audience black. Remember Mrs Thornton's pillow, chequered like the keys of a piano? The anecdote does to Mrs Thornton's pillow what anecdotes do to *Othello*: turn an instrument of infinite possibilities into a binocular spectacle of black and white.

3

Romeo and Juliet: Central casting

Be some other name

In 1744, the forty-one-year-old Theophilus Cibber played Romeo opposite a fourteen-year-old actress named Jenny, which prompted some mixed reviews. David Garrick wrote that he had 'never heard so vile and scandalous a performance in my life . . . the girl, I believe, may have genius; but unless she change her preceptor [her Romeo] she must be entirely ruined.'[1] The theatrical scribbler John Hill went even further, writing that he pitied poor Jenny for having to play opposite a 'person whom we could not but remember, at every sentence she delivered concerning him, to be too old for her choice, too little handsome to be in love with, and, into the bargain, her father'.[2] I should have mentioned that.

While this seems creepy today it's far from anomalous. *Romeo and Juliet*, a play famously focused on a couple with problematically *different* last names, has, for much of its performance history, featured actors who share the same one. It puts a different spin on Juliet's well-known plea: 'Oh be some *other* name.'

Over the last 400 years this quintessential play of young heterosexual love has featured fathers playing to their daughters, mothers to their sons, daughters to their mothers, brothers to their sisters, sisters to their sisters, two Romeos to one Juliet, six Juliets to one Romeo, men playing to men, women to women, and even the most polymorphously perverse of all possible casting choices, a husband playing to his wife.

The play is somewhat unique among Shakespeare's canon in featuring such odd couples. We find little like it in the cast lists of Shakespeare's other power couples – Antony and Cleopatra, Gertrude and Claudius, Brutus and Cassius .... Something about *Romeo and Juliet* seems not just to beckon for such casting but to be positively asking for it. When Covent Garden staged an 1814 after-piece to the play called 'Brother and Sister', they not only flirted with redundancy but also encapsulated the play's performance history, which will seemingly do whatever it takes to keep its star-crossed lovers crossed by its stars.[3]

For much of its history, then, the play has prompted among its producers something very like what it suggested to John Ford in *'Tis Pity She's a Whore* (1629), which essentially recasts Romeo and Juliet as brother and sister. What occurred to Ford, and many thereafter, is that star-crossed lovers are okay, but star-crossed siblings are a scandal. Ford cannily corrected Shakespeare's juvenile tragedy ('juvenile' not because its protagonists are so young but because its catastrophe hinges on a postal boner). The production history of *Romeo and Juliet* – abetted by a team of chuckling anecdotes – has attempted to do for the play what it won't do for itself: provide the scandal that Shakespeare leaves out. *Romeo and Juliet*'s anecdotal history is therefore marked by octogenarian Romeos and adolescent Juliets, by murdered Mercutios and rival Romeos, by pregnant and nursing Juliets, and by the enduring theatrical question of how high to set the balcony.

The anecdotes all perform the same work, however. They 'correct' for the play's structural oddity, and in so doing unwittingly tap its source. For Shakespeare's principal source,

Arthur Brooke's novella *Romeus and Juliet,* treats the 'unhonest desire' of 'unfortunate lovers' who by means of an 'unhonest life' hasten to the tragic end of an 'unhappy death'. There is little 'unhonest' about the desire between Shakespeare's leading teens. True, they circumvent their parents' wishes. We don't usually call that, 'tragic'; we usually call it, 'Friday night'. John Ford ratcheted up the conflict by separating *his* central couple not by different names, but by the same one – the first couple in history to divorce over irreconcilable similarities – and the performance history of *Romeo and Juliet* has followed Ford ever since.

While it's hard to know what audiences across the ages have thought about incestuous casting, criticism of the mid-nineteenth-century's greatest Romeo, Charlotte Cushman, who performed opposite her sister Susan, provides a signal instance. Reviewing the Cushmans' *Romeo and Juliet*, George Fletcher objected to the 'disgustingly monstrous grossness of such a perversion'. Makes you sorry you missed it. But Fletcher's revulsion at the Cushman family players is precisely what Ford tried to provoke with *'Tis Pity*, a vasovagal reflux at the play's perversions. The irony should speak for itself, but I won't let it. Here it is the casting – not the play – that draws the outrage that Romeo and Juliet's coupling fails to elicit. It takes incestuous casting to turn reviewers into Tybalts, to make us raise our eyebrows rather than stifle yawns at the story of two teenagers sparking in the dark.

Audiences obviously adore the play – as its robust performance record reveals – but the theatre seems annoyed with its central couple, as though there's something irritating about the transcendental idealism of Romeo and Juliet's mutual love. Perhaps it's the play's hasty attempts to normalize relations between the red-hot lovers, to convert erotic fascination into sanctioned wedlock. According to at least one anecdote, the Friar 'is the part which SHAKESPEARE himself, according to tradition, used to perform'.[4] Even if this isn't so, Shakespeare is figuratively the gentle friar, determined against all odds to bring these two together. Anecdotes, on the other hand, attempt to ungentle Shakespeare, to cross-cast the star-crossed lovers in order to outrage us. On the other hand, anecdotes may simply push back at the idea that Franciscan friars – enjoined by their order to unmarried celibacy – make the best marriage counsellors.

But if Shakespeare defused Brooke by making his young lovers so likeable, he left an unexploded grenade by making them so young. As the play weirdly belabours, Juliet is thirteen, which is . . . young. Generations of teachers have had to explain this one, with version of 'people were shorter back then'. But they weren't *that* short. And if you ever want to see a page sweat, open the Variorum *R&J* to act 1, scene 2. In the classroom or study, Juliet's youth is rationalized into the historical past (and history is old after all) or trampled into a non-issue beneath a thousand footnotes. On the stage, however, her body must manifest, and somebody must do the manifesting.

It took ages for the stage to come around to the idea that it might cast a thirteen-year-old girl to play a thirteen-year-old girl. Whether prevented by child-labour laws or the stage's own edicts against working with children (or animals, or Junius Brutus Booth), central casting is the last place *Romeo and Juliet* has looked for its central cast. Extraordinarily, it may not have been until the 1960s that Romeo and Juliet were played by actors of the sex and the age nominated by the text. Though an obvious piece of promotional puffery, the souvenir programme that accompanied Franco Zeffirelli's 1968 film boasted, 'Olivia Hussey, a shy, petite brunette, at 15-years-old is the youngest actress ever to play *Juliet* professionally.'[5] This is almost certainly not factually the case, to cite only the fourteen-year-old Jenny Cibber. But in the friction between Olivia Hussey's astonishing last name and the assurance that she's 'shy', we locate the embarrassing collision between theatrical means and fictional ends. With *Othello*, theatre could hide its red face under black, but since its premier *Romeo and Juliet* has had to find approximate bodies to cover up the play's shame. As this book has suggested, such approximations almost always produce anecdotes – particularly when approximate fits turn out to be ill-fitting.

If *Othello*'s anecdotal history toggles between alteration and alternation, *R&J* plays in the space between the 'appropriate' and the 'approximate'. During *Romeo and Juliet*'s first run, for instance, a mature male Romeo played to an adolescent male Juliet. No news here, of course, since such was the case for all romantic couples on the Elizabethan stage. This was a relatively short-lived phenomenon for most plays, however. By the end of the seventeenth century the stage was sexually integrated and most romantic couples – Shakespearean or otherwise – were played by 'appropriate' bodies. Yet *Romeo and Juliet*'s central couple remained a turbulent ripple in the slow, steady flow towards 'naturalistic' casting. Romeo and Juliet remained approximately, rather than 'appropriately', cast long after other plays appropriated actors of the 'correct' sex and age. In the 1590s, Richard Burbage played Romeo when he was pushing thirty to an adolescent boy in his middle-teens, and theatre has memorialized this cross-generational, cross-gender casting of its famously star-crossed lovers by keeping its casting perpetually crossed.

It is in perfect keeping with the stage history of *Romeo and Juliet*, then, that roughly 200 years after the play's premier the stage found a thirteen-year-old actor precocious enough to play at Covent Garden, and then promptly cast him as Romeo against the fifty-year-old Juliet of Sarah Siddons. In the early nineteenth century, the London stage enjoyed – or suffered, depending on your tolerance for precocity – the brief craze of the 'Young Roscius', the thirteen-year-old William Henry West Betty, more often called 'Master' Betty, in cheerful despite of his minority. Betty caught the acting bug at the age of eleven while in Dublin watching Siddons play Elvira in Sheridan's *Pizarro*. He first made a splash in 1803 as Young Norval in John Home's *Douglas* but quickly graduated to mature parts, such as Hamlet. He went on to make a number of star turns and in 1805 played Romeo to Siddons' Juliet at Covent Garden, prompting a review that found him not quite house broken: 'The Young Roscius made his first appearance last night in *Romeo* . . . He was, however, not quite "at home" in the love-scenes, and yet many of the speeches were delivered with an interesting softness which in an older performer might have been mistaken for feeling.'[6] ('Mistaken for feeling' is one of those perfectly candid assessments of acting that most reviewers are too polite to employ.)

It is the love scenes, of course, that trigger the uneasiness here – the implication being that the Young Roscius was perfectly at home killing Tybalt and then finally himself. But here, a married and mature Juliet – old enough to be Romeo's mother[7] – plays to an adolescent boy, inverting the play's original casting, where a mature Romeo played to an adolescent Juliet. As sketched out in the introduction, *Romeo and Juliet*'s stage history has always been one of inversions, as its closing line predicts. Whatever the title may promise, the play's final line casts Juliet first before it bothers with Romeo. In an 1893 overview of *Romeo and Juliet*'s stage history, for instance, the *Commercial Advertiser* recollected a reviewer who preferred one theatre's Romeo, and another's Juliet: at Drury Lane, he saw 'Romeo and Juliet' but 'At Covent Garden,' said a critic, 'I saw "Juliet and Romeo"'[8] The anecdotal history of *Juliet and Romeo* reminds us that it will always take inversion to make a couplet of the couple.

Old Montague

Like most child stars, the Young Roscius flamed out fast. He spent the bulk of his later years learning to live outside the spotlight (when he tried to re-light it some years later the critics turned against him, deciding that fifteen minutes was quite enough. There is nothing more embarrassing than a child star who grows up and reminds us that we fell for him). Master Betty was survived, however, by a tradition of mature or even over-ripe Romeos. For the Betty-and-Siddons match notwithstanding, the more common move was to cast an older Romeo against a younger Juliet. As a critic in 1750 burped, 'What, the *soft*, the *youthful Romeo* represented by the *rough*, *black, hard-featured Digges*, in appearance too old for *Juliet*'s father!'[9] Even when Romeo is not actually his Juliet's father – and is in fact *too* old to be her father – his age is reckoned in paternal terms, turning a discrepancy in the actors' age into a figurative act of incest. A cartoon from *Punch* in 1913 lampoons the trend, while blaming the shortage of young actors on the war.[10] Juliet blooms on the balcony above while Romeo bows on bandy legs below. It's fairly clear that Romeo will have no satisfaction on this or any night. This Romeo couldn't reach that balcony if he'd been born there. The National Theatre's 2011 update of Dion Boucicault's 1841 comedy, *London Assurance*, gathered the whole tradition into a single joke. Sir Harcourt Courtly breaks the news to Cool, his servant, that he's to marry a rich girl of eighteen, which prompts a cool reply:

> SIR HARCOURT: You do not approve of her relative youth?
> COOL: On the contrary, there can be no fault with *her* youth sir. Love is the domain of the young. Shakespeare's Juliet was thirteen
> SIR HARCOURT: How old was Romeo?
> COOL: Fifty seven.[11]

The inside joke's so in it's out. Theatre history has often preferred an obsolescent Romeo to an adolescent one, exchanging Young Roscius for Old Nestor. After all, nothing succeeds like excess in the theatre, and so it produced in the early 1800s 'The Nestor Roscius Aged Ninety Five!!!', who, we are promised,

> will make his second Appearance in ROMEO, in which Play an additional NURSE will be introduced, a precaution which was rashly neglected at some late representations, but of which a judicious Audience could not fail to have approved both from its striking Novelty, and from its still more striking Utility.[12]

The novelty of another nurse emphasizes the second childishness of age, which, as the *Punch* cartoon subtly suggests, sanitizes any hint of a sexual dimension between the lovers. In the anecdote's actuarial account of the play, Juliet's inappropriate youth gets rolled over into Romeo's uncomfortable age.

While anecdotes may not know what to do with sexually mature thirteen-year-old heroines, they do know how to treat foolish old men who go on chasing girls when they should be rocking chairs. Anecdotes respond to thirteen-year-old brides by converting *Romeo and Juliet* from a juvenile tragedy into a pantaloon comedy, a form the theatre knows full well.

> Mr Alexander, at this time a man over fifty years of age, played all sort of parts, but he was essentially a low comedian . . . Miss Jean Davenport . . . on one occasion acted *Juliet* to the *Romeo* of Alexander. This proved too much for the Glasgow people to endure. Hand-bills were distributed throughout the city, which read: 'Murder at the Theater Royal! Alexander as *Romeo*.' The populace came armed with clubs, sticks, etc., and seldom, I suppose, was a scene like it ever witnessed in a theatre. When *Romeo* made his first appearance the spectators hooted, yelled, and shouted, 'Go home, Alec!' . . . When [Friar Lawrence] said, 'Come forth, thou desperate man' (referring to *Romeo*), there was a roar. After *Romeo*'s speech, 'Fall upon the ground as I do now, / Taking the measure of an unmade grave,' Alexander fell in such a comic manner that the audience was convulsed. They shouted, pounded the floor with their sticks, and cat-called until *Romeo* could stand it no longer. He rose up; from his prone position, came down to the footlights, and spoke as follows: 'Ladies and gentlemen.' [A voice from the gallery: 'Oh, go home, Alec.'] 'I'll give five pounds,' said Alexander, 'if some one will point out that blackguard in the gallery.' [Another voice: 'It was me, Alec.'] 'Hold your tongue,' roared Alexander, 'and don't incriminate yourself. Ladies and gentlemen, I have built you

> a beautiful theater.' [Yells.] 'I know I am not so young as I was.' ['No, no,' and roars of laughter.] 'But, thank God, I can play the part.' At this there was a general row, and Alexander went back to his position, again stretching himself upon the stage. The disturbance continued throughout the evening . . . When my father and I were leaving the theater after the performance, we saw a crowd in front of the building, with Alexander in their center, sword in hand, endeavoring, as he said, to protect his property from injury at the hand of a lot of 'blackguard ruffians.' We hurried home. Next morning it was discovered that during the uproar some one had managed to find his way to the roof of the theater and had given one side of the face of Alexander's statue a liberal coat of whitewash. A reward of five pounds was offered for the apprehension of the culprit, but he was never discovered.[13]

By the end of the anecdote, the hand-bill's 'Murder at the Theatre Royal!' sounds more like an incitement than an indictment. An amusing story about theatrical impropriety becomes a shaming ritual that ripples with violence. The harmless catcalls *inside* the theatre sound more sinister out front – as Alexander takes to his guard to protect his property. In fact, the story's curious concern about property rights – 'go home, Alec', the audience shouts; but 'I have built you a beautiful theater', he protests – retails a familiar narrative, in which a wealthy burgher believes his property entitles him to the town's blushing Juliet. If the crowd's reaction seems incommensurate with the crime of over-parting ('clubs and sticks' seem a bit much), it only reaffirms the point that Alexander learned to his shame that night. Just because you built the theatre doesn't make you Romeo. Boy was his face white.

Some actors never learn, and go on playing Romeo until the bitter end. A haunting story from the late 1700s about the last stage of Mr Reddish's life demonstrates the way the role remained a point of yearning, even unto the point of death.

The Middlesex Journal in July of 1786 offers up an 'ANECDOTE *of the late Mr* REDDISH, *the Player*.'

> When the late Mr Reddish's indispositions of mind rendered him incapable of fulfilling his duties at the theatre, and he was by his inability reduced from a salary of twelve or fourteen pounds a week, to an income of seventy pounds a year from the fund, some of his friends made interest with the manager to grant him a benefit. The play advertised was *Cymbeline*, and Mr. Reddish was announced for Posthumus. He was to pass an hour previous to his performance at a house where I was asked to meet him. He came into the room with the step of an idiot, his eyes wandering, and his whole countenance vacant. I congratulated him on his being enough recovered to perform. 'Yes, Sir,' replied he, 'I shall perform, and in the garden scene I shall astonish you!' – 'In the garden scene, Mr. Reddish? I thought you were to play Posthumus.' – 'No, Sir, I play Romeo.' – 'My good man,' said the gentleman of the house, 'you play Posthumus.' – 'Do I,' replied he; 'I am sorry for it. However, what must be, must be.' At the time appointed, he set out for the theatre. The gentleman who went with him, for he was not capable of walking without a guide, told me, that his mind was so imprest with the character of Romeo, he was reciting it all the way; and when he came into the Green-room, it was with great difficulty they could persuade him he was to play any other part. That when the time came for his appearance, they pushed him on the stage, fearing he would begin with a speech of Romeo. With the same expectation I stood in the pit close to the orchestra, and being so near, had a perfect view of his face. The instant he came in sight of the audience, his recollection seemed to return, his countenance resumed meaning, his eye appeared lighted up, he made the bow of modest respect, and went through the scene much better than I had ever before seen him. On his return to the Green-room, the image of Romeo returned to his mind, nor did he lose it . . . After that time he never performed.[14]

The anecdote mercifully spares Reddish – and the reader – the shame of his astonishing the audience with the garden scene when they're expecting *Cymbeline* (the 'garden scene' we now call the 'balcony scene', an architectural alteration taken up below). What must be, must be, realizes Reddish. He's in a late Romance, not a juvenile tragedy. Still, anecdotal history teaches us, there is no greater delusion among aging actors than that they're still suited for Romeo, particularly when they're on the verge of being posthumous.

Young Capulet

If Romeo actors are often too old, Juliet's are often too young. One of theatre's tiredest canards is that, in a 'criticism credited to Ellen Terry: "No actress can play Juliet until she is old enough to play the Nurse."'[15] This old saw cuts both ways. The mature actress will fail to convey Juliet's girlish dash; the immature one, her wisdom. A defender of Fanny Brunton's 1785 Juliet, played when Brunton was sixteen, eloquently testifies to Juliet's dilemma. Her critics, he wrote, punished her, 'Because she at the age of sixteen has not the experience of an actress of thirty . . .'[16] Actresses step into this precocious ellipsis and often have a hard time acting their way out. The problem is that Juliet acts older than thirteen, and so, whatever the actress's age, Juliet will always be beyond her years. When it comes to casting Juliet, the play presents another inversion, turning the part into a trap.

A gilded trap, of course. What actor could say no to Juliet? The role is full of delicious speeches and dynamite scenes. John Gielgud tentatively suggested that Romeo is overrated – 'It may be heresy to suggest that Romeo is a great name, but not a great part'[17] – but no one says this about Juliet. But if no one says the part's not great, critics will tell you if the actress isn't. And it's often the age gap between actor and role that draws attention to the actress's appearance since, to repeat the canard in a more barbed form, 'it has been said of Shakespeare's *Juliet* that no actress was sufficiently experienced to play the character till she was too old to *look* it'.[18] George Jean Nathan called the idea 'buncombe', part of theatre's 'ersatz profundity'. He instances successful Juliets from young to old, from Mary Anderson's seventeen-year-old sensation to Helen Modjeska who played Juliet into her forties.[19] In rebutting the argument he reaffirms it, however, since he ends up citing the approximate ages of these appropriate Juliets. The success of an actress in the part of Juliet is always calculated relative to her age.

Theatrical chatter therefore repeatedly pinions Juliet with her age, the dilemma being – as a reviewer of Fanny Kemble's Juliet put it – she's '[i]n growth a woman, tho' in years a child'.[20] In 1789 Covent Garden advertised that Juliet was to be played by a 'YOUNG LADY',[21] but theatre reviewers continue to quarrel over precisely how young is young, despite the play's specificity. The Nurse says that Juliet's thirteen, and she says so roughly thirteen times, but an 1816 reviewer revised this notion.

> It should be considered that *Juliet* is but a mere girl, only fifteen, or, as the players will have it, eighteen, who falls in love at first sight, and loves with childish fondness and vehemence. We have heard the speeches in the balcony-scene, delivered precisely as we may imagine they would be by an antiquated coquette of five-and thirty, rather than by a green love-sick girl, alike incapable of restraining her inclinations or disguising her wishes.[22]

The Nurse says she's thirteen, the critic that she's fifteen, the actors that she's eighteen, and the imagination – whose wishes are pretty thinly disguised here – that she's a thirty-five-year-old coquette. (That thirty-five can be called 'antiquated' is a reminder of the depressing climate in which women actors have long plied their trade.) Reviews like this read like transcriptions of critics' wishful thinking, triggered, it seems, by the chastity panic at what goes on behind the balcony.

Critics, that is, can't quite bring themselves to make Juliet thirteen, and the closer they get the more circumspect – or savage – they grow. In the 1780s a critic praised an appropriately aged actress, since she, 'with respect to her age, comes nearer to the child of Shakespeare's fancy than perhaps any one that has attempted the character; being in reality, just what the author supposes her to be, something under *eighteen*'.[23] Thirteen is certainly something under eighteen, but by failing to specify Juliet's age the critic sanitizes the implications of the 'child of Shakespeare's fancy'. An early twentieth-century reviewer comes closer when he writes that 'Juliet was fourteen' but sneers that 'any mathematician can now tell how old Miss St Albans is'.[24] His chronological precision – which is still imprecise – comes at Khyra St Albans' expense. Unlike the Nurse, critics cannot bring themselves to say how old Juliet is. Very occasionally critics will listen to what the play tells them about Juliet's age, but only so they can savage the actress for the crime of growing up. Theatre history's mathematicians subtract Juliet's age from that of the actress and always find her wanting.

A more generous reading of theatre reviewers is that they're pushing back against the play's implication that Juliet's engaged in underage sex. The obsession with the actress's age is, then, an expression of anxiety not an aesthetic judgment. This is not just an anachronistic back projection of modern norms onto early English practice, since Renaissance medical treatises detailed the perils of childbirth to mothers so young. Juliet has always been – and will always be – underage. Centuries of criticism therefore hover nervously over Juliet's age and – consciously or not – couch their criticism in terms that actively belie the play. Like critics who praise Othello's well-coloured performances, critics of Juliet often single out her chastity. In 1790, Mrs Pope's Juliet was 'altogether so chaste and interesting a performance' and was followed by the 'more interesting or chaste performance' of Mrs Spencer in 1797. Fanny Brunton, mentioned above, was, despite or no doubt *because* of her youth, praised for her 'chaste spirit of hymeneal affection'. Just as the last thing you might want to say about Desdemona is that she's 'colourless', the last thing you might want to say of Juliet is that she's 'chaste'. But the last thing we should say is so often the first thing on our mind. The play makes us wonder what to make of Juliet's age, and criticism seems to resent being made to think on it.

Of course, as *Othello* teaches us, the only way truly to guarantee a woman's chastity is to kill her first and praise her after, as a late eighteenth-century critic of Juliet suggests: 'As a beauty, we fancied her most when dead – and this model might serve for improvements while living.'[25] The critic may not be entirely in control of his sentence, which suggests that the actress play dead even while living, since her corpse outshines herself. This tradition of Juliet appraisal sets up an anecdote told of Margaret Mather, who took the cue of the critic and resembled in death what she aspired to in life:

> Margaret Mather made her last appearance as Juliet in the death scene of the famous love tragedy yesterday afternoon. Robed in the jeweled gown that she has worn so many times in her notable impersonation of Shakespeare's sweet heroine, she was lowered to her final rest in Elmwood cemetery before the eyes of a larger audience than ever greeted her in life.

Her last audience was her largest, but there was no hope of a curtain call. But there's a wrinkle to this neat fable, since Juliet was not her final part. Like old Mr Reddish above, Mather expired in the late Romance, *Cymbeline*. She died as Imogen, but was buried as Juliet.

> Margaret Mather died last Thursday at Charleston, W. Va., from an acute attack of Bright's disease, from which she had been suffering for some time . . . On Wednesday evening she appeared in Charleston as Imogen in the opening acts of Cymbeline at the Burlew Opera House. In the cave scene it was noticed that she began to omit her lines, and to sway and stagger. She finally collapsed and was carried off the stage . . . Nurses and several physicians did their utmost to

> save her life, but she was beyond medical control and remained in a comatose condition until five o'clock on Thursday afternoon, when she passed away peacefully, surrounded by her entire company . . . Miss Mather was buried in the gown she wore as Juliet.[26]

To be yet more precise, she did not die as Imogen but as Fidele, the faithful page boy Imogen impersonates. It is unclear whether she was carried off the stage by her fictional brothers who thought she had died or by stage hands who feared she was dead. Both Imogen and Juliet feign death, and wake beside dead husbands – at least Imogen thinks so. Yet another version relates that, 'She had assumed the part of Imogene. In the cave scene, where she first appeared as the boy Fidele, she was taken suddenly ill and was borne into the rocky retreat. Many of the spectators thought it part of the play – a bit of admirable acting. The last word she spoke was "Fidele".'[27] If the spectators thought her being carried into the cave was 'part of the play' who could blame them since it is? The anecdote realizes the similarity, and, as with Reddish, allows Mather to make her final appearance not in a late Romance but in a youthful tragedy. Mather is buried as Juliet, forever faithful, thirteen forever.

This strain of chatter and anecdotal lore – like the tradition of senescent Romeos – helps process the stage's unease with Juliet's youth, a youth that Shakespeare innovates and insists upon by diverting from his source (though, as a critic in 1757 put it gently after reviewing Shakespeare's treatment of that source, 'There is Reason to think Shakespear was not Master of the Italian Language').[28] The anecdotes shift our attention from the uneasy spectacle of Juliet's minority to the ludicrous image of Romeo's old age or the biological maturity of the actress. Juliet may be thirteen forever, but actors and actresses alike grow up. A poignant tale of Romeo and Juliet reunited across the ages offers us – as so often – an alternative ending to tragedy's dire reckoning. If Master Betty was not quite 'at home' in the love scenes, mature actors offer a domesticated version of what would have happened had the star-crossed lovers lived. A story told about the great Juliet of the 1860s, Eliza O'Neill, finds her reunited with her young Romeo:

> There is a pretty story told of her meeting Charles Kemble in a private parlor long after her withdrawal. 'Ah, dear Juliet!' cried the Romeo of seventy-five. Whereupon the Juliet of sixty-five embraced him with a pretty, half-real, half-dramatic tenderness, quaint yet touching in white-haired Montagus [sic] and Capulets who had loved and lived and died together, night after night, almost half a century before.[29]

The account normalizes relations, shows us the couple in their twilight years – the troublesome gap between thirteen and thirty narrowed into negligibility as two white hairs embrace in domestic tranquillity, half-real, half-dramatic, altogether normal, all-together forever. Now *that's* a pretty tale.

Something old, something new . . .

As Shakespeare's gentle Friar seems eager to insist, one way to normalize sexual relations between the central couple is to marry them. Recalling his own *Romeo and Juliet* of the 1930s, Laurence Olivier writes, 'The theatre is replete with emotional legends; it is not surprising that those playing Romeo and Juliet are supposed to present a more stirring partnership if they develop the same passion between themselves as that which they are emulating.'[30] 'Buncombe', George Jean Nathan might retort, but the 'emotional legend' of Romeo and Juliet completing off stage what they fail to do on has some precedent, and some staying power. A 1916 newspaper caption beneath a photo of Edward H. Sothern and Juliet Marlowe as Romeo and Juliet reports, 'It was the Shakespearian Revival and the Passionate Love Scenes These Two Played That Drew Them at Last Into Real Love and Marriage.'[31] The caption's knowing 'at Last' winks at the couple's long theatrical partnership, which began in 1904 and led to their 1911 marriage. If the star-crossed love of passionate teens presents an odd emulation for a pair of seasoned actors, it reassures the reader that even doomed young love can be eclipsed by companionate marriage.

While *Romeo and Juliet* does not seem the most promising of marriage models, anecdotes about Edwin Booth suggest he used it as a dating opportunity, meeting both of his wives in the part. Joseph Jefferson, beloved by nineteenth-century America theatre-goers for his portrayal of Rip Van Winkle, recalled Booth's marriage to his first wife Mary Devlin: 'She was for three years an inmate of my house, and afterward became the leading lady of my company. One night I told her to prepare to rehearse *Juliet*, as she was to play the part to Booth's *Romeo*. At that moment I had a premonition that Edwin Booth and Mary Devlin would become man and wife.'[32] Telling a young woman to rehearse Juliet before she goes to bed might not make the most comfortable night-cap, but Jefferson's 'premonition' was borne out in two respects. Devlin did marry Booth. She was twenty, he just three years her senior, and the marriage apparently a passionately happy one. She left him a widower after just three years, however.

Booth was apparently shattered by Devlin's death, and returned to central casting to find her understudy. But Booth's second marriage, to Mary McVicker, the step-daughter of J.H. McVicker, a Chicago theatre manager, proved more enduring but less satisfying than his first (the matter of Booth's endurance and McVicker's theatre will come back to haunt us in the next chapter of this book). In Booth's obituary *The Baltimore Sun* reported that he met McVicker 'when she was a child. In 1867, when he was playing at McVicker's Theatre, Mary McVicker made her appearance at Booth's request as *Juliet* to his *Romeo*. Their mock wooing terminated in romance.'[33] The *World* gave a comb-over to this bald narrative, eulogizing Booth's marriage in rosy terms at the time of his death:

> A pretty story is told of the courtship of Edwin Booth and Mary McVicker. According to the story he and she

> were playing together in the sweet old love-play of Shakespeare. He was Romeo; she was Juliet. The pretty tale of the old theatre-goers of twenty-odd years ago has it that the stage Romeo and the stage Juliet forgot their acting in the love they felt for each other, and made not stage love, but real love during the balcony scene. This same old story further says that during the whole course of the play Edwin Booth was telling pretty Mary McVicker the old, old story, that was just as old even when gentle Willie Shakespeare wrote of Romeo and Juliet. And the same old retrospective gentlemen and ladies will tell you that Romeo and Juliet has never been done in our day as Booth and Mary McVicker did it in those days, nearly twenty-five years ago.[34]

The author's strategy seems to be to say 'old' so often that you'll forget how young Juliet is (McVicker was eighteen, Booth thirty-four). The anecdote casts a twilight twinkle over the courtship, whereas Booth and McVicker had worked together for some time and lived together privately for over a year before they were married.[35] For that matter, McVicker had played a number of parts opposite Booth, including Desdemona to his Othello and Ophelia to his Hamlet, parts during which Booth presumably told his leading lady some other old stories. As ever, Romeo and Juliet provides the emulative model for those actors intent on making a career out of romance.

To make a pretty tale out of *Romeo and Juliet*, you have to forget the ending. So while this 'pretty story' selects *Romeo and Juliet* as the plot in which Booth and McVicker's love could bloom, it can't quite shake the sense of the belated. Even its sweaty nostalgia can't cover up the fact that by selecting *R&J* as the emulative model, the love must end in death. Indeed, another correspondent, on the occasion of Booth's death, remembers McVicker as a 'very brilliant and accomplished girl, who will be remembered as having played *Juliet* to his *Romeo* with grace and sweetness', adding, however, that they 'were separated before her death'.[36] Try as they might to polish the past, these anecdotes relate a love that 'terminated in romance' and led to a separation before Juliet's death. In so doing, they honour the 'death-marked' love detailed in *Romeo and Juliet* and remind us that while anecdotes end, the play goes on.

These tales of Edwin also remind us that the Booths did not make a speciality of happy endings. John Wilkes's last appearance on the stage – but one – was in the character of Romeo. He had volunteered 'for the occasion of Miss Avonia Jones' benefit', the *Washington Union* reported on the day of Lincoln's assassination.[37] (Avonia Jones had in 1858 played Juliet to her mother's Romeo, the start of a career of disastrous matches.) John Wilkes had been scheduled to play Romeo again, a week after the assassination, with brothers Edwin as Mercutio and Junius as Friar Lawrence, though *Julius Caesar* was the more obvious vehicle for the Booth boys to air their grievances. It was not, however, an engagement that never was but one that was not meant to be that brings John Wilkes to the brink of a happy ending. A year after the assassination, a newspaper recalled:

> The first time John Wilkes Booth played Romeo was to Miss Kate Bateman's Juliet, in Moutgomery [*sic*], Ala. It was an immediate success, and at that period Booth thought seriously of accompanying Miss Bateman to England, which, if carried out, would have saved a good man to the country, a great actor to the stage and possibly changed the political destiny of a nation.[38]

Had Juliet proved more alluring, Booth would have been diverted from what the *Bostonian Magazine* called his 'unfortunate subsequent career'.[39] If Romeo had followed his Juliet to England, he still might not have played Romeo on 22 April 1865, but *Our American Cousin* might have made it to curtain on 15 April.

Romeo must die

Histrionic and violent, the battling Booth brothers are the first family of the American stage – if not the first family of American history. Had they selected *Romeo and Juliet* rather than *Julius Caesar* as their family drama, perhaps they would have turned their swords on one another rather than on Caesar. *Romeo and Juliet* would have served the brothers well. For all its emphasis on romantic love, the play has a history of fratricidal rivalry, even fratricidal violence. As with one strain of *Othello* anecdotes, a tradition follows *R&J* across the ages that turns just another story of star-crossed lovers into one about what happens when stars cross one another.

From its early performances, the play became an allegory about ambitious actors. Not long after *Romeo and Juliet* premiered in the mid 1590s, John Marston satirized play-house gossip, particularly a theatre-haunter named Luscus, from whose lips 'doth flow / Naught but pure *Iuliat* and *Romeo* / Say, who acts best? *Drufus* or *Roscio*?'[40] Marston transposes 'Romeo and Juliet' to make it rhyme with rival actors. The couplet leaves out Juliet altogether, turning 'Romeo' into the last word in acting. These various acts of inversion and substitution point up the play's history of rivalry. Frank Benson, for instance, recalls his early years at the Lyceum, when he played Paris to Henry Irving's Romeo. His memoirs remember that he

> broke every rule of etiquette by going up to the great man, seated on a chair in the wings: 'A very beautiful part, that of Romeo,' quoted Paris airily. Irving looked up sharply, annoyed doubtless at the presumption of a beginner interrupting his rest and talking in the wings. 'Yes! And the odd thing about it is that every damned young fool who has been on the stage two minutes thinks he can play it.'[41]

Not to question Benson's analysis – he was there after all – but Irving's annoyance was born of a king's certainty that every pretender wants his crown. Benson's airy indirection was a direct threat, and his vagueness all the more ominous. Irving knew what Benson wanted, not the beautiful leading lady but the beautiful leading part. It's not for love but advancement that Paris courts Juliet.

The anecdotal history of *Romeo and Juliet* is distinguished then not just by quasi-incestuous couples, and inter-generational couplings, but by rival Romeos who compete for the love of the audience. The 1750s featured the 'Battle of the Romeos', with Spranger Barry versus David Garrick at Covent Garden and Drury Lane respectively. Critical reactions differed violently, leading to the anecdote that some audiences found Barry superior in the early love scenes but Garrick more fit for the end. Thus, or so goes the account, 'some of them supported this opinion by frequently leaving Covent Garden in the middle of the play to see it finish at Drury Lane'. The audience plays the fickle Juliet. Barry's lovely in the garden, but it's Garrick they want in the end.

Garrick may have won that skirmish, but the battle was far from settled:

> Barry was in no part so eminent as in Romeo. At the time when he attracted the town to Covent Garden by his admirable delineation of the character, Garrick found it absolutely necessary to perform himself as Romeo at Drury Lane, in order to obtain at least some share in the attention of the public, and to divert into his own coffers a driblet of the stream of gold which was rolling into the treasury of the rival house. Garrick, however, wanted the physical advantages of Barry, and, great as he was, would perhaps have willingly avoided such a competition. This, at least, seems to have been the prevailing opinion; for, in the garden scene, when Juliet exclaims, 'O Romeo, Romeo! wherefore art though Romeo?' an auditor in the pit archly gave the explanation of this fact by replying, 'Because Barry has gone to the other house.'[42]

Juliet has to settle for the arms of Garrick, since her other ardent lover has gone over to the other side. Even when

Romeo and Juliet are alone, there's always another man in the garden.

The rivalry was augmented by the fact that Barry and his Juliet, Susanna Cibber (the aforementioned Theophilus's estranged second wife – I said it was incestuous) had originally performed under David Garrick's direction at Drury Lane before decamping for Covent Garden. Garrick, motivated by either piqué or publicity (probably both), responded by mounting an *R&J* of his own with George Anne Bellamy, who had played Juliet earlier at Covent Garden. You're way ahead of me: two playhouses, both alike in dignity . . . The rivalry raged for twelve straight days, leading to the following bit of doggerel in the *Daily Advertiser*: 'Well what tonight says angry Ned as up from bed he rouses, Romeo again! and shakes his head, Ah! Pox on both your houses!' What the doggerel fails to mention is that 'Romeo again' implies the same of Juliet, but she's vanished from the scene, an impertinent part in the play-without-the-play called *Romeo and Romeo*.

Laurence Olivier encapsulates the tradition by making it perfectly clear that what the actor wants is Romeo, not Juliet, who's simply the stardom every Romeo courts: 'That year [1935], no less than four jealous juveniles in London all saw themselves in the part of Romeo. It would be unpardonably coy if I did not disclose that the four were John Gielgud, Robert Donat, Ivor Novello and the doubtful character who bears my name. The last three aspirants were all jealously agreed that the first would be the least well cast of us all.'[43] Donat, Novello, and Olivier might have agreed that Gielgud was the least well suited for Romeo, but that does not mean they were happy to share the spotlight with each other – the first step was to convert the quadratic equation into a triangle, but that was presumably just the first step. As Gore Vidal once said, it's not enough that we succeed, others must fail.

Shakespeare had a nearly Euclidean fondness for triangles, and anecdotes introduce another element to the play that he excised from his source, jealous juvenilia. For Arthur Brooke's novella includes a male rival for Juliet's affection (an actual rival, not the anodyne Paris). In Brooke's version Mercutio is not just Romeo's friend but a rival for Juliet's esteem. *Romeus and Juliet* features a scene in which Mercutio and Romeus sit flanking Juliet, each holding one of her hands. Ultimately, Juliet prefers Romeus because Mercutio's hands are cold as ice, suggesting that it was not the excellence of Romeus's poetry that won the day but the superiority of his circulatory system. After all, it is not usually Paris who threatens to have Romeo's part – nor even the outside threat of Romeos playing at the other house – but an insidious rival much closer to home, Mercutio. Among the earliest and most well-known anecdotes of *R&J* is the alleged act of infanticide that Shakespeare practised on his character. John Dryden recounts and rebuffs the narrative, thus previewing the call and response of the anecdote across the ages:

> *Shakesper* show'd the best of his skill in his *Mercutio*, and he said himself, that he was forc'd to kill him in the third Act, to prevent being killd by him. But, for my part, I canot find he was so dangerous a person : I see nothing in him but what was so exceeding harmless, that he might have liv'd to the end of the Play, and dy'd in his bed, without offence to any man.[44]

Dryden suggests that Mercutio was no threat to his progenitor, but overlooks Mercutio's danger: it was not an act of parricide but fratricide that Shakespeare prevented by authoring the character's exit.

A reviewer in 1895 flags the threat. Just because the play is named after you, doesn't necessarily make you the lead:

> Charles Hanford as Mercutio Was the Hero of the Play. By a strange perversion of Shakespeare's play, the merry Mercutio was the hero of 'Romeo and Juliet' at the Academy last night. Charles B. Hanford carried this role, and although his scenes were brief, his matchless elocution and acting made it the leading male part of the play. Mr Spencer is

> entirely unsuited for the part of Romeo. Not only is he awkward in the garb of a young gallant, but he is so throughly imbued with the spirit of stage villainy that he makes love as Iago might.[45]

Mercutio's gain is Romeo's loss – stardom is a zero-sum game. Hanford's performance wrests a 'strange perversion' of the play, making Mercutio the leading man and turning Romeo into a skulking Iago, every inch the other man driven by jealousy and with murder on his mind.

As John Gielgud tentatively suggested, the problem with Romeo is that though it's a 'great name', it might not be a great part. In a play that quibbles over nomenclature, the other name that Romeo might be is 'Mercutio'. After all, it's a 'juicy part', as one critic called it in 1895, to which a Mr Levick one night 'applied a sort of artistic lemon squeezer'.[46] Perhaps the role is so enticing since Mercutio is, according to John Hill in 1751, 'a comic character, tho' introduc'd in tragedy'.[47] In any event, Romeos across the ages have had to contend with Mercutios who come for their girl, in this case one called Stardom. When he played Romeo at Smock Alley, Dublin in the 1760s, Thomas Sheridan could read the writing on the wall and didn't like what it said, so he transferred Mercutio's 'fine description of a dream to the part of Romeo, merely because he would monopolize so fine a speech to himself'.[48] Thomas Sheridan – and his more famous son Richard Brinsley – knew something about theatrical monopolies, being both in the management game. With respect to Romeo, Sheridan understood that the quickest way to profit was to monopolize the lines. In this case, Mercutio's loss was Romeo's gain. One way to silence Mercutio is to take his words away.

One other way to share the profits is to alternate ownership. Famously, John Gielgud's production of the play in 1934 saw Gielgud and Laurence Oliver alternating as Romeo and Mercutio to Peggy Ashcroft's Juliet, a performance frequently read – with Olivier's help – as a proxy rivalry between acting traditions: Gielgud standing for the grand tradition, Olivier the coming thing. This fatuous debate masks the as-pertinent point that the revolving cast rehearsed Brooke's scenario of Mercutio and Romeo competing for Juliet's favour. Olivier writes, 'I suppose I must have sensed a sort of possible rivalry between us, that might last all our lives, I don't know,' while Gielgud rejoins, 'I was so jealous, because not only did he play Romeo with tremendous energy but he knew just how to cope with it and select.'[49] Perhaps because it was the family line, Gielgud knew his theatre history, and that threats to Romeo could come from all quarters:

> Much as I loved the part of Romeo, I knew by this time how difficult it was, and that a good Mercutio might easily eclipse me. I had once seen that happen in 1919, in a disastrous production of the play, in which the Juliet of the American actress Doris Keane and the Romeo of Basil Sydney were over-shadowed by the successes of Ellen Terry as the Nurse (her last professional engagement) and Leon Quartermaine, who played Mercutio so finely. The audience had shouted for him at the end of the first night performance, but he was modest enough to slip away directly after his death scene.[50]

As Shakespeare must have learned, just because Mercutio doesn't make it to the curtain call does not mean that he won't steal the show. But the anecdote makes it clear that the stakes are high for Juliet as well. Contesting actors may want to turn the play into a locker-room contest over whose part is bigger, but Juliet's a factor in the play's arithmetic too (though the laddish tradition of theatrical anecdotes usually want to subtract her). We could, after all, read the Gielgud, Ashcroft, Olivier dynamic though the prism of another play, written just two years prior to Gielgud's production, *Design for Living*, in which Noël Coward ultimately argues that a romantic triangle is not a problem to be solved but an equation to be savoured.

Romeo and Juliet's anecdotes have determined that a game played for a *pair* of stainless maidenheads is disappointingly low stakes and so have found ways to up the ante. The history of *Romeo and Juliet* in performance has continued to fuss with the annoyingly tidy equation enshrined in Baz Luhrmann's title, *Romeo + Juliet*. After all, in the play he occupies, Romeo is not a one-woman man, so why should the actor be?

> In 1877 Mr. George Rignold played Romeo; but . . . this Romeo was not content with fewer than six Juliets, numbering Mesdames Neilson, Dyas, Davenport, Granger, Wainwright, and Cummings. Had there been six Romeos nobody would have had a right to complain, except, perhaps, the shade of Shakespeare; but this six to one business strikes us as being somewhat comical, and we suppose that all concerned will admit that they were seeking a sensation rather than the advancement of the dignity of their art.[51]

Six Romeos and six Juliets would have troubled no one since that would even the odds, but six Juliets plus one Romeo is an odd equation, one that, in this accounting, adds up 'somewhat comical'. Odd equations usually equal comedy; it's the even equations that don't add up. In any event, the performance history of *Romeo and Juliet* is distinguished by anecdotes that consistently make the odds longer and longer or at least odder and odder.

Six to one might equal comedy, but two Romeos to one Juliet is downright embarrassing. Ten years earlier than Rignold's Romeo, on a different continent, and in another form, we learn that one night,

> Monsieur Michot absented himself from the theatre, giving such short notice that no substitute could be found. The opera of *Rigoletto* had in consequence to be played instead of that of *Romeo et Juliette*. The manager, thoroughly discontented, ordered M. Blum to study the role of Romeo, and play it on alternate nights with M. Michot. Unwilling to submit to this arrangement, M. Michot dressed for the part of [Romeo on]

> the evening fixed for the first appearance of M. Blum. At the opening of the piece Juliet was embarrassed to find herself in the presence of two Romeos. At length M. Blum retired and M. Michot went through the performance.[52]

The embarrassment of facing two Romeos is an expression of theatre's problematic surplus, in that there are always more actors than parts, and never enough stardom to go around. It's a source of constant wonder that the name of the American acting union doesn't dissolve from irony alone: in the end, there is no such thing as actors' equity.

Unromantic altitudes

Yorick's skull, Desdemona's pillow, Juliet's balcony – the objects have materialized over the years to give significant forms to the plays' inchoate longings. The objects are overdetermined of course – a case, if ever there was one, of too few signifiers chasing too many signifieds. Whatever else the objects hold in common, performance history calls for them far more often than the play texts ever do. *Hamlet*, at least, requires its skulls (though how many? That's both the question and the rub). But the pillow and the balcony are pure figments of theatre's imagination. Or impure ones, since both the pillow and the balcony simultaneously disclose and obscure what goes on in the bedroom, the epicentre of deaths both little and large. When we consider the etymological origins of 'balcony' – *bel cony* – it's no wonder it forms the smutty centre of the play's anecdotal attention. Shakespeare modestly calls for a window – to give us just a glimpse at Juliet – but anecdotes demand to see her balcony.

Maybe Marjorie Garber is right. Real estate is the way that old people talk about sex, so to talk about Juliet's *bel cony* we talk about her balcony.[53] Or maybe the chatter takes its cue from Juliet's proto-capitalist metaphor for sex as property acquisition. 'I have bought the mansion of a love / But not possess'd it' (3.2.26-27), she says, sounding like every homeowner who's closed on a house but not yet moved in. In any event, the 'balcony scene' is the most famous in the play and has, over the years, become a hieroglyph for romantic love – reproduced on stage, film, and in paintings and illustrations. But like many of Shakespeare's most famous locations – the battlements of Elsinore, the seashore in *Twelfth Night*, the heath in *Lear* – the balcony is never mentioned in the text of *Romeo and Juliet*. It is, instead, a figment of the play in performance. In fact, the first printed text of *Romeo and Juliet* in 1597 clearly indicates that Juliet appears aloft, at her 'window' as Romeo says. And in the eighteenth century, the scene was known as the 'orchard' or 'garden scene' – emphasizing the prelapsarian innocence of young love. (Perhaps to a generation raised on Baz Luhrmann, the encounter will be known as the 'swimming-pool scene'.) Despite the fact that the balcony is an addition, it has nevertheless become the literal site and the symbolic centre of the play. Mounted on a scaffold of anecdotes, the balcony emerges to put an obstruction in the way of Romeo and Juliet. In short, architecture provides what the art leaves out, an external means of keeping the two lovers from instantly mauling one another while simultaneously showing us what the play prissily obscures.

The performance history of *Romeo and Juliet* is full of chatter about the balcony, which gives theatre an excuse to discuss in detached, technical ways the play's central preoccupation. *Romeo and Juliet* is not unique in this respect. It happens quite often with Shakespeare's plays in performance where a staging challenge will align with the plays' thematic pressure. As discussed in the previous chapter, the long history of *Othello* in performance is marked by anecdotes about Othello's blackface makeup 'rubbing off' on Desdemona, which exercises (or exorcises) the play's anxieties about racial transfer. The history of *Hamlet* is full of stories about the use of a real skull, which ends up restaging what Hamlet calls a 'necessary question of the play', which is his certainty that there's a difference between seems and is but his ultimate frustration that he cannot tell the difference. Or, as the next chapter details, the history of *Richard III*, which is full of actors injuring themselves by miming Richard's disabilities, which rehearses the play's histrionic conundrum about the abilities of actors. These theatrical problems align with the plays' thematic ones, and provide theatre professionals with opportunities – however unwittingly – to wade into, but usually against, the plays' prevailing currents.

Similarly, the balcony in *Romeo and Juliet* forces playmakers to stage both the lover's separation and their attempts to overcome it, giving them a physical obstacle that the play does not otherwise provide. The famous design team 'Motley', who fitted out the landmark Gielgud/Olivier/Ashcroft production in the 1930s, regarded the balcony as, in their words, 'The main thing that sets off how you think about the play.' They are designers, of course, but it is still remarkable that they describe the balcony (not Shakespeare's text, nor its performers) as the primary index to the play's meaning. Across the years, the precise height of the balcony has, therefore, produced some hilariously serious and seriously hilarious debate about its proper altitude.

John Gielgud pointed out, for instance, that the problem with a low balcony is that it makes Romeo's ascent too easy – it's all too clear what satisfaction he could have tonight. Peter Brook apparently overcorrected for this problem with his famous 1947 RSC production, placing the balcony quite high, which led *Punch* to complain that the bedroom scene was played at an 'unromantic altitude'. Edwin Booth pursued something in this line and made Juliet's house over 'sixty feet in height, and had two balconies one above the other' (one for each wife).[54] There's just no pleasing some folks, however, and critics will complain both high and low. In 1868, at Sadler's Wells, 'the balcony is reduced in height until Juliet is within reach of Romeo, who, if he chose, might lift her into the garden. This is altogether wrong. It is clear from the language Romeo employs that Juliet is above him.'[55] The question of whether Juliet is above Romeo is clearly one of architecture but just as clearly one of interpretation, to which a generation of critics, actors, designers and directors have had to apply their erotic altimeters.

Operating on the theatrical principle that if you can't delight your audience you might as well disappoint them, some twentieth-century productions have brought Romeo and Juliet back down to earth. An RSC production in 1980 displeased the critics, since, 'having the lovers clutch each other at ground level in what looks like a shabby alley deprives the situation of all its symbolism'.[56] It doesn't, of course, deprive it of *all* its symbolism – the image of Romeo and Juliet fumbling one another in a furtive alley seems more in line with Shakespeare's source, which saw in their passion something 'unhonest'. The staging has symbolism, all right, but it's all wrong in the eyes of this critic. In any event, it's worth keeping in mind that the symbolism to which the critic is responding is largely a product of the play's performance history, not its text. But the critic is right to note that this moment of architectural symbolism is vital to our conception of the love of Romeo and Juliet – the play needs to put *something* between them, at least several yards of air space.

The bind for producers today – held hostage to this most iconic of images – is that they risk placing the balcony at an unromantic altitude or grounding it at street level, where Romeo can get his grubby mitts on his teenage target. You *could* take the approach of the 1988 Temba production, with Juliet on the stage and Romeo aloft: 'What light from yonder basement breaks?' In sum, the balcony has become so central to the play's conception of its protagonists' passion that it can feature as a measure of Romeo's attractions. The nineteenth-century actress Hannah Pritchard, when asked whether she preferred David Garrick or Spranger Barry, replied, 'Had I been Juliet to Garrick's Romeo, – so impassioned was he, I should have expected that he would have come up to me in the balcony; but had I been Juliet to Barry's Romeo, – so tender and seductive was he, I should certainly have jumped down to him!'[57] In the end, nothing in the play comes between Romeo and Juliet but decorum and a balcony, and it doesn't take much of a leap to overcome either.

Hannah Pritchard intuitively registers something odd about this scene, which is that balcony (or window) scenes on the Renaissance stage are usually a prelude to elopement. They usually end with Juliet descending her safe house for the thrills of romantic love – as Pritchard hints, it's almost always the woman who's willing to take the leap for her Romeo below. There's *Two Gentlemen of Verona,* whose balcony scene is prepped for but averted. There's the 'balcony scene' in *Merchant of Venice*, where Jessica robs her father's house before eloping with Lorenzo. Even with *Othello*, the balcony figures as a stage cipher for elopement, as Iago and Roderigo 'court' Brabantio from below with tales of his daughter's Venetian escape. Or consider the scene from Christopher Marlowe's *The Jew of Malta*, from which all of Shakespeare's balcony scenes derive. In *The Jew of Malta*, Barabas sees the beautiful Abigail above at the window and calls out, 'But stay, what starre shines yonder in the East? / The Loadstarre of my life, if Abigail' (2.1.680ff). Abigail is his daughter, of course. I should have mentioned that. And it is from the window in *'Tis Pity She's a Whore* that Annabella first spies Giovanni and calls out 'See! what blessed shape / Of some celestial creature now appears! – What man is he?' The answer is, of course, 'your brother'. These 'balcony' scenes are haunted by elopement and incest. But Romeo and Juliet don't elope nor is their love incestuous or even scandalous. (Juliet suggests that she's prepared to follow Romeo throughout the world, but apparently not to Mantua, at least not in the summer, when it's choked with apothecaries peddling drugs to nervous tourists.) The point to make here, however, is that in the vast majority of balcony scenes it is ultimately the woman who comes down from her pedestal for the enticements of a man who's clearly beneath her.

Directors and designers can bicker over what elevation to set the balcony, then, but history has an anecdote for every altitude. If a director decides to bring Juliet down to earth, the balcony has obviously been set to Romeo's satisfaction.

> On Miss O'Neil's first representation of Juliet in the capital of Ireland, the following ludicrous circumstance occurred: – The balcony in the garden scene was particularly low; Conway, the Romeo of the night, was uncommonly tall, and, in delivering the lines – 'Oh! that I were a glove upon that hand, / That I might touch that cheek,' laid his hand upon the balcony. A fellow in the gallery immediately interrupted him. 'Get out with your blarney,' he said; 'why don't you touch her, then, and not be preaching Parson Saxe there?'[58]

Whether placing the blame on Parson Saxe or Friar William, the anecdote raises the central objection. Shakespeare's plays shudder with acts of violence – suicides, child slaughter, cannibalism, the word 'nuncle' – but they draw the line at pre-marital sex. Balcony anecdotes course with a common complaint: why not allow the central couple some non-contractual coupling?

Attempts to raise the balcony don't do much to raise the tone. The options are limited. Bring Juliet down to earth, and Romeo can get his hands on her, put her on a pedestal, and he'll look up her skirt.

> For want of a proper side scene, the lady, who enacted *Juliet*, was under the irksome necessity of delivering her amorous extasies from a ladder, which was placed purposely against the O.P. Wing— [John] EDWIN being then but a sort of novice in making love, and not knowing the delicate customs of *Mantua*, placed himself too immediately under the fair object of his idolatry, who was obliged in consequence to pay more attention to her petticoats than her author, to prevent the puny inamorato from espying the nakedness of the land.[59]

The anecdote obviously gets it wrong, in assuming that Romeo's a Mantuan rube, but it gets the main thrust right. The reason that Romeo is underneath Juliet's balcony is that he wants what's underneath.

The preoccupation with Juliet's balcony animates the play's oldest anecdote, which produces what the play otherwise obscures.

> There being a Fight and Scuffle in this Play, between the House of *Capulet*, and House of *Paris*; Mrs. *Holden* Acting his Wife, enter'd in a *Hurry*, Crying, O my Dear *Count*! She Inadvertently left out, O, in the pronunciation of the Word *Count*! giving it a Vehement Accent, put the House into such a Laughter, that *London* Bridge at low Water was silence to it.[60]

The anecdote inadvertently exposes the ultimate object of the play's inquiry. In so doing, it exemplifies the way that theatrical chatter can express what criticism – or the play – can't bring itself to say. Mrs Holden blurts out what's on the play's mind. Juliet's too young to talk about it, and Romeo's too shy. 'Counts' are 'dear' in the play as well, since – as the play's language of mercantilism suggests – the price paid for them is far too high. The fact that there is no House of Paris does not discredit – in fact it underscores – the way the anecdote offers an alternative account of the play, one that features a competing house, an absent 'o' and a 'Dear *C-unt*', which is in the anecdote's estimate what the play is all about.[61]

Shakespeare might be gentle, but anecdotes are not, and will always turn a blushing maid into a fallen woman. An early twentieth-century headline reports that 'Miss Haswell as Juliet Falls from Balcony and Is Injured. / Actress Takes Twelve Foot Plunge at Allentown, Pa., and Audience is Dismissed.' The story details the events on the night in question:

> Miss Percy Haswell, Shakespearian actress, was injured at a matinee performance at a local theatre to-day when she fell twelve feet from the stage balcony in 'Romeo and Juliet,' striking the floor with her head. She was playing the part of Juliet, and she and John E. Kellard, the Romeo, were playing the love scene when the balustrade on which she was

> kneeling gave way. She was stunned and the audience was dismissed. Miss Haswell was taken to her hotel, where she is under the care of two physicians. She is suffering principally from shock. She is the wife of George Fawcett, who also is on the stage.[62]

At least she's married, so there's that to cushion her shock. The odd closing detail reassures us that her husband was – like his fallen wife – on the stage, but not the same one as Haswell and Kellard. The account irresistibly triangulates the event, suggesting that Juliet's fall is somehow related to her playing around with another man.

The idea that Juliet is actually married, and therefore not quite the ingénue she seems, is a point of emphasis for anecdotes that insist on bringing her back down to earth.

> On Friday, December 24, 1814, *The Stranger* was performed for the benefit of Charles Kemble. During the fourth act, Mrs Cruse, who performed Mrs. Haller, appeared much agitated. The audience attributed it to the pathetic nature of the character, and applauded her highly. When, however, the bell rang for the fifth act, they were informed that Mrs Cruse was very seriously indisposed, and the character was finished by another actress. In the interim, Mrs Cruse was delivered of a child in the ladies' dressing-room. Only the night before, she had played Juliet.[63]

The events appear to be unrelated. But it turns out from this anecdote that Juliet's not just already married but expecting, which will ground any courtship, or turn a teen romance into a cuckold comedy. A similar episode goes into yet more detail.

> In Wigan, a little town . . . occurred a laughable circumstance. The juvenile leading lady, a good actress and very pretty woman by the way, and a young mother, was cast to play Juliet, in 'Romeo and Juliet.' Her baby had been placed in her dressing-room for security, and to be near the mother.

> But just before the balcony scene the young tyrant became unruly and impossible to control. What was to be done? A mother's tact hit upon the true soothing syrup. She nestled the infant to her breast, and from that moment the young villain became silent as a mouse. Being called, she hastily mounted the rostrum that supported the supposed balcony, throwing a lace scarf over her shoulders, which concealed the little suckling; and leaning over the balcony, with her other arm pensively placed upon her cheek, she looked the picture of innocence and beauty. The scene opened and went glowingly. But alas! Juliet has to appear and disappear three times, and in her effort to do so gracefully, and yet conceal the child, she stumbled against the iron brace that held up the frail structure. Down fell the balcony, and lo! The love-lorn maiden was discovered with a baby at her breast – seated on a tub, that served for a stool, and at her foot, accidentally placed there by the thirsty carpenter, was a quart pot. The said carpenter was discovered on all fours, steadying with his back the rickety-structure above. Shrieks of laugher from all parts of the house greeted the tableau, and of the play no more was heard that night.[64]

Hamlet might struggle with problems of the real, but nothing daunts the theatre like the ideal. Juliet is a thirteen-year-old virgin, and Romeo not much older and certainly no wiser. They meet in a sonnet and depart in an aubade, for God's sake. The anecdotes bluntly point out that Romeo is actually fifty-seven, Juliet thirty-five, and that just off stage there's a mouth to be fed. The carpenter? He's there to remind us that however high you put the balcony, it will always come up short.

Duck!

Wherever theatre sets the balcony, anecdotes can always go lower.

> One time when Mrs Mantell was playing opposite that famous of Shakespearian interpreters, her husband, a very awkward moment happened in the balcony scene. One of the stage hands had acquired a live duck through a raffle. Unable to take it home before the performance, he shut it up in a room on one of the upper tiers at the side of the stage. Unaware that this room had the feathered occupant, some one opened the door. In a mad scamper out waddled the duck to the edge of the floor. Instead of saying 'nice ducky' and trying to make friends with it until some one could bring the sack, the blundering person gave chase. Flapping and squawking with fright, the duck flew out in the Capulet garden just at the zoological moment when Romeo, desirous of flying off with Jule [*sic*], was fervently gushing, 'I would I were a bird.'[65]

If you talk that way to your wife, you probably deserve a maniacal duck. Seriously, a bird? What grown man talks that way? But Romeo isn't a grown man. If the play is as imprecise about his age as it is exact about Juliet's, one thing is perfectly clear. He's at just the right age – and in just the right situation – when saying such a thing might give him satisfaction. Older men, the *Washington Star* argued in 1893, have 'more horse sense than to be prancing around balconies in the middle of the night and climbing fire escapes by the light of the moon'.[66] It might take a young man to act that way, but older actors often hang onto the reigns just as long as they can, which is often longer than they should.

Audiences in the English Renaissance apparently got a kick out of watching adolescent boys pretend to be grown women – and pretend to be grown men for that matter, as the intermittent success of the boy companies attests. But the history of *Romeo and Juliet* in performance seems to catalogue a trans-historical unease with older actors aping adolescent amour. The anecdotes that swirl about *R&J*'s central casting organize the resistance to the embarrassing approximations that the play requires of actors. In some perfectly representative way, the duck anecdote interrupts the play's insistence on transcendental teenage love. The play might call for a hopping bird – a metaphor for a love just about to take wing – but anecdotes quack back. You can talk of gardens all you want, but the theatre operates in a fallen world.

way, the duck encounter dramatizes the play's undercurrent of transcendental romantic love. The duck might embody a hope but a [illegible] just about to take [illegible] quickly back. [illegible] but the theatre operates in a fallen world.

4

Richard III: Oedipus text

Olivier's Dick

I'll buy you a drink if you've heard this one before. One time Laurence Olivier was invited to a charity event, where he agreed to read a bit of the Bard for the assembled luminaries in aid of a deserving cause. Taking the stage, Olivier opens his edition of Shakespeare and commences to 'read', 'Now is the winter of our discontent . . .' when from out of the audience a voice brays, 'Larry Oliver! Larry Oliver! Sing "Bolero"!' Nonplussed, Olivier pauses and gazes into the crowd. 'Please,' he says, 'I'm trying to recite the opening from Shakespeare's early masterpiece, *Richard III*. And despite my poor efforts, this audience seems eager to hear it.' To supporting applause, Olivier begins again. 'Now, is the winter . . .', 'Larry Oliver! Larry Oliver! Sing "Bolero"!' Olivier pauses, as before, and scolds the anonymous voice. 'Sir! Please! *Richard the Third* by William Shakespeare. Cease to interrupt!'

'Now is the . . .', 'Larry Oliver! Larry Oliver! Sing "Bolero"!' Olivier loses his patience, snaps shut his book and flares his nostrils, 'Look, I am trying to recite the opening to William Shakespeare's *Richard III* and quite against the laws of decorum and good manners you continue to interrupt! Please desist!' He begins to return to his book, but adds, as an afterthought, 'Besides, even if I *were* to accede to your impertinent request, "Bolero" is an *instrumental* number, and I could hardly sing it for you. Now, let there be no more interruptions!' Grand round of supporting applause. Olivier opens his book once more, this time sharply so. Clearing his throat and gathering himself, he begins: 'Now is the . . .', 'Larry Olivers! Larry Olivers! . . . Show us your dick!'

This is one of the weirdest anecdotes I have ever heard. It is not clear why the punch line is funny, or even that it is, other than its crass incongruity. Olivier. Shakespeare. 'Bolero'. Your dick? Submerged somewhere in its inert comedy, however, is the fact that Olivier is at least trying to show the audience his Dick.

I heard this un-citeable anecdote from an actor who heard it from his father. I asked his father for his version and received a slightly different account, in which it's 'Malaguena' that Olivier's asked to sing – and to which he sniffs that he 'rarely takes requests'. The punch line is the same, however, and so both this anecdote and the way that I heard it end up making a similar point: sons will always differ from their fathers, just as actors will with their authors. This anecdote joins the one that opened this book and the one that closes this chapter to offer the same argument – by interrupting Richard and making him lose his place the anecdotes give the actor what all of them secretly want: the chance to compose themselves.

Richard's whose self again?

Richard III may be a history play, but the anecdotes it generates are all revenge comedies. As detailed here and in the introduction, Richard anecdotes often interrupt Shakespeare's most famous opening line, and stage history is full of tired jokes that wrinkle Richard's opening salvo – 'Now is de vinter of our discontent made glorus summer by de son of New York'; 'Now is the winter of our discontent made glorious summer by this leg of pork'; 'now for the winter of our disco event', etc.[1] – as actors alter or go off the script, which is the single most effective way to cope with the dispiriting fact that everything they have to say has been written down for them. Another Richard – Burton this time – complains of this in his diary, where he describes acting as 'sheer drudgery', largely due to the 'indignity and boredom of having to learn the writings of another man, which nine times out of ten was indifferent'.[2] 'Now is the winter . . .' is hardly indifferent, but it is un-different, so utterly familiar as to provoke ire. Antony Sher complains in his diary that it seems 'terribly unfair of Shakespeare to begin his play with such a famous speech. You don't like to put your mouth to it, so many other mouths have been there.'[3] An actor may elsewhere make an audience forget that he's reciting the 'writings of another man', but during 'Now is the winter . . .' everyone knows who's holding the pen.

A reviewer asked in 1867, 'Cannot some mutual friend – if any such there be – effect a reconciliation between [Edwin] Forrest and Shakspere? They are notoriously enemies, and never meet without exchanging blows. . . . If this thing goes on, either Forrest must annihilate Shakspere, or Shakspere will annihilate Forrest.'[4] History has given it to Shakespeare on points, but the hostilities seem to erupt anew every time *Richard III* is staged.

The play has therefore spun off an unusually coherent body of anecdotal adaptations that stage the antagonism between an actor and his author. Who comes first? Father or Son? Author or actor? William the Conqueror or Richard the Third? The antagonism is due not just to the part's physical challenges – it is, with Lear, Shakespeare's most punishing part – but the logical extension of the play's solipsistic dramaturgy. Richard professes in *Henry VI, Part 3* an ambition for kingship based on his own antipathy to kinship: He has 'no brother'; he is 'like no brother', he is, he says, 'myself alone'. His regnal ambition is, furthermore, self-nullifying. Pursued to its logical end, it would leave him king of graves, since every subject is a potential threat. Resolved to be a solo act, Richard murders his way through the play of his name until there's no one left to kill, except the author.

In their eagerness to break free of the script, actors often author their own adaptations by retailing anecdotes that wander off the text. In so doing, they participate in the great tradition of Shakespearean adaptation. While many of Shakespeare's plays have enjoyed or suffered alternative versions, the fundamental antagonism of the effort – in which an adaptor attempts to differentiate his labours while signalling his allegiance – often finds expression through the case of *Richard III*. In 1676, John Dryden, in the epilogue to his and D'Avenant's adaptation *The Tempest or the Enchanted Isle*, manages his anxiety through the spectre of the play: 'The Ghosts of Poets walk within this place, / And haunt us Actors wheresoe'r we pass / In visions bloudier than King Richard was.'[5] Dryden obliquely uses the tent scene in *Richard III* to imagine the ghosts of authors past, who haunt not just writers but 'Actors'. In either case, adaptations – and particularly *Richard III* – operate in the shadow of what a New York critic, a century later, called 'the great original':

> In London, as in this city, the caricaturing of some incidents in a classic story, or the ludicrous representation of historic events, will receive greater notice than the performance, by actors holding a creditable position, of Shakspere's best plays. Indeed, in the effort to gratify this debased appetite, even the great dramatist's creations are not sacred, and 'Richard Ye Third' often secures a larger attendance in many a theatre than the great original.[6]

The phrase was catching, since in 1820 a critic celebrated the return to the stage of Shakespeare's text, which Cibber had 'mangled'. The 'great original has now come forward'.[7] It's fairly apparent what the 'great original' represents – the patriarchal creator in whose shadow all actors abide.

It is fitting, therefore, that the anecdotes that best register the timbre of antagonism that scores *Richard III* revolve around a punch line that Shakespeare did not write. A number of anecdotes resolve into the line that, 'Richard's himself again'. The line comes from Colley Cibber's adaptation of *Richard III*, which held the stage for nearly 200 years – from 1700 until the late nineteenth century (despite any number of attempts to supplant it with the original, a deferred Oedipalism that history successfully beat back for a time). Waking from his dream before the battle of Bosworth field, Cibber's Richard famously howls, 'Conscience avant! Richard's himself again' (5.5.85).[8] The best way to signal that Richard's back in charge is to quote a line from Shakespeare that Shakespeare didn't write.

Theatre history is liberally sprinkled with assertions of Richard's self-possession and the substitution of the word 'Richard' for whomsoever the anecdote treats. Following John Philip Kemble's illness in 1815, a paper writes, 'We therefore trust, that we shall not only have soon to say, "Richard's himself again," but that his numerous friends and admirers will, before the close of the season, see him take the field with his wonted cheer and alacrity of spirit.'[9] Even Richard Burton – who never played the part – used Cibber's line to mediate on his return to self-possession. In his diary on 28 July 1975, Burton writes, 'Stopped booze and Richard is his shaky self again.'[10] Burton returned to his wonted spirits, but this palimpsestual meditation upon an actor's self-possession grows increasingly blurry as Burton uses Richard Gloucester via Colley Cibber via William Shakespeare to articulate Richard Burton's return to sobriety. It's enough to give you the spins.

The line has proven so flexible that it floated free from *Richard III* and came simply to express an actor's return to the audience's favour. Following one of Edmund Kean's many scrapes with propriety, he appeared as Shylock at Drury Lane, when 'his ears were assailed by what he was not accustomed to, loud hissing, and cries of "Off! Off!"' According to the tale, Kean stepped forward to the edge of the stage and offered a heartfelt apology that he had composed himself. 'General applause followed, with loud cries of "Richard is himself again!"' The line is remarkable enough since Kean was playing a usurious money-lender not a usurping tyrant, but the anecdote prefaces itself with the information that 'just before the curtain rose his Highness the Duke of GLOUCESTER entered his box'.[11] The seemingly inapposite punch line overlaps with reality and suggests that even when the play isn't *Richard III*, the Duke of Gloucester is always in the house.

As a line, 'Richard's himself again' may be great, but it's hardly original. It's Cibber's riff on Shakespeare's assertion of Richard's self-identity: 'I am I' (5.5.139). (It is telling too in the terms outlined here that Colley Cibber apparently couldn't quote Shakespeare's 'I am I', since he wrote his Richard in ink not irony.) Both lines flirt with tautology, but also dilate the split loyalty of the actor to character and self. But within the tautology – or at least the redundancy – is a buried but circular syllogism, a self-fulfilling one: Richard is an actor; I am Richard; ergo, I am an actor. What the tautologies and syllogisms tend to leave out is the author, so that this moment of Richard's self-composition becomes an opportunity for an actor to give birth to himself.

Lord Byron left something out when he first saw Edmund Kean as Richard, writing, 'Richard is a man, and Kean is Richard.'[12] This assessment, as in so many tales of Richard, leaves an odd man out. Richard is not a man but a fictional character, co-written by actor and author. But these moments indulge in a fantasy of 'autogenesis', as though 'a man were author of himself' (5.3.36), as Coriolanus puts it, quoting his author. After Cibber's version claimed the stage, 'Richard's himself again' quickly became the actor's catchphrase of autogenetic creation, and it proves remarkably flexible. Once, when Junius Brutus Booth was playing Richard in 1817,

> [a] branch of laurel which was thrown from the boxes during his fine performance in the tent scene unluckily caught his eye. This seemed to discompose him for the moment – it was however only for a moment; for Richard immediately became 'himself again'.[13]

It's not entirely clear what or whom constitutes 'himself' in this account, which is precisely the point. The laurel celebrates Booth, not Richard (or Cibber or Shakespeare) and so discomposes him, un-writes the character to reveal the actor whose credit is ransomed at the character's expense. The thrown laurel throws the actor, but only so that he may return to the script, in which Cibber requires him to claim to be himself – but this time 'himself' equals Junius Brutus Booth not Richard Gloucester, though the anecdote's point is that it cannot tell the difference.

But if Richard is 'himself again', who was he when he wasn't? An actor, obviously, since the moment peels back the character to show the body beneath. 'Richard' is, in these anecdotes, just another word for 'actor' (and as detailed below in 'Dickie Three Sticks', Richard is not just an actor, Richard is *the* actor, and vice versa). Another anecdote of Junius Brutus Booth finds the mad patriarch of the Booth family deep in his cups before a performance of *RIII*. In the memoirs of the nineteenth-century eccentric George Jones – self-styled 'Count Joannes', the 'actor, author, and counsellor of the Supreme Court' – we learn that he played Richmond to Booth's Richard upon New Year's Eve. By the time the Battle of Bosworth Field came around, Booth was 'drunk as a lord, and searching behind the scenes to fight and kill the "Earl of Richmond"'. The anecdote concludes with a fight to the death.

> Never in the history of the stage was there such a real combat as that which followed, and had I not been one of the most calm and skillful of swordsmen, I should have been cut to pieces and died upon the field, instead of 'Richard III.' As it was, I merely defended myself from his furious attacks, and as he could not touch me he became more enraged and frantic; foam at his mouth, and curses upon his lips. The audience, 2,000 persons, 'applauded to the very echo, that should applaud again,' all believed that there never was such a simulated combat as that before them; but it was, in fact, a reality they applauded. At last, he

> becoming exhausted from his maniac attempts to kill me, I thought it was time for me (professionally) to return the compliment, and consequently I gave him the coup de grace, or blow of death, as I thought. Believing that he would fall, 'I took the stage,' when, quick as a flash, he followed me, and aimed a blow at my head. I suddenly turned and disarmed him, seized him by the throat, threw him, and held the madman down, at the same time saying to him: – '"Richard III", are you dead?' 'Dead?' he replied, 'No! You infernal "Earl of Richmond" Down! Down! To hell, and say I sent you there!' I gave a signal to the prompter to drop the curtain, and Mr. Hamblin, Mr Anderson, and myself lifted the exhausted body of the dead King and took him to his room, and an hour elapsed before 'Richard' was himself again.'[14]

Here the parricidal mania of an overweening actor gives way to fratricide, an attempted one at least. It's not enough to kill the author, the other actors have to go as well – itself an adumbration of the play. The audience ate it up, according to the anecdote, which quotes Shakespeare to praise Cibber's play (the 'applause' line is from *Macbeth*). The account resolves once more to the refrain that Richard was 'himself again', meaning that Booth had sobered up, which further implies that he was not himself when he was drunk. But if Booth wasn't Richard when he was on the stage, who was? At the same time, the stock anecdotes about Booth's insobriety trade on his persona onstage and off as a drunk. In the anecdotal dramas of Booth's career, he's never more himself than when drunk, never more himself than when he's playing Richard, and so never more himself an actor when playing Richard drunk.

There's another player in the crowded contest between author and actor, and that's the audience. 'Richard's himself again', may be a verdict the character arrives at, but the audience will often be the judge of whether the actor's living up to himself, as a letter to the *Daily Advertiser* reports in December 1860:

> Some of your elder readers may remember the anecdote of Edmund Kean when at great expense he was brought down to Kilkenny. The audience received him as rapturously as the great tragedian could desire, but there their applause ceased. The two first acts of *Richard* were received with solemn silence; the actor felt it, and was so dispirited that the audience began to murmur. The manager called for, and accused of having deceived the good folks of the city of the cats, and brought down some stick from the Dublin boards, instead of the great actor. In vain he assured them that this was the veritable Edmund Kean. They did not believe him; and then he told them the cause – they had not applauded. The audience took the hint, and in the next and following acts Richard was 'himself again.'[15]

Kean was unbelievably bad, so bad that not only did the audience not believe in the character, they did not believe in the actor. Richard becomes himself again only after the audience was persuaded to believe – with Lord Byron – that Kean is Richard, and, more importantly, that Kean is Kean. Edmund Kean was, it seems, not himself that day, but only because the audience did not give him the recognition he craved. Like Tinkerbell in *Peter Pan*, Kean needed to be clapped back to life.

However cloying Kean's neediness, the anecdote is overt where others are more coy. Richard is the part where actors get to be themselves. Complaining that an actor is just 'playing himself' is among the lazier barbs that critics throw (you try it). Maybe the wish is father to the thought, or criticism the parent to desire. If so, Richard is the premier part in which wish and thought meet, as a late eighteenth-century anecdote about 'Mr Whitely' reveals:

> No man's name is better known among the erratic tribes of Thespis, than Mr Whitely's; the anecdotes arising from his singularity of disposition are innumerable: – this gentleman (formerly the manager of a company who performed in Nottinghamshire) having constantly an eye to his interest,

> one evening during the performance of Richard the Third, gave a tolerable proof of that being his leading principle. Representing the crook'd back'd tyrant, he exclaimed: 'Hence babbling dreams, you threaten here in vain, Conscience avaunt – That man in the brown wig there has come into the pit without paying – Richard's himself again!'[16]

What comes between Richard's conscience and himself is a concern that the audience might be paying attention but nothing else. The anecdote's pun about the 'leading principle' of the leading principal perfectly expresses the collusive agendas of the star player – one eye on his part, the other on the bottom line. The anecdote expresses, however, the underlying expectation of the audience: what they paid for – all but one – was to see Mr Whitely's 'singularity of disposition'. Once he expressed it, Richard was back to his old self.

'Singularity of disposition' might just be a fancy phrase for 'star', and Richard is nothing if not a star turn. In these terms, Richard Burbage, not Shakespeare, is the great original – though the 'William the Conqueror' anecdote puts the matter to question. All the actors that follow Burbage therefore collaborate with the audience not just against the author but against other actors. For much of theatre history, Richard was the role in which male actors proved their mettle, though in the last fifty years or so Hamlet has succeeded Richard. Both characters die without heirs, however, and a crowd of pretenders is always eager to take up the sword. George Fredrick Cooke was once late for the stage, and found that though the writer may be dead, his rival was quick:

> Poor COOKE was on Monday delayed so long on his way to town in a stage coach, that he kept the dramatic stage waiting for some time. This gave great displeasure to the company. KEMBLE offered to take the place of COOKE; but soon after the absent Gentleman made his appearance, and being rallied a little, Richard soon became himself again, and got through his part with tolerable credit.[17]

Cooke and Kemble had crossed swords before – though Kemble would ultimately have the last word, as we saw in the *Hamlet* chapter, since he played with George Cooke's skull. Here, however, Cooke gets the last laugh, or at least the credit, since, in the anecdote's syllogism, the antecedent of 'himself' is Cooke, not Kemble, and certainly not the crook-back (and certainly not the writer). The point of the anecdote is, however, to ask on behalf of all aspiring actors, if you're not going to be himself, do you mind if I give it a go?

Following his star turn as Richard III, Antony Sher ran into the great original himself. At the opening of the Barbican in March 1982, Sher had a backstage encounter with 'Father Time'. He and a group of luminaries were gathered, eagerly anticipating the arrival of the Queen. Instead, he met the King:

> The Royal arrival was imminent . . . I turned to beckon my flagging group and almost immediately crashed into someone heading in the other direction. I say crashed, but it was soft and cushioned as befits a collision with Destiny. The recipient of my careless shoulder was an old man with a white beard and rimless spectacles. The face was vaguely familiar, the voice even more so. 'Are you trying to kill me?' he asked . . .

'Yes', Antony Sher did not say to Laurence Olivier.

> The Queen arrived, but my encounter had so stunned me that I was pointing in the wrong direction, expecting her to come down the stairs instead of up them, and missed seeing her altogether. It didn't matter, for I had just brushed shoulders with Richard III.[18]

Even when he's being conversational, Sher has a knack for the mythic. Gentle condescension, phony reverence, the brusque shoulder – you get the feeling that's the way they talked around Colonus. The king's face, after all, looked vaguely familiar.

At the time, Sher writes, he put the encounter 'down to drunkenness' but later suspected it had to with a 'Greater Scheme Of Things', as though they are mutually exclusive. If a 'singular disposition' is another word for 'star' or, better, the 'It' that stars are alleged to possess, the 'Scheme Of Things' is another word for 'Myth'. The function of Sher's myth-making tale is to counter the knowledge that there have been, are, and will be many Richards. One thing that is clear from Sher's scheme of things is that stardom is a singular disposition, in which one star rises as another descends and heads off in the other direction. Another thing that Sher is clear about is that Richard should watch his back.

Heart-throbs and hamstrings

Because, if you don't watch your back, you'll never see who's gaining on you.

> One morning Kemble, crossing the stage before rehearsal, heard shouts of laughter from the green-room. Inquiring the cause he was told, 'It's little Kean acting Richard III.' Throwing open the door he beheld his company grouped about a shabbily-dressed lad who was spouting the speeches of Gloucester in imitation of himself. For this deed he was summarily banished from the theatre by the irate Kemble who possessed little kindness and no sense of humor.[19]

If there's one thing actors hate, it is finding out they aren't inimitable. (Anecdotes abound about David Garrick's incomprehension when he encountered imitators, in whose imitations he did not recognize himself.) What cost little Kean his job was imitating not Richard but 'himself', a third-person singularity named Kemble who could not bear to be imitated. The story of Kean's summary dismissal (he'd return, predictably, to become Richard himself again) could have been about any role, but Richard is where a covey of acting anxieties convene, anxieties concerned with originality and imitation.

The collision of originality with imitation often expresses itself in the form of a genuine crisis: actors have simultaneously to be both the original and copy, both parent and child. They have, in short, to give birth to themselves. When Mr Young debuted as Richard III in 1813, the reviewers praised his originality in autogenetic terms:

> Nor did his manner appear to us as borrowed from any antecedent example; for he seemed to marshal the results of his own feelings, in his own way, (AS EVERY PERFORMER SHOULD,) and did not fail to illustrate his text well; and that was a professional triumph, which may justly entitle him to take his stand in the same class with Mr. KEMBLE himself, and exclaim, without presumption, I am an actor also.[20]

The review runs into some telling contradictions. Praising Young (the name is almost too redolent) for his originality, for owing nothing to his predecessors in the role, the reviewer concludes that Young's originality is in the class of Kemble, which allows him to announce his birth as 'an actor also'. 'I am an actor also' is as self-contradictory as 'Richard's himself again' is tautological. The theatre is rarely embarrassed by contradiction, however, so that Young's originality should be the pattern for 'every performer', who should all be so original and by so doing become actors also. Performers should compose themselves in such a way to be simultaneously legible and unique – all the while, of course, illustrating the author's text. Actors are expected to become inimitable through acts of imitation.

That Richard should provide a site for these contradictory impulses has everything to do with Richard's disability. Actors express their inimitability through Richard not because Gloucester is inimitable but because he's inimitative – disabled by his physique from imitating others. While Richard may dissimulate, he may not simulate. Grounding the circuit of theatrical exchange, Richard is where acting stops. He is the end of all acting.

Under normal conditions, what primarily marks a body as an actor is its ability to be anybody, even or especially a body less able than its own. Richard III is not, however, the exception that proves the rule, but the exceptional example *of* that rule. Able actors feign Richard's disability, a form of impersonation that actors have long relished but that has more recently become a point of contention. 'Cripping up is the twenty-first century answer to blacking up,' a character says in Kaite O'Reilly's 2002 *peeling*, a play written about – and exclusively to be played by – the disabled. The author's objection – echoed by others – is less that able actors perform disability than to the assumption that no disabled actors are available.[21] O'Reilly likens the case to Othello, played in blackface for so many years. The analogy between black actors and disabled ones is tricky, to say the least, since it flattens nuances peculiar to both constituencies. Still, the success of the four-foot-five star actor Peter Dinklage, who played Richard III at the Public in 2004, makes O'Reilly's point for her: stars come in all colours and sizes.

For most of Richard's performance history, Richard was – and still is – performed by the able-bodied. Furthermore, the chatter around the play reveals the relish performers take in mimetic difficulty. The physical difficulty of disabling an able body – and the chance to ostentatiously draw attention to that difficulty – allows virtuosic displays by able-bodied actors, who signal their ability by disabling themselves. This idea is lampooned in the 2008 film *Tropic Thunder*, where Robert Downey, Jr, playing an actor in blackface named Kirk Lazarus, critiques a film made by Ben Stiller's character, who is also an actor. In that film, Stiller went what Lazarus calls 'full retard', immersing himself totally in the character of a mentally deficient man named 'Simple Jack'. The spectacular irony of an actor (Downey) playing a blacked-up actor (Lazarus) critiquing Ben Stiller's character for 'cripping up' too fully in a fictional film glosses the performance history of *Richard III*: the role requires not the performance of disability but the performance of the performance of disability. Never go full Richard.

Though it has recently become politically contentious, the scrutiny the play brings to the body is not remotely modern. One of the earliest references to Shakespeare's *Richard III* comes from the 1602 play *The Return from Parnassus*, where 'Richard Burbage' and 'Will Kemp' come to Cambridge to audition some actors. In a moment that looks forward to Sher's run in with Olivier, Burbage auditions his usurper:

> *Burbage*. I like your face, and the proportion of your body for *Richard the 3*. I pray, M. Phil. let me see you act a little of it.
>
> *Philomusus*. 'Now is the winter of our discontent
> Made glorious summer by the sonne of Yorke'[22]

Burbage interrupts Philomusus there – he knows how it ends after all – but what makes Philomusus so promising a Richard is the 'proportion of [his] body'. It's impossible to know from the text alone whether Philomusus's body is shapely or misshapen, but the verdict of history has largely been one-sided. It takes a well-formed body to perform deformity. This verdict is rendered more clearly in 1750, when John Hill relates an anecdotally precise if blunt diagnosis of the effect a disabled actor had upon an audience:

> [We] have had a proof that even the peculiar bodily imperfection which is mentioned in the play [*RIII*] itself as belonging to the hero of it; and which we even expect the performer shou'd counterfeit to us by bolsters and bandages, yet if he be unhappy enough really to possess it, he offends us in the representation . . . There is some where about town a person of the name of Machen, who has been long the darling of the theatres at the Blue Boar, the Tennis Court in James-Street, and sometimes of the Bartholomew-Booths; and who has of late been honur'd with the title of the lame

> actor of low comedy in Mr. Foot's drolleries . . . It is his misfortune to be lame of one leg; which is so much shorter than the other, that the highest heel he can wear is not enough to raise that side of his body to a level with the rest. Tragedy is the darling passion of this player, and he concluded, from this natural imperfection, he was the fittest of all men to perform the character of Richard III, which Shakespear himself (with how much justice we do not presume to say) has figured to us as lame. Vast were the expectation of applause with which this man had flatter'd himself, when he should come to that part of the character where this peculiar natural defect, by which he thought himself qualified to perform the part, should come on: But what was the event? The audience, when he hop'd across the stage as he spoke the line, 'Dogs bark at me as I halt by them,' instead of the applause he listen'd for, burst out into a loud laugh. They could never reconcile themselves to have an original impos'd on them, when they expected or desir'd no more than a copy. There is a seeming contradiction and absurdity in judgment of the world on the occasion: but it is only such, 'tis not a real one.[23]

Machen is naturally imperfect when the audience wants him to be artificially so. His disability, he thought, made him fit for the part but, cruelly, is just what the audience found laughable. Machen's disability only proved he wasn't acting. He is therefore doubly damned by his 'peculiar natural defect'. He's better off sticking it out as the 'lame actor of low comedy' in, again the name is too bad to be true, 'Mr Foot's drolleries'. But, in a contradiction, even an absurdity that Hill points out, artful imperfection is applauded while natural imperfection is not. The anecdote lays bare what the performance tradition of Richard so often mystifies – we don't want the original imposed upon us, we want the copy. The only actors who get to be 'Richard himself' are the ones who obviously aren't.

In a telling companion to the failure of Machen, an amateur actor who 'once volunteered to play *Richmond*' had his lameness pointed out to him, though it does not seem to have halted the performance:

> He was lame, having one leg shorter than the other. He began his opening speech, '–Thus far into the bowels of the land have I marched on without impediment;' when a rude unfeeling fellow interrupted him with, '*Hopped* on, you mean;' to which, with a polite bow, *Richmond* replied, – 'Thank you, sir; I *hop* corrected;' and proceeded with the performance.[24]

Machen's 'hop' brought down the house, but this Richmond – having conceded that his limp was not a put on – is allowed to proceed. Of course, he wasn't playing Richard, for whom the limp is usually reserved. We might expect a vast compendium of actors wrong-footing it across history's boards. The limp is the part's signature effect, after all. For that matter, the prosthetic hump that Richards employ should provide an opportunity for deflating gags, like Peter Shaffer's Shakespearian actress in *Lettice and Lovage* who repurposes Richard's hump as Falstaff's stomach. Prosthetics almost always provide anecdotes an alibi – wigs, noses, makeup – but while it is dangerous to argue from a lack of evidence, Richard's hump has not raised much hilarity (though Simon Callow described the 'hump acoustic' he produced while playing Richard for the World Service of the BBC). Even Falstaff's fat-suit has produced more belly laughs.

There are many tales that treat Richard's limp, but they rarely play it for laughs. Instead, the anecdotes all play upon the role's physical risk. Perhaps here, at last, we find an element of performance that theatre won't trivialize. But the theatre has something more important in mind than safety, and that's publicity. A variant of the 'mask that sticks' stories, tales of ham-strung actors worry over – and in so doing celebrate – the fear that an able actor may become less so by playing the disabled King. As quoted in the introduction, Terry Hands passed on, or invented whole cloth, a bit of theatrical fake-lore to give this legend legs. Recorded by Antony Sher when he embarked on his role as Richard, Hands

> tells me that when Robert Hirsh did it for him in his *Comedie Francaise* production, he limped on alternate legs from night to night, with two sets of costumes. 'You might like to think along similar lines. I've been advised by an osteopath that irreparable damage can be done to the pelvis otherwise. It's a little known historical fact, but apparently after the original production Burbage said to Shakespeare, "If you ever do that to me again, mate, I'll kill you."'[25]

Hands credits the lore to the Great Original, in this case Richard Burbage, who – in a 'little known historical fact' – decided that once was enough. Once, however, is usually sufficient. It's not for nothing that Oedipus is a cripple. The point of the anecdotes is to advertise that the actor is in harm's way, ready to risk his ability for the sake of the audience. The anecdotes are pre-emptive advertisements, a bit of publicity, to constantly remind us that the disabled King is always played by the most able actor.

Actors will therefore go out of their way to advertise a fear of injury. In this case, anecdotes function as part of the media apparatus that publicize a production. When Kevin Spacey played Richard in 2012, a wire story circulated nearly verbatim across multiple platforms of the lengths to which Spacey went to avoid injury.

> He tells chat show host Ellen DeGeneres, 'A lot of thought went into what I was going to do because I talked to a bunch of actors who played Richard III before I did and they all said to me: "Be careful . . . I threw my neck out, my back, my knee, my leg. . . ." I didn't want to hurt myself over all of those performances and, you know, massages were a good thing, but at the very end of the play, they hung me upside down after Richard is killed and that was great. They put these big ankle things on and lifted me up and you could hear the

> audience going "Oh" – they were, like, a little scared about it, and I was like, "This is the most awesome thing". After crumpling up all night long, it was the best stretch ever.'[26]

This is an exemplary twenty-first century theatrical anecdote, filtered through pixels until it's rubbed smooth. Like most good theatrical stories it combines a pinch of market savvy, a dose of theatrical lore, a whiff of deprecatory self-regard that dissolves into a 'just get on with it' shrug, as Spacey enjoys a leisurely stretch at the audience's expense. At the moment the audience audibly expresses their fear in a collective 'Oh', Spacey flips the switch. He may have genuinely feared for his hamstring, but the audience knows the limp's a put on. Finally, at the point where the audience thinks his body is *actually* at risk, Spacey can relax and just hang out – a literal and figurative conjugation of the suspension of disbelief.

It's worth pausing for a moment to think about the reflexive gesture to the past that this story contains. Cautionary tales about Richard's physique always leverage the past – the bunches of actors 'who'd played Richard III before' – as a cautionary reminder of what can happen to a tightrope walker who works without a net (or an offstage masseuse). At the same time, the gesture acknowledges that every Richard's a copy in a long, long line of Richards and therefore helps to process a performer's historical burden. All those actors, across the years, who have famously played Richard. It's enough to bend any back. To acknowledge the past is to attempt to break from it. The reason Spacey talked to a bunch of Richards, at least putatively, was to avoid repeating their mistakes.

Richard's limp – like Yorick's skull, like Juliet's balcony, like Desdemona's pillow – becomes a place to talk about a topic fundamental to theatre. Acting is an embodied art, and so the actor's body is always on the line. As with 'Richard's himself again', the role floats out of the play and becomes a way for actors to talk about injuries. A bit of cod etymology – or fishy philology – even suggests that the actor's usual good-luck wish of 'break a leg' comes from *Richard III*: 'Some attribute the line to a performance of Shakespeare's *Richard III*, where the famed 18th century British actor, David Garrick, became so entranced in the performance that he was unaware of a fracture.'[27] However far-fetched, the explanation assigns Richard a role in one of theatre's typically contradictory rites: an expression of good will disguised as a curse. Or the other way around. The most cynical reading of 'break a leg' might see in it an expression of labour anxiety. If you break a leg, I can play him myself.

Even when the play isn't *Richard*, then, Gloucester is always in the room. In 1948 on tour in Australia, Olivier wrecked his right knee, and though he was playing in Sheridan, Richard was to blame: 'At this precise time I had a torn cartilage in my right knee; my limp in *Richard*, in constantly fatigued conditions, had set up a weakness in the "straight" leg, and one evening in the dance at the end of *School [for Scandal]* it just went.'[28] A reviewer at the time – one 'J.B.' writing for the *Sydney Morning Herald* – offered an alternative version:

> It was unfortunate that, during a matinee performance of 'King Richard III,' Olivier injured his right knee, but continued; he subsequently appeared in later performances of the play supported by a 'T-shaped' crutch. It was remarked that 'instead of the virile and active King, he became a twisted, bitter man who hated his infirmity.'[29]

From the reviewer's standpoint in any event, it's no contest between Shakespeare and Sheridan. Shakespeare did it to Richard again and so he gets the blame, or the credit.

Olivier's account sounds like a gripe, but it's actually a boast. Only stars get to injure themselves as Richard since only actors of name get to be himself again. Richard Burton, after putting his foot through a television after a performance where he was booed as *Hamlet* and then fought with Elizabeth Taylor,

> arrived at the theatre on the following evening with a decided limp. He insisted on playing the performance with

> the limp and said, 'Some critics have said I play Hamlet like Richard the Third anyway, so what the hell is the difference?'[30]

Burton doesn't detail what it means to 'play Hamlet like Richard III' other than that he played Hamlet like a star, which he was, which means in this case that he 'insisted' upon playing Hamlet with the limp just as though he had a choice. As with Olivier, even when the limp is genuine it still seems like a put on. By lacerating his foot on the shards of a TV screen and then arguing with Taylor – an even greater star – Burton limped onstage to play Hamlet, and Richard was himself again. Like a drunk J.B. Booth almost murdering his Richmond, Richard Burton was never more himself than limping through *Hamlet* after trashing a hotel room following a fight with Elizabeth Taylor.

The most famous hamstring in Richard's recent history is the one that Antony Sher snapped while playing the Fool in *Lear*. In his diary about playing Richard, *The Year of the King*, Sher gives a grim description of a crippling injury and offers an anecdote for an orthopaedic age:

> Halfway through the evening performance of *King Lear*. We'd done the first storm scene. I was alone on stage, coming to the end of the Fool's soliloquy. Goosestepped to the front of the stage, 'FOR – I – LIVE – BEFORE – HIS – TIME', aware that I was slamming my feet down harder than usual . . . swung into the little dance – BANG! My first thought as I fell was, 'Fucking floorboards!' I looked round. No hole in the stage. No floorboard sticking up. Then what had hit the back of my leg? What had made that noise? A bullet? Dazed, I looked towards the audience for the assassin or some explanation. Realised I was sitting on the floor, had missed several cues, the music was unwinding around me, I tried to rise, fell again.

The tendon had unravelled up the back of his leg 'like a venetian blind.'[31] The transition from sidekick to star for Sher started with a blown-out Achilles. But Sher was just getting in character, all part of what the diary calls the 'Achilles mythology'. Sher's ascent to Richard's throne began with him propped up on crutches and ended with him using crutches as a prop. It provides some fitting framing material when late in the diary his crutches snap.

Injury and disability fold into performance what usually waits until the curtain call, when the exhausted actor appears before us 'like a champion weight lifter or hunger artist', as Roland Barthes has put it.[32] We generally reserve our applause for the end, when we thank the actor for consuming his body in the course of a performance. Our applause is meant to replenish him, or at least urge him to go get some much-needed rest. Richard's deformity – the limp, the hunch, the contorted arm – allows the lead actor to appear before the curtain for the entirety of the play. The role of Richard is a curtain call that lasts the whole play long.

The iconic image of Sher's Richard pictures him propped on two crutches, which, as Sher explains in his memoir, were meant to evoke the image of Richard as 'spider'. Sher doesn't look much like a spider in the photographs. He looks like an actor with a couple of props. Of course the crutches *are* just props, or the props are just a crutch. They are there to remind you that he does not need them. In fact, today's Richards often use properties from crutches to braces to orthopaedic boots to make sure we do not miss the point. Where a legless man might rely on a prosthetic merely to allow him to limp, here the able actor arrives at the same place but from the other end. Devices designed to ambulate the disabled become props to encumber the actor. The point of all this was driven home by Ian McKellen in the stage and film version of 1995. He confined his disability to a disabled arm, which afforded him virtuosic feats of single-handed cigarette lighting, and so on. A feigned disability gives the star a chance to show he can act with one hand tied behind his back.

As anecdotes seem to recognize, this is grotesque, and so they strenuously remind us that the actor is genuinely at risk. Sher doesn't need the crutches, but he might if he does not use them, and so anecdotes disable criticism by, among others, the disabled. Ironically, whether a result of increased sensitivity to the disabled, or a reaction against *Richard III*'s suggestion that a malformed body reflects a malformed character, Richards on the stage today often use crutches, braces, or prosthetics and end up suggesting that deformity's a put on.

However sustained, a limp is a star sign reserved for history's Richards. Simon Callow learned this the hard way, when he tried to inflate a small part into a large one. Playing a small role in *Galileo* under John Dexter's direction, he hit upon a big idea:

> It seemed to me hugely to the advantage of the play that the little monk should have a social and physical reality. I communicated my insight to John. 'Could I not,' I asked, 'have some physical disability as a result of malnutrition?' 'And where,' he asked, 'will you have the parrot, on the left shoulder or the right?'[33]

The monk was little, and so it was 'hugely to the advantage of the play' – not to mention Callow – that Callow disable him. By adding a physical disability, Callow aspired to add a 'physical reality' to the play, but the physical reality here would not advantage the play but Callow. What Callow was hungry for was stardom, and learned one of theatre's weirdest enthymemes: limps are for stars.

Olivier put this premise to the ultimate test, following his stunning debut as Richard at the Old Vic in 1944. He writes:

> I felt, if you like, what an actor must finally feel: I felt a little power of hypnotism; I felt that I had them. It went to my head, as I said, to an extent that I didn't even bother to put on the limp. I thought, I've got them anyway, I needn't bother with all this characterization any more. It's an awful story really.[34]

Even Olivier's egotism failed him, as he cops to the awfulness of the story – without specifying precisely what he finds so awful about it. He was merely testing a postulate, after all, by trying to prove the reverse. If the limp makes you a star, does stardom make you limp? Since Olivier was decidedly a star, does he even need to affect a limp for the audience to discern it? Olivier does not report on the results of his awful experiment, but he was punished for his hubris, at least anecdotally. During the filming of *Richard III* in 1944, Olivier hired an archer to shoot at him from below.

> One of UK's top archers was employed for this stunt. The horse was padded, but the arrow missed its mark and wounded Laurence Olivier in the lower leg. However, this scene worked to Olivier's advantage, as the Battle of Bosworth scenes were the first to be shot for the film. For the rest of the shoot, Olivier did not have to fake Richard III's famous limp.[35]

The story strains credulity, since if Olivier did this it was hugely stupid. Still, Olivier's various memoirs and interviews are filled with a masochistic commitment to active acting – his famous Hamlet dive onto Claudius from nine feet above, his hanging from his heels at Coriolanus's death, him brained by a camera while filming *Henry V*. Olivier is always advertising his recklessness and often limped through performance, hobbled by his total commitment to performance. His account of Richard going to his head suggests that standing up straight on his own two feet is one of the actor's only acts of revenge against an author who's trying to hamstring him.

Booth's trunk

A 2013 exhibition at the Folger Shakespeare Library called 'Here is a play fitted' featured among its artefacts and photographs Edwin Booth's costume for *Richard III*. Particoloured in red and blue, the tunic features the royal coat of arms of Richard's day, British lions quartered with French *fleurs-de-lise*. One shoulder of the coat is heavily padded, to indicate Richard's hump. It's a fairly tatty costume, small and threadbare. The lions look preposterous; indeed they're facing the wrong way. However unremarkable the costume, the display was magnificent. Due to a trick of the light, the visitor could see him or herself projected onto and therefore into Booth's costume. To look at the costume was to try on the costume.

Furthermore, rather than laying the costume flat, the curators embodied it with a headless form, providing the volume that draws our attention to the human heart that once beat beneath the fabric. The dress form stood for all that was present, and all that is absent. In fact the whole exhibition was spooky, a haunted house of theatre history – prompt books sprawled open, abandoned by absent actors; a discarded dagger fresh from a murder scene; costumes draped upon headless figures. In this particular costume's case, the viewer found, or didn't, the missing trunk of Edwin Booth.

The costume's accompanying placard read, 'Costume worn by Edwin Booth in the role of Richard III. Embroidered velvet, ca. 1870's. Edwin Booth wore this surcoat over a set of armor during the Battle of Bosworth field in the final scenes of his productions of *Richard III*.' What made this object worthy of our attention, worthy of the considerable conservatory efforts taken to preserve, maintain and display it was the verifiable fact that Booth wore it, and wore it more than once. The artefact survived its actor, and it is through it that we remember him. There is a powerful irony in this instance, however, for the costume remembers something Booth tried to forget. The following story suggests that the power of a costume to evoke presence can prompt destruction as well as preservation – and that conservation and vandalism come out of the same impulse. The story about another missing trunk suggests as much, as recounted by the actor and writer Otis Skinner to *The American Magazine* in the 1920s. Get a drink. This is a long one.

There is one glimpse of his brooding spirit that stands fixed in my memory. It did not come from his own lips, but from those of an old property man who had begun active life as a general errand boy about Booth's Theater that stood on Twenty-third Street. He was called 'Garrie.' His chief occupation was as 'basket boy,' in which capacity he conveyed the costumes and properties of the actors to and from their lodgings and the theater. Mr Booth was very fond of Garrie, and employed him frequently in his own personal service . . . At some time prior to the great tragedy at Washington [Lincoln's assassination] the theatrical wardrobe and personal effects of John Wilkes Booth had been confided to the care of John McCullough, between who and the former there had grown up a close and sympathetic acquaintance, and conveyed by him across the Unites States border into Canada . . . [T]his wardrobe trunk was in his possession during his Canadian engagements, before and after the assassination . . . It was a number of years later, in 1873, that Edwin Booth learned of its existence, and it was forwarded at his request by McKee Rankin, the actor . . . I will tell the story, as nearly as I can remember, just as Garrie told it to me: 'It happened early in '73. The day had been one of storm and drifting snow, one of those belated days in New York when winter forgets to become spring. Mr Booth had a snug suite of apartments high up over the stage, in which most of his time was spent between his hours of business and acting in the theater. 'Richard III' was on for a short run and had drawn a fine audience that night in spite of the storm. And say! How he had played! . . . On leaving his dressing-room about twelve o'clock, he gave me orders to wake him at three in the morning . . . I mounted the stairway to his apartment, where, over a spirit-lamp in the library, I proceeded to make some strong coffee. This done I opened the door of his bedroom. He was breathing heavily in a dead sleep . . . Then I shook him gently by the shoulder and told him the time. As I expected, he sat up dazedly and reach about for something to throw at me; but it was only a moment that his wits wandered . . . After drinking two cups of [coffee] he asked about the weather . . . I helped him into his coat (he had lain down partly dressed), and took the lantern. 'Where are we going, Mr Booth?' I asked. 'To the furnace-room, Garrie,' he said. So I led the way down the stairs, across the black stage, and into the cellar. The theater building was erected before the days of general steam heat, and the furnace-room was a cavernous place of vaulted brick, which held the big, old-fashioned heater that warmed it . . . I lighted a single gas-jet, and it made a bright spot in the gloom. Over near the furnace I saw an unusually large trunk, almost like a packing-case, tied with ropes; there were seals on it, some on the cords, some at the edges where the cover and the body of the trunk met. 'I shall want an ax, Garrie,' said Mr Booth. There was one in the corner by the coal-bins, and when I had found it I was told to cut the cords of the trunk and knock off the top. This was but little work, for the box was rickety and old. The lid was soon off, and out came the smell of camphor and musty fabrics. There they lay, the costumes of John Wilkes Booth . . . For a few moments he stood looking down at the things then he laid the wigs and swords aside on the overturned trunk cover, and commenced taking out the costumes. The first was a Louis XVI coat of steel-blue broadcloth, embroidered with flowers in silk – probably John Wilkes's Claude Melnotte coat, I thought, and was aching to ask, but I said nothing. He turned it about at arm's length, as if he were fancying his brother's figure in it, and perhaps remembering when he saw it worn last. Then he handed it to me. 'Put it in there,' he said, pointing to the heater. I opened the furnace door – the coals were all red and blazing. I paused for a little – 'twas such a shame to destroy so handsome a garment – and looked back at him, but he was as still as a statue – just waiting. There was no help for it – I threw it in. It settled down on the blaze with a sort of a hiss – a bit of the lace at the sleeve caught and the coat was in flames. We watched it without a word until it was nothing but a spread of red film in the blue coal flames. A satin waistcoat, a pair of knee breeches, and several pairs of tights were next taken out, and they followed the coat . . . After that there was a black-beaded Hamlet hauberk, which M. Booth turned affectionally about before he passed it to me. It needed but little guessing to know how hard it was for him to part with it. Then there came some 'shape' dresses of the Elizabethan period, and some fine silk hose and velvet shoes. They may have been worn for Iago . . . There were cavalier's costumes . . . These had seen much service and showed their wear, for John Wilkes's most successful performance, with the exception of his Richard III, had been in the romantic plays . . . These . . . went to the funeral pyre. Then his Roman things for Marc Antony . . . his costumes for Romeo, Shylock, Macbeth, and a gorgeous robe for Othello made of two East India shawls, so fine you could have pulled them through a lady's bracelet. It was agonizing, living through these mementos, while without a word Mr. Booth inspected each article, touched it fondly as if it were his own flesh and blood, before handing it to me to be burned . . . Finally he drew out of the trunk a long, belted, purple-velvet 'shirt,' ornamented with jewels and gilt lace, and a like-colored robe made to attach to the shoulders. Both garments were much creased, and in places the fabric was worn threadbare. He held them out for a moment, then sat down on the edge of the trunk with the costume on his knees. For fully a minute he didn't move, and as he sat looking at the costume, his eyes filled with tears, which ran down his cheeks, falling on the tinseled trappings. After a while he glanced up at me, as if for the first time he was aware that anyone was near him. 'My father's!' he said, his voice hoarse and shaking. 'Garrie, it was my father's Richard III dress. He wore it in Boston the night I first went on the stage as Tressel.' 'Don't you think you ought to save that, Mr Booth?' I ventured to ask. He became quieter. 'No – put it with the others.' In a few minutes it was nothing but ashes. I felt as if I had assisted in a crime. He didn't linger so long with the various articles after this, except now and

> then to pause over a costume as if he were puzzling his brain to recall what part it had been used for . . . When the bottom of the trunk had been reached and the last garment, a couple of finely wrought daggers, broken scraps of stage jewelry, and various odds and ends, which, strangely enough, included a pair of women's pink satin dancing-slippers, were thrust in on the coals, I threw in the wigs and even the swords that lay upon the cover – they would break and melt before the fire could be mended again. At the last I was directed to knock the trunk to pieces, and these, with the cords that bound the box, were the final contribution to the flames. We stood for a few moments, silently watching the snaky rims running through the feathery ashes and the sword blades glowing to a molten heat, then he bade me shut the furnace door. The sacrifice was complete – complete with one exception – a simple wreath of bays tied with a broad white ribbon. 'Twas his one memento. 'That will do,' he said quietly. 'We will go now.' I looked at my watch. It was nearly six . . . What emotion had arisen during that scene in the furnace-room had sunk to the depths, and his face had found again its old, set look of gentle melancholy. We came up to the stage and crossed to the stairway leading to his rooms. 'You needn't come, Garrie. Thank you,' he said. I ventured a 'Good morning, sir,' but he merely nodded, and I stood at the foot of the stairs with my lantern until I heard his door shut above.' This is Garrie Davidson's story of how Edwin Booth placed the seal on the tomb of his brother's memory.[36]

Sometimes forgetting the past is what allows the present to live with itself. As usual with such stories, the details are in some dispute. Following Junius Brutus Booth's death, his eldest son, Richard, 'challenged the accounting and handling of J.B.'s estate, particularly the "professional wardrobe of Mr Booth"'. Booth's widow – Richard's mother – countered that the wardrobe was essentially worthless, and in any event after her husband's death in Kentucky, 'all of it that was ever returned was contained in two trunks forwarded by the Adams Express'.[37] Moreover, as the *New York Journal* reported nearly a dozen years after *Edwin* Booth's death, his daughter auctioned off his wardrobe, including,

> Hamlet, Richard III., King Lear and Richelieu Robes in Five Trunks That Have Lain by Fifteen Years – Wigs, Pipes and Other Mementoes Listed. For fifteen years, ever since Edwin Booth died, five theatre trunks containing the greater part of the actor's wardrobe have been lying in the basement of a house at 12 West Eighteenth street, in the possession of his daughter, Edwina . . . In one of the trunks is *Hamlet*'s robe of black velvet trimmed with rare purple lace and jet, which was used by Booth for many years. Then there is the *Richard III* suit which he used when he succeeded his father in the portrayal of that character. The coat is ornamented with fleur de lis and animals worked with gold thread, while the robe is of black fur with a foil embroidered collars . . . Another famous garment which he wore as *Richard III* is a royal state robe of purple velvet and gold trimmed with ermine.[38]

The *New York Sun* somewhat disputes the account, and reports that,

> Mr. Booth's 'Richard III' outfit, used also by his father, was split up into so many different lots and disposed of to so many different buyers that it will probably never be reassembled . . . As the bidding was going on an old admirer of Booth turned away choking. 'It reminds me of the Roman soldiers shaking dice for the clothes in the story of the Crucifixion,' he remarked.[39]

Burned or bought, auctioned or bartered, the costume itself 'will probably never be reassembled'. Still, through it all, the father abides, even as his son's garments are played for at dice.

It is impossible, in other words, to know if Garrie's story is factual. It is, however, unquestionably true. And what is true about it is that it ripples with the play for which the costume was intended – a play about the emergence of an unlikely son from a family of violent, histrionic, and aspiring men. Like Richard before Bosworth, Booth was haunted by spectres of history, which violently implicated both the American family and his own. The anecdote about Booth's trunk relates his destruction of his brother's and father's theatrical remains, an attempt to lay the ghosts, then, not just of his brother's crime but also of his father's luminous but lunatic theatrical presence. The same magazine in which this story appears featured a cartoon of Booth as Hamlet confronting a ghost, with two lines of dialogue in captions: '*Spirit of the Elder B—h.* – I am thy father's Ghost. / *B—h the Younger*. – I'll call THEE Hamlet, Father.'[40] After this funeral by fire, Edwin emerges purified and isolated, free from the welter of fraternal and filial relationships that haunted his history. After the fire, he is no longer 'Booth the Younger'. He has no brother, he is like no brother, Edwin Booth is himself again and himself alone. No artefacts survive to verify this anecdote, since its point is their destruction. The evidence went up in smoke. All we're left with is a story that's just too good to be true. Or too true to reduce to a question of fact.

And here's another story that's too good to be true. When Edwin Booth *was* 'Booth the Younger', his first appearance on the stage was as Richard III in the cellar of his family's Baltimore townhouse in the early 1840s. A performance for which he lacked a costume. At least at first. A boyhood friend recalls:

> Our initial performance was Richard III, owing to a predilection of Edwin Booth . . . Our resources and our bank accounts . . . were meager. But a happy thought occurred to Edwin. His father had not at that period played Shylock for some time, and in the attic . . . was an old Shylock costume. Thither sped the young Richard, found the costume, and we cut out . . . large spangles . . . for armor. These he fastened on to a piece of oil-cloth, and tied it on over his

> shoulders for armor . . . But we little recked that meanwhile a special request had been made for the elder Booth to give a performance of his Shylock . . . Mr Booth hunted up his old dress . . . and found that it was missing. . . . Meanwhile we were in full blast – our 'house' good, our mettle its keenest. Edwin was declaiming grandly in his oilskin armor, fine to behold: 'A horse! A horse!' etc. Enter the elder Booth foaming with rage. Not knowing him, the [doorman] demanded . . . his three cents admission; and the . . . magnetic tones reached the younger Booth. It was the voice of his parent, as he well knew, and forgetful of all histrionic triumph, he turned and fled precipitately for the first means of exit – a window in the back, whence he hoped to escape down the alley. The opening, however, proved too small. 'Richard' was held midway, and his father, in a towering passion, reached the stage and belabored him unmercifully.[41]

Booth is left hanging, like so many anecdotes, interrupted in mid-play. Here the son dismantles his father's costume to fabricate one of his own, a primal scene framed over thirty years later by the one in which that same son now grown into stardom incinerates the remnants of his family line – burning their theatrical remains as though, the anecdote reports, they were his own 'flesh and blood'. Sparing from the funeral fire one single exception – a simple wreath of laurel bays with which to crown his ascension.

The problem for Richard, crudely put, is that even after he crowns himself he knows he's not the Great Original. His attempts to author himself, it turns out, are simply feeble imitations of the men who authored him. Well before Edwin Booth tried to immolate his past through the spectre of Richard III, his father had gotten there first, even before Edwin was born. One night, during a production of *Richard III*, Booth was interrupted by an unscripted messenger:

> Just as the second act was about to commence a messenger covered with dust rushed behind the stage, and before he

could be stopped was in earnest conversation with the tragedian. 'What?' said Booth as he pressed his long fingers on his broad, white temples, as though he tried to clutch the brain beneath, 'dead, say you? My poor little child – my loved, my beautiful one?' And then, seeing the curtain rise, he rushed on, commencing: 'She has health to progress as far as Chertsey, / Though not to bear the sight of me,' &c. The beautiful scene between *Anne* and *Gloster* was never better played. The actor, 'the noblest of them all' when he chose to be, gave the words of the bard with thrilling effect, but there was a strange calmness about his manner that told that his mind was not upon his character. Still, the multitude applauded until the old roof rang again, and those behind the scene stood breathless with eager delight. The third act came out, but Booth was nowhere to be found . . .

It was a bitter cold night, and the farmer, as he drove his wagon to market, was startled from his reverie as he saw a horseman wrapped in a large cloak – and as it opened it disclosed a glittering dress beneath – ride rapidly past him. It was Booth in his *Richard* costume! Madness had seized him, and, regardless of everything, at the still hour of midnight he was going to pay a visit to his dead child. Drawing his flashing sword and throwing his jewelled cap from his head, he lashed his horse's flank with the bare weapon until the animal snorted in pain. The tall, dark trees on each side of him touched his heated brow with the silver-frosted branches, and, thinking they were men sent in pursuit, the mad actor cut at them with his sword and cursed them as he flew rapidly by. At last, after a gallant ride of two hours, the horseman came in sight of a country graveyard, and, as he saw the white tops of the monuments peeping through the dark foliage like snowy crests upon the bosom of the black billow, he raised a shout wild enough to have scared the ghosts from their still graves. He dismounted, and away sped the riderless horse over hill and dale. It was the work of a moment (and the insane are cunning beyond all imagining) to wrench the wooden door from the vault

> containing the body of his child. He seized the tiny coffin in his arms, and with the strong arms of a desperate man he tore open the lid, and in a moment more the cold blue lips of the dead child were glued to the mad actor's! The next morning some member of the tragedian's family heard a wild strain of laughter that seemed to proceed from his sleeping room. The door was forced open, and Booth was discovered lying on his bed, gibbering in idiotic madness and caressing the corpse of his little one.[42]

It seems facile to speak of this as an 'anecdote', as it does with so many concerning the Booths. None of the stories are laughing matters, and even the light-hearted one about Edwin's debut ends in a fit of violence. It makes for a disturbing picture, Junius Brutus Booth, having lost his horse, lying in a vault in rural Maryland, dressed as Richard III and caressing the body of his dead son. The family attracted dozens of stories, but again and again the Booths face life and death while costumed as Richard III.

The recursions of history nearly came back to bite Edwin Booth, as one final story relates, this one, appropriately, about an artefact, though one not featured in the Folger's exhibition. Edwin Booth fashioned it to remember all that he tried to forget in the flames of January 1873. And it's another anecdote of an interrupted Richard. For fifteen years after his brother interrupted *Our American Cousin*, and over ten years after he tried to burn away the memory of that awful night, Edwin Booth was himself interrupted, during, as is by now somehow predictable, somehow inevitable, somehow even too good to be true, a performance of *Richard III*, possibly one in which he wore the very costume on display at the Folger library.

You may not have heard about the assassination of Edwin Booth, and that is due to what the costume lacks, which is a hole. Because in this case, history missed. First, the facts; then, the inevitable anecdotes that followed. From a contemporary newspaper:

> The public will be surprised and pained to hear that an attempt was made last night to assassinate Edwin Booth, the well known tragedian, while he was enacting the character of *Richard III*, at McVicker's Theatre, Chicago [which belonged to the father of Booth's second wife]. There were two shots fired by a man in the right hand gallery. Mr. Booth then rose and started toward the left wing of the stage, pointing out the would-be assassin. The man was at once seized, and except for the intervention of officers, would have been roughly handled. The prisoner states that his name was Mark Gray, that he is twenty-three years of age, and is a dry goods clerk of St Louis. He said he had been three years preparing to kill Mr Booth. He was surprised at his failure, which was the only part of the attempt that he regrets.[43]

Another newspaper adds that the 'intending assassin sat . . . with the pistol concealed in his sleeve, and in his left hand holding a copy of the play, which he had evidently been following with the dire purpose of firing only at the right time'.[44] No wonder actors hate it when audiences have the script.

The various newspaper accounts and illustrations disagree on a number of particulars, including the motive – some said a girl, some said that Gray preferred a rival actor, others that Gray thought Booth was his father, another who feared that Gray 'shot at Mr Booth not as an enemy but as a critic, and actors may ask themselves in some alarm whether this method of expressing disapprobation is to become general'.[45] The location of the shooter is uncertain – gallery, box, wings – as is the number of shots, as is, interestingly, the play being performed. Most report that Booth was playing Richard III, others that he was playing Richard II or even, in one fairly implausible account, a play called *Richard I*. There is even some reason to believe that the assailant, at least, thought Booth was playing Richelieu in which part he preferred another actor. Whatever the discrepancies, the fact that an assassination was attempted and failed is verifiable. The truth that it represented the return of all that Booth tried to repress is left for us to ponder.

Anecdotes inevitably followed. They relate that Booth preserved one of the bullets that lodged in the scenery just over his head. He kept it as a talisman, an artefact that he wore on his watch-chain, and engraved upon it 'From Mark Gray to Edwin Booth'. Some fifteen years after his brother shot Lincoln and a decade removed from his attempt to purge the past, Booth came to practise the arts of preservation.

One last thing. The inscription on the bullet – 'From Mark Gray to Edwin Booth' – may have reminded him of all that he had tried to forget – that history will always have a bullet with the name of Booth upon it. But that isn't all there is to the inscription. Booth also engraved a date – one on which all the newspapers agreed the assassin tried and failed. That date surely reminded Booth, as it can us, of something else, which is that William the Conqueror will always come before Richard III. The bullet gave the year, 1879, but it also included the date, 'April 23'.

5

Macbeth: An embarrassment of witches

The unfortunate comedy

In the mid 1780s, Thomas Davies – one of David Garrick's first biographers – described a series of accidents that marred a production of Shakespeare's play, not least the death of the actor who played the King, who 'caught a distemper which proved fatal to him, by wearing, in this part, a too light and airy suit of clothes'. As a consequence, the play was 'termed, by the players, the unfortunate comedy, from the disagreeable accidents which fell out several times during the acting of it'. Thomas Davies is describing a production of *All's Well that Ends Well* that didn't. The play's insanely optimistic title asks for trouble and on this occasion got it.[1]

Macbeth is usually the 'unfortunate' play, the one stalked by superstition and haunted by disaster. And yet, as the opening suggests, it has not always been unfortunate. In fact, the tradition of *Macbeth*'s supposed curse is surprisingly recent and surprisingly thin. For roughly the first 300 years of *Macbeth*'s history, the anecdotes that follow it uniformly fail to mention the curse that allegedly has always hung over the play. This is the more notable when stories record disasters. On 20 August 1671, for instance, Thomas Isham recorded a fatality in his diary at a showing of *Macbeth*, writing:

> It is reported that Harris has killed his associate actor, in a scene on the stage, by accident. It was the tragedy called 'Macbeth,' in which Harris performed the part of Macduff, and ought to have slain his fellow-actor, *Macbeth*; but during the fence it happened that Macduff pierced Macbeth in the eye, by which thrust he fell lifeless, and could not bring out the last words of his part.[2]

In this case it was a dagger that Macbeth saw before him, but Isham does not linger over the difference between a player who 'ought to have slain his fellow-actor' and one who actually did. Instead, he describes a theatrical mishap and sensibly calls it an 'accident', the kind of thing that can happen when two grown men swing sharp objects at each other. Perhaps Isham moved outside theatrical circles and had not heard that the play was cursed and so does not see the accident as evidence of anything other than itself. Or perhaps *Macbeth* was not cursed, at least not yet.

Twenty years later, Gerard Langbaine witnessed another *Macbeth* that got out of hand, where imaginary daggers turned into real ones:

> At the Acting of this Tragedy, on the Stage, I saw a real one acted in the Pit; I mean the Death of Mr. Scroop, who received his death's wound from the late Sir Thomas Armstrong, and died presently after he was remov'd to a House opposite to the Theatre in Dorset-Garden.[3]

Gerald Langbaine *did* move in theatrical circles – in fact his life's work was to draw theatrical circles, as in his *New Catalogue of English Plays* (1688). Yet he draws no connection between the curse on *Macbeth* and the death of

Mr Scroop, although the event is pregnant with portent, not least Langbaine's uncanny account of one late man who turned another latterly.

In 1792 a production of *Macbeth* turned into an unfortunate comedy of errors:

> The tragedy of Macbeth was advertised for a performance at this theatre last night; and as Holman was disabled by illness, the part of Macbeth was allotted to Harley. Unluckily Harley was also indisposed, and it became absolutely necessary to make an entire change in the performance of the evening. Mr Hull endeavoured to explain the cause of the alteration to the audience, but they were too restive to listen to him, and called for Lewis. Lewis at length came forward and developed the mystery, proposing *The Farmers* and *The Merry Mourners*, which the audience, after some murmuring, consented to receive. To make the whole a night of disaster, Macready made a third apology on account of Quick, who, in hurrying to the Theatre, fell, and materially bruised his knee.[4]

Macbeth after Macbeth falls by the wayside, and though the account mentions how unluckily things fell out, it never mentions the curse.

Even Quick is not exempt from a spill, though his clumsiness was catching, since just three years later in 1795, this time at Drury Lane, Sarah Siddons' Lady Macbeth fell under the curse:

> *Macbeth* was the performance of Tuesday evening, and obtained a crowded house. The acting of Mrs Siddons in Lady Macbeth was exquisite; . . . In the supper scene, in descending from the Throne, Mrs Siddons unfortunately fell forward upon the stage, in a manner that gave the impression of her being very materially hurt. The audience were for a moment in a state of anxious suspense, which was testified in a manner highly honourable to their feelings, and flattering to the character of the distinguished object of

> their attention. She recovered in a few seconds, and proceeded in her part with all her wonted energy and power.[5]

The story is one of Siddons' fall and rise, not one of how she was tripped up by a curse. The correspondent does not dwell upon the matter, but neither does he mention that *Macbeth* is uniquely unlucky, though Siddons' sprawl gave him every chance to do so.

Even when a production goes utterly, totally, magnificently awry, providing the perfect occasion to bring up *Macbeth*'s haunted history, older anecdotes fail to mention it. Frank Benson recalls a production of *Macbeth* in Stratford-upon-Avon in 1900 in which everything that could go wrong did.

> As sometimes happens when one is particularly anxious all should go right, on that night everything went wrong. Weir, who usually gave an impressive mystical rendering of the First Witch had, in the afternoon gossiped with convivial friends over healths five fathoms deep. He came down to the footlights in a friendly, cheery way, beamed vacuously at the audience, and then, in a confidential whisper, informed them that 'The cat has mewed three times.' . . . To make matters worse, Herbert Ross, who was blessed – or cursed – with a keen sense of humour, fastened the cauldron to Weir, so that in the fourth act the First Witch found himself pursued all over the stage by a bowl of liquid fire and sulphourous fumes. To the intense delight of Ross, the poor man kept appealing to him as to whether he had 'got 'em' or not. I was proud of my new business in having a small tea-bell sounded as a signal from Lady Macbeth that it was time for the murder to be accomplished. Unfortunately, as I was preparing for my great exit, the man in the flies thought the bell was the signal for lowering the curtain, and down it came in the middle of the scene . . . When the stage should have been dark it was light, and vice versa.[6]

The closest Benson comes to superstitious speculation is his comment that a fellow actor was 'cursed' with a keen sense of humour, yet he brings down the curtain on the anecdote without mentioning the play's more general doom. It was simply a night on which *Macbeth* turned into an 'unfortunate comedy'. Steeped in theatrical lore and an anecdote monger himself, it never occurs to Benson to blame the disasters of opening night on *Macbeth*'s curse rather than on Murphy's Law.

The transfer of *Macbeth* from stage to celluloid did not make it immune to accidents, though it remained so to superstition. In 1916, Herbert Beerbohm-Tree produced a silent film of *Macbeth*. If ever there was a way to avoid saying 'Macbeth' out loud in a theatre, the solution might be to make a silent movie. Yet, though it was marred by accidents, no one thought to blame its troubles on a curse. The *Motion Picture Mail* mentions in 1916, for instance:

> One day [Tree] stole away from the studio to keep a luncheon engagement. As he left his host's bungalow he slipped and fell against the mudguard of his motor. When he was lifted up blood was streaming from a ragged cut under his eye. A physician quickly patched him up, he worked all the afternoon and evening with makeup concealing the wound.[7]

No mention of the curse. Macbeth's Macduff had equal luck, as the *New York Sun* reported:

> The . . . principal parts, a score in number, were played by thoroughly experienced motion picture actors. To show what the latter can and will do by way of devotion to their art, Wilfred Lucas, who played Macduff, suffered a broken wrist while rehearsing the fight with Macbeth. In order to avoid having to give way to a substitute when the picture was taken, because a Macduff in splints was obviously out of the question, Lucas refused to permit his physician to

> allow the bones to knit. Day after day he endured excruciating agony through the four weeks that elapsed before the fight could be staged. Then he plunged through it maddened with pain, and crept out of the scene to accept the medical attention he so greatly needed.[8]

No mention of the curse. The story is about an actor's pluck, not a production's luck, a tale of an actor's devotion to his craft rather than a story about *Macbeth*'s haunted history. A one-eyed Macbeth and a short-handed Macduff silently duelling for the camera's benefit should provide a fitting image for *Macbeth*'s troubled history. But it didn't.

Finally, around 1921, James Hackett – Lincoln's favourite Macbeth – did break a leg while playing the lead, furnishing a perfect opportunity for a correspondent to invoke the curse, if only he had known about it.

> I look back with much personal complacency upon the impersonation of the 'fearful king' which Mr Hackett gave at the Criterion Theatre in this city a few seasons ago . . . [I]t would doubtless have enjoyed a long and well-earned run, had not Mr Hackett met with an accident that seriously crippled him, and caused the withdrawal of the piece after too few performances.[9]

A broken leg will obviously limit a long run, but the point here is that, time and again across the years, *Macbeth*'s anecdotes come to a conclusion without coming to the conclusion that the accidents they relate are symptomatic of a curse.

While *Macbeth* has prompted anecdotes since early in its history, then, for the first 300 years those anecdotes fail to mention that the play was in any way unfortunate. Even the horrific Astor Place riots of 1849, sparked by the rival Macbeths of Edwin Forrest and Charles Macready, did not produce any chatter about a curse. We are nevertheless assured today that the curse is ancient and ubiquitous, that 'there is one superstition so old, so all-consuming, so intimidating, that just about everybody in the theatre believes it. . . . *Macbeth* is the unlucky play of the theatre and has for four centuries carried in its wake a truly terrifying trail of disaster and bad luck.'[10] (Just about 'everybody in the theatre' would have to exempt, as Dennis Bartholomeuz points out, 'Irving, Macready, Kemble, or Garrick',[11] who never mention the curse.) The source of this claim for antiquity and ubiquity, *The Curse of Macbeth*, is a popular book by a working actor with a story to tell (and a product to shift) and might be excused its exaggerations. Yet even serious scholarly work peddles the line that '*Macbeth* has always been considered an unlucky play', though 'always' in this case would have to ignore the first 300 years of the play's stage life.[12] As the Cambridge Shakespeare in Production edition of *Macbeth* concludes, there is no evidence that the play was considered unlucky in the eighteenth or nineteenth century, although 'by 1937 it was common knowledge'.[13] Until relatively recently, then, there was no injunction against saying 'Macbeth' in a theatre nor the idea that the play suffered from bad luck or that its performers were more than normally doomed for having gone into theatre in the first place. For the vast majority of *Macbeth*'s history, the theatre did not know that the play had always been unlucky.

It is probably fruitless, and somewhat pointless, to run down the origin of the superstition, though suspicion might hover around the Old Vic production of 1937, featuring Olivier as Macbeth under the direction of Michel St Denis. (If we follow our nose a bit further, we might suspect that the *Macbeth* superstition smells not of brimstone but the 'inspired recklessness' – Kenneth Tynan's words – of the Old Vic's impresario Tyrone Guthrie, who knew a thing or two about marketing.[14]) Lilian Baylis's death coincided with the 1937 production, and the coincidence of her death (not to mention her dog's), a poorly received production, and a run of bad luck in the play's preparation seems to have consolidated the play's unfortunate reputation. (St. Denis was in a taxi smash up, the sets were too big and had to be cut down, the opening was postponed when Olivier lost his voice and then nearly his life when 'a stage weight weighing twenty-five pounds crashed down on to the seat' he had just vacated, 'crushing it to fragments. He had missed death by seconds.'[15] Had Olivier not left his seat, the history of the modern theatre would be very different, as would, of course, the history of Laurence Olivier.) If this production is not the origin of the superstition – and it almost certainly is not – it was the moment at which it seemed to come true. Given the echo effect of theatrical chatter, and the contemporary – and subsequent – publicity about the production's bad fortunes, we could date 1937 as the moment that *Macbeth* became always unlucky.

It would be just as easy as it is pointless to prove the 'curse' is a sham. It is exactly as true as those who believe it. It's far more interesting to speculate what question the 'curse' answers. Why, in short, have accounts of *Macbeth* across the ages been brought together in the last hundred years in a uniquely concentrated form? All plays, at least those performed with the frequency of Shakespeare's most popular ones, rival *Macbeth*'s long incident report of disaster and accident. Jody Enders has asked, after reviewing several legendary stage disasters, 'One begins to wonder why there is not a curse of *Hamlet*, *Othello*, or just plain Shakespeare.'[16] Or *Henry VIII*, for that matter, since every time the play is performed the theatre burns to the ground. Why has theatre history decided that *Macbeth* is uniquely cursed?

One obvious answer, which is not obviously wrong, is that the play is full of curses, superstition, and witchcraft. It might seem therefore altogether 'natural' that *Macbeth* should be thought superiorly so. In this account, however, the anecdotes simply abbreviate the play, redundantly supplementing the play proper. The argument of this book has been, however, that the most persistent anecdotes do something for the play that the play won't do for itself. In these terms, the invented curse of *Macbeth* must be a form of special pleading, an answer to a gnawing sense that the play left something wanting.

The superstitions around the play probably grow out of the fact that *Macbeth* is remorselessly rational. The play, in the end, is disappointingly un-mysterious. Or at least it relentlessly demystifies itself. Macduff is *not* 'not of woman born'; he's the product of a Caesarean delivery. Birnam Wood's ambulation is *not* supernatural; it's a bunch of soldiers with twigs. Even the witches disappoint. They are not omni-spectral, they've merely read ahead. 'When shall we three meet again,' they ask, as we see them meet for the very first time. They sound an awful lot like a Committee on Committees, whose mandate is that meetings take place. They are the stuff of middle-management, not of middle-earth. In these terms, the curse restores what the play disowns, producing more lies that sound like truth since *Macbeth* is a play dedicated to putting the rabbit back in the hat.

A curse is not an anecdote and neither is a superstition, but the superstitions of *Macbeth* are fabricated out of anecdotal material. Some combine of agents have looted *Macbeth*'s history for anecdotes and then marshalled them to a conclusion. In that respect, history has beaten this book to the punch since I have argued throughout that Shakespeare's most durable anecdotes express something a play hints at but suppresses. *Macbeth*'s anecdotes have already been conscripted, then, to collectively articulate – even insist on – a central idea: that the play is cursed. History has already written the chapter on *Macbeth*, the conclusion foregone in that one of the few things that everyone knows about *Macbeth* is that it has always been bad luck. To an extent unmatched by any other of Shakespeare's plays, theatre history has got its anecdotes organized, formally arrayed them in such a way that any incident remotely unfortunate that happens during a production of *Macbeth* now has a foregone conclusion. This chapter therefore functions differently than those that have come before. If preceding chapters attempt to tally a play's anecdotes to see what they add up to, this chapter unweaves the fabric of fiction woven around *Macbeth* to try to understand why the modern history of *Macbeth* insists on believing an unbelievable thing.

If the previous chapters told a new performance history of Shakespeare's most canonical plays, this one must deal with an old one first.

Of curses and kilts

If curses arose to re-mystify *Macbeth*, it remains to ask why the play suddenly seemed in the early twentieth century to require a superstition that previous centuries did not. After all, from its first performance in 1606, the play's treatment of the supernatural was readily apparent – though tempered by adaptations for much of its history. Yet for roughly three centuries it seemed sufficiently spooky. It is somewhat beyond the scope of this book – and the resources of its writer – to understand the total array of historical forces that might explain why the mystery went out of *Macbeth* early in the twentieth century. (History, like hell, is murky.) The rise of realism is obviously part of the story. The witches make little sense within the realm of naturalism, thus a supernatural supplement gives the play a hall pass. It is also just possible that in the cold light of modernity, *Macbeth* seemed all too plausible.

Perhaps it was scientific rationality that summoned up a superstition, an investment in wonder for a wised-up age. And nothing challenges modernity more than three bearded hags who – with the assistance of an eye of newt and a blasphemer's finger – spin prophetic riddles. But if the effort to press-gang *Macbeth*'s anecdotes in service of a supernatural agenda is relatively recent, the 400-year performance history of *Macbeth* has long struggled to explain the play's supernatural actors, the witches. The witches might embarrass modernity, but they have long done so for the stages that had to embody them. Read against *Macbeth*'s long history, the curse looks like only the most recent effort to account for the weird sisters. From a long view, *Macbeth*'s stage history can be read as a series of attempts to posses the witches.

The history of *Macbeth* in performance can be divided into four periods, which have dropped away from the play like stages of a rocket as it has moved through time: Jacobean, Restoration, Antiquarian, Superstitious. The first to go was the Jacobean stage, which can now be found bobbing in the front matter to the play's critical editions. Though no evidence can place the play in front of James, it can be alleged to flatter the king's interest in the occult, although a play about a Scottish regicide might not be the *first* one you'd choose to flatter a Scottish king. Nevertheless, James' own study of witchcraft, the *Daemonolgie*, and the period's witch trials are often invoked to sufficiently establish that witches were just something that everyone believed in 'back then'. The witches, in this argument, are a quaint residue of a benighted time, an historical curiosity that would nevertheless dazzle their first audience who would gape in credulous wonder. They are just one more way in which the early moderns were weird (or 'weyward', depending on your edition). The second stage, the Restoration, substituted spectacle for the spectral, producing an operatic version of *Macbeth*, complete with cavorting witches. The perceptive Pepys was dazzled but puzzled that the 'divertisement' of operatic witches should grow to such a 'strange perfection' despite the play's 'deep tragedy'.[17] The notion seems to have been to make the witches magical by making them musical. The fantastical supplanted the supernatural, turning the witches into a shallow divertisement that showed how deep the tragedy was. The witches were unbelievable but ostentatiously theatrical, an index to theatre's ability to make its own magic.

One thing the Restoration did not restore was Shakespeare's text. Once more sober minds banished the dancing witches – often played for comic kicks by the companies' clowns – they were still faced with an embarrassment of witches. Charles Macklin was among the first, in 1773, to banish the comic hags and launch the next stage, the Antiquarian *Macbeth*. He nevertheless had to account for the sisters, and his answer was 'history'. Not the Jacobean history of the play's stage origin but the 'barbaric splendours of early Scottish history' including the 'old Caledonia dress'.[18] Macklin's innovation emerged in the midst of an antiquarian rage, which dominated productions of *Macbeth* until the turn of the nineteenth century, reaching its apotheosis in the productions of Charles Kean, who appended a supplement to his playbills that defended the play's eleventh-century settings by citing his antiquarian sources.

Henry Irving doubled-down on this impulse, with all the resources of his Lyceum army, combing the museums 'for every article of costume, weapon, furniture and domestic utensil down to every nail, button and blade'.[19] Irving scoured Scotland in search of inspiration, and his antiquarian approach to *Macbeth*, like Macklin's, substituted ancient Scottish history for the play's Jacobean one. Like the Jacobean strategy, the Antiquarian one turned to history to explain the witches, back before all the wonder went out of the world.

Irving was hailed as a 'veritable genius of stage management' for casting as his witches 'three tragic actresses, instead of, as heretofore . . . the low comedians of the company'.[20] This regime held the stage until supplanted by another antiquarian impulse, this one for the conventions of the Elizabethan stage under the revivalist William Poel and his pupil Harley Granville-Barker. Just as one nail drives out another, one history replaced the other. Though the Elizabethan revival did not entirely take, it cleared the stage for unlocalized, expressionistic, or modern settings. Stripped of their historical trappings, however, *Macbeth*'s witches challenged the modern stage to make some sense of them. With the Jacobean, Restoration and Antiquarian stages of history fallen by the wayside, the stage was set for the emergence of the curse, which needed to create an historical genealogy to mystify itself. Otherwise this 'ancient' curse would look suspiciously modern. The history of *Macbeth* in performance is a history of ersatz histories, a constant labour to forge an excuse for the witches.

With the curse of *Macbeth*, then, we encounter that remarkable phenomenon, an invented tradition that seemed to be instantly true. An 'invented tradition', in the famous formulation of Eric Hobsbawm, is one that might 'appear or claim to be old' but is 'quite recent in origin'.[21] Thus invocations of the curse inevitably include a fake genealogy. Citations of the superstition endow it with a deep tradition, stretching back to an original account of 'Hal Berridge', a boy actor who died just prior to his premier as Lady Macbeth in 1606. Through a telling slippage, journalists cite this apocryphal event as the 'first mention of the curse' though the curse was not actually mentioned, it seems, until the twentieth century.[22] Invented traditions require actual history. *Macbeth* was performed around 1606, and Lady Macbeth was played by an adolescent boy who died at some point, though not, of course, as a result of his appearance in the play of *Macbeth*. The history of *Macbeth*'s run of bad luck is a lie that sounds like truth.

Invented traditions are not arbitrary. They speak to certain needs. What's more, invented traditions like the curse of *Macbeth* constitute 'a set of practices . . . of a ritual or symbolic nature, which seek to inculcate certain values and norms of behaviour by repetition, which automatically implies continuity with the past'.[23] The practices of *Macbeth*'s curse are by now well known. They include the injunction not to say the word 'Macbeth' in a theatre – unless while rehearsing or performing the play when it can scarcely be avoided – and even a remedy to undo the spell should one transgress (it requires the transgressor to leave the building, spin around three times, spit, curse, and then knock to be allowed back in. Additionally, one may recite bits of *Merchant of Venice*, as though, oddly, it were *Macbeth*'s opposite). In relatively rapid fashion – sometime between the two world wars, when Hobsbawm notes a number of such traditions emerged – an aggregate of theatrical energy articulated a fully fleshed out set of practices, replete with back story, that reaffirmed certain values every time the practices were repeated. The curse of *Macbeth* becomes true every time someone believes in it.

So pervasive is the idea of the curse that attempts to explain its origin shudder under their own incoherence (while doing no harm to its durability). One popular version of its origin is that *Macbeth* was often rolled out as a sure-fire thing by struggling theatre companies. Donald Sinden offers a conventional explanation, which takes him,

> back to repertory theatre days when each town and village had at least one theatre to entertain the public. If a play was not doing well, it would invariably get 'pulled' and replaced with a sure-fire audience pleaser – Macbeth guaranteed full-houses. So when the weekly theatre newspaper, *The Stage*, was published, listing what was on in each theatre in the country, it was instantly noticed what shows had NOT worked the previous week, as they had been replaced by a definite crowd-pleaser.[24]

It is an ill kind of logic that turns everything into evidence of itself. *Macbeth* is unfortunate because it has been so fortunate to theatrical purveyors across the years. Sinden had real doubts about the play's reputed misfortune, and the proven popularity of the play on the stage should discredit the idea that it could ever be thought unlucky. Superstition is at home to paradox, however; they dress out of the same trunk. *Macbeth* is unlucky because it has proven so lucky. Trying to disarm superstition with logic is like showing up at a knife fight with a stick of butter.

At the same time, the invented tradition reclaims *Macbeth* from its history of burlesque, in which the witches were frequently lampooned. In these terms, the superstition redeems *Macbeth* for the tragic canon, elevates it to the level of *Hamlet*, *Lear* and *Othello* (which, to be fair, all also have a history of adaptation and burlesque, and while *Hamlet* does feature a ghost, ghosts have always been more respectable than witches). Above all, history provides a straight face to mask the red one that the buffoon tradition of *Macbeth*'s witches produces. Reflecting upon *Macbeth*'s comic legacy, a reviewer of Henry Irving's 1898 production hopes its comic treatment is a thing of the past, which of course it is, but the reviewer wants to make sure it stays there. Under the heading 'The Macbeths of Yesteryear', the correspondent for *The Sketch* writes:

> They Lacked the Historic Sense Which You Will See At The Lyceum . . . Every playgoer who has had any experience of the old stock companies must recollect that the Weird Sisters were represented by the Low Comedian, the Old Man, and the Old Woman of the company – generally a fairly grotesque trio. This, it may be hoped, is a thing of the past.[25]

'History' is the antidote to comedy. *Macbeth* has a history, of course, a performance history of low-comic treatment, but that is the wrong kind of history that actual history must work to replace. The kind of history that audiences will encounter at the Lyceum will draw on Irving's archaeological search for the play's 'actual' Scottish origins, which will temper the play's lapses into buffoonery, which we can only hope is a thing of the past.

The irony is that the history the correspondent hopes will replace *Macbeth*'s grotesque one is, itself, a sham. It is more than coincidence that the phony history that follows *Macbeth* includes the insistence that it be called 'The Scottish Play'. For Scotland has, as Hugh Trevor-Roper brilliantly showed, been subject itself to a long history of invention. The Highland culture that Irving drew upon actually serves as the example *par excellence* of ersatz history, of 'invented tradition'. The 'ancient' kilt was invented in the mid-eighteenth century by a Quaker industrialist of English origin, and the clan-specific tartan was a stroke of marketing genius by William Wilson and Son of Bannockburn to capitalize on a Royal visit in 1819. Such is the force of this invented tradition that following Boswell and Johnson's tour of the Hebrides in 1785, Boswell could already write, 'The very Highland names, or the sound of a bagpipe, will stir my blood and fill me . . . with pity for the unfortunate and superstitious regard for antiquity . . . with a crowd of sensations with which sober rationality has nothing to do.'[26] Nostalgia sounds like a bagpipe, apparently, and Boswell's reaction to the Hebrides reads like a prescient history of *Macbeth* in performance. Kilts are famously instruments of exposure, but one thing they successfully cover is their own phony history.

The skeins of all these invented histories – 'real', and unreal, theatrical and otherwise – married in a 2013/14 *Macbeth*. When Kenneth Branagh mounted his mud-and-blood, men-in-kilts production, *The Guardian* dutifully reported that the play had claimed another victim:

> [A] cast member was taken to hospital after last Wednesday's performance at the deconsecrated St Peter's Church with unconfirmed reports suggesting that he was struck by Branagh's sword. The as yet unnamed actor – not one of the show's stars – was hit in the opening battle scene and received medical attention from an on-site paramedic before returning to the performance. After the final curtain, he was taken to hospital.[27]

At least it wasn't a star. The paper is careful to include the detail of the 'deconsecrated St Peter's Church' – we report, you decide. Nevertheless, between the kilt and the curse, what audiences saw was a production draped in sham, which is one way to reconsecrate the play for a deconsecrated time.

Invented traditions might seem, at worst, a harmless scam. There are usually good reasons why people prefer implausible histories to plausible ones. But the problem with invented traditions is that they can obscure actual ones. The putatively ancient superstition around *Macbeth* has retroactively made its anecdotes all mean the same thing. The curse of *Macbeth* has become an onomastic Order that colonizes its anecdotes and predetermines their meaning. In this instance it deprives *Macbeth* of its history in the theatre, tidying its unruly profusion into a foregone conclusion. And yet, *Macbeth* has an anecdotal history that serves as something other than a precursor to a curse.

One way to unwind the curse, or to see the play's anecdotal history without the already arrived at conclusion that they are evidence of ill luck, is to turn back the clock, to work backwards into the centuries before the play was doomed, to a time when the cauldron scenes were sources of hilarity, not dread, when spectral daggers were material ones, and when the play's supernatural imaginings were fodder for theatre's mordant wit.

Tangible properties

Alongside *Hamlet*'s skull and *Othello*'s handkerchief, *Macbeth*'s dagger might be Shakespeare's most famous prop. And as with Yorick and Desdemona's wayward token, it is the dagger's absence that makes it important. 'Is this a dagger I see before me,' Macbeth asks, and in so doing delivers theatre's version of *cogito ergo sum*: What am I looking at? Theatre becomes itself by wondering what's there, and Macbeth's address to an absent dagger invites questions of ontology, epistemology and phenomenology. As well as a cat.

> When [William Rignold] began the famous soliloquy, 'Is that a dagger I see before me?' a cat sedately strolled out upon the stage to form his opinion on the subject, and the presence of the harmless, necessary animal as it investigated the stage and the auditorium and peered down to see if there were any mice in the orchestra, was not found to assist the solemnity of the act.[28]

The anecdote is an antidote to theatre's self-seriousness. For if the cat is harmless, it is also necessary, since the cat – which stepped right out of the adage as well as *Merchant of Venice* – points out that while the dagger of the mind is not a real one neither is the one that Macbeth will soon draw. The cat is the only thing on stage that isn't pretending to be something else. The scene, in other words, attempts to outline theatre's reality postulate: Macbeth's imaginary dagger reifies the one he draws. (The imagined dagger is 'in form', but not in fact 'as palpable / As this which now I draw' [2.1.40-41]). The cat's investigation discovers that the dagger Macbeth draws is a dagger of the mind as well, since it is just a prop, with which Macbeth will commit an offstage murder that the audience will just have to imagine.

The cat discovers no difference between a hand-drawn dagger and an air-drawn one. Though the distinction between a real dagger and a phony one dominates another widely circulated anecdote, one often cited, of course, as evidence of the curse. During a production of *Macbeth* in Amsterdam in 1672, 'the actor playing Macbeth substituted a real dagger for the fake one and with it killed Duncan in full view of the entranced audience'.[29] The anecdote appears, nearly verbatim, on dozens of websites and in scores of theatrical programmes. Yet no discoverable version ever points out that the script calls for Duncan to be killed off stage, not 'in full view' of the audience, entranced or otherwise. The anecdote rewrites the play to show us something the play will not. It also reminds us that when Macbeth returns from the murder of Duncan he carries at least two daggers – 'Why did you bring *these* daggers from the place?' Lady Macbeth scolds – by which point we have forgotten that he left the stage with one. Or was it two? One real, one imagined, both fake since it does not take a real dagger to kill an offstage actor.

Like daggers of the mind, superstitions, curses and invented traditions are also all forms of willed belief in unbelievable things, and Macbeth's imagined dagger forms a sign for all manner of things that have to be believed to be seen. In so doing, the dagger scene spurs a legacy of theatrical chatter about *Macbeth*'s intangible properties. In the grandest terms, the dagger is a riddle that asks theatre's fundamental question: what are we looking at or what are we looking for? The air-born dagger forms a focal point for anecdotal accounts that negotiate between the seen and the unseen, the tangible and intangible, and the sublime and the ridiculous. *Macbeth* is an eager host to such anecdotes since it is, among all of Shakespeare's plays, the one most whole-heartedly committed to disillusionment.

The space between the sublime and the ridiculous is where theatre stores its props, though the dagger-of-the-mind has rarely taxed theatre's property masters. You just have to act like it's there. Yet it is always in the staging of illusion that the theatre comes closest to disillusioning the audience, which is, by extension, a source of ready hilarity. The difference between the air-drawn dagger and an actual one sets up a nineteenth-century anecdote about a literal-minded property master named Phil Stone, who insisted that an envisioned dagger be made visible.

> With him, dramas are altogether represented, by their 'properties;' in fact, they merge their names in the articles of the scene; thus, with Stone, 'The Merchant of Venice,' becomes 'the casket piece;' 'Macbeth' sinks into 'the cauldron and brooms;' – though, by the way, an incident connected with this tragedy is illustrative of the professional anxiety of our hero: by some chance, he once stood at the wing when Kean exclaimed, 'Is that a dagger that I see before me?' at the same time, as Phil thought, glaring reproachfully at him. Stone, in an agony of impatience, threw himself on his defence – turning to the prompter, he exclaimed, 'By——. Mr. Wilmot – it wasn't in the list!' It took considerable pains to convince him, that the actor meant visionary steel; and though convinced, Stone remained of the opinion, that the 'air-drawn dagger' ought to have been among the tangible properties.[30]

The joke is on Stone, his myopic insistence that visionary steel be made tangible. But Stone's obdurate literalism eloquently articulates the theatre's 'professional anxiety'. From Stone's perspective *Macbeth* is reducible to cauldron and brooms, the tangible shams that embarrass the play's spectral ambitions.

Stone never got the chance to materialize his ambitions on stage, but a property master nicknamed 'Props' – in keeping with the literalism for which these men are legendary – had his eyes fixed on stardom. From a book with the promising title

Blobson's Dire Mishaps in a Barnstorming Company comes a tale of 'Props' that does not disappoint:

> 'Ah! Blobson,' said he, while sitting in their room, trying to keep themselves warm by getting as near as possible to a dying fire in a sadly decayed sheet iron stove, 'one day, I will surprise you with the innovations I will make in the rendering of "Macbeth."' 'Why, what do you mean?' said Blobson. 'Why, sir,' said Props, 'I intend, when I come on, in the dagger scene, the audience will see the very dagger that "Macbeth" speaks about.' 'That would be wonderful; in fact, I have never heard of such an innovation. Is it your own idea?' 'All mine; and I intend to have it patented. You see, when "Macbeth" orders his servant to retire, he locks the door to prevent the entrance of eaves-droppers and, on turning around in the direction of the king's chamber, he sees the imaginary dagger and speaks as follows – now watch me and I'll show you how it goes – 'Props: "Is this a dagger which I see before me, the handle toward my hand? Come, let me clutch thee! I have thee not and yet I see thee still! Art thou not, fatal vision, sensible to feeling as to sight? Or art thou but a dagger of the mind, a false creation, proceeding from the heat-oppressed brain? I see thee yet; in form, as palpable as this which I now draw! Thou marshallest me the way that I was going and such an instrument I was to use. Mine eyes are made the fools o' the other senses or else worth all the rest. I see thee still and, on thy blade and dudgeon, gouts of blood which was not before. There is no such thing. It is the bloody business which informs thus to mine eyes."'
>
> 'By this, you will observe, nobody in the house sees the dagger he speaks of, consequently the audience is obliged to take "Macbeth's" word for it. Time and again I have watched an audience through a peep-hole in the property room, when the play was given and, when "Macbeth" speaks of the imaginary dagger, I have seen plenty of the people in the auditorium look in the direction "Macbeth"

> was looking for the dagger spoken of, and the impression on their faces showed downright disgust in being fooled in looking for something that never existed. One night, at a town we stacked up at, "Macbeth" was played and, when "Macbeth" spoke of the imaginary dagger, a big country lout yelled out: "That's an old chestnut! I got caught on that once and you can't get me to look for your old dagger again." The audience commenced to roar and yell and that ended the night's performance. My method is, to make a reality of this scene.' 'How will you proceed? You must certainly speak the same lines and, if you do, you will be subject to being ridiculed as have others,' said Blobson.
>
> 'I will speak the same lines but my dagger business will be different. I will have a dark stage, to start with a drummond light on the fly gallery; my dagger will be suspended from above the flies and will be worked by the prompter. When I give the cue and I clutch at it it is there, the light being thrown on it from above. The audience see the dagger, see that I am really jumping at it, skating around after it as it were; that it is the simon pure article; that there is no humbug about it; and I win my applause and any spare bouquets that the audience may have. How is that for an original idea?'[31]

Not bad. Stone and 'Props' are just thinking like a witch. Just as there is no such thing as a motherless man or a walking wood – since men, like trees, have roots – there is no such thing as a dagger of the mind. Well before the chatter of the curse came to dominate *Macbeth*, the dagger scene gave anecdotes a chance to delight in its fundamental phoniness. If the witches end up demystifying *Macbeth*, theatre history has been along for the ride, worrying over the maintenance of its various signs of wonder and by exposing them, exposing them.

Notwithstanding Stone's consternation, Macbeth insists the dagger is imaginary. But though it may be disembodied, it is not bloodless. It is covered with gore, Macbeth reports, 'which was not so before' (2.1.47). The dagger, which was not there to begin with, did not have blood on it at first but now – although the dagger is still not there – is covered in blood, which is also not there. This is the sort of stuff that anecdotes cannot leave alone:

> The following anecdote is told of a certain irritable tragedian. He was playing Macbeth, and had rushed off to kill Duncan, when there was no blood for the Thane to steep his hands in. – 'The blood! The blood!' exclaimed he to the agitated property-man, who had forgotten it: the actor, however, not to disappoint the audience, clenched his fist, and striking the property-man a violent blow upon his nose, coolly washed his hands in the stream of gore that burst from it, and re-entered with the usual words, 'I have done the deed – didst thou not hear a noise?'[32]

The anecdote offers a backstage pass that lets us see what Macbeth is really up to. He isn't murdering Duncan, who is cooling his heels until the curtain call, he's exchanging his bloodless daggers for bloody ones. He isn't murdering a king, the anecdote reminds us, he's hitting up the property man for some blood.

You can always count on the property man to give blood rather than miss an opportunity to make the audience see what they might just as well imagine. The absurd limits to which anecdotes go to scapegoat the property man become clear in another tale told on Mr Stone, the angel of theatrical literalism. 'Stone discovered the blood in which Macbeth on his exit, smeared his hands, was the blood of a king; when, ever after, he made it, with a fine prodigality of rose-ink, of a richer dye than the blood used in common.'[33] Again, the joke might seem to be on the extent of Stone's absurd literalism – or the idea of drawing blood from Mr Stone – but the anecdote reminds us that, in this play at least, it's the property man who has the blood of a king.

Alfred Hitchcock was apparently fond of muttering to himself in crowded elevators, 'Who would have thought the old man had so much blood in him?' and *Macbeth*'s meditation on just how much blood the old man has in him and what colour it should be produces a sustained chatter about the difference between blood and blood. (Macbeth reports that it is 'golden', a point Stone seems luckily to have missed.) David Garrick's Macbeth was famed for its intensity, and his power is measured by a story that reports his ability to convince even a fellow actor that he is not acting:

> One little green-room anecdote is a proof of the wonderful effect he produced in 'Macbeth,' even if we accept it with a more than ordinary large grain of salt necessary for the reception of theatrical anecdotes. He was one night playing it, and when he said to the murderer in the banquet scene – 'There is blood upon thy face,' the other, as he acknowledged himself, was so thrown off his guard by the intensity of the look and earnestness of the manner, that he put his hand up, with a start, and said, 'Is there, by G—d?' thinking he had broken a blood-vessel.[34]

Garrick never leaves the script and still convinces the actor that he's telling the truth. The grain of salt does not sour the anecdote, it spices it, preserving, as ever, the theatre's prerogative to find the greatest source of amusement at the very point where it pulses with life.

Peter O'Toole could never be accused of missing a chance for a joke, even when it was on him. His disastrous *Macbeth* at the Old Vic in 1980 – 'Not so much downright bad as heroically ludicrous' – reached its nadir, or apogee, at a moment the audience found bloody hilarious: '[W]hen Peter appeared after the murder drenched in blood from head to foot, there was a burst of laughter. Peter, expert comedian that he is, waited at the top of the stairs for the laughter to subside before exclaiming, "I have done the deed," which brought the house down.'[35] O'Toole, like Garrick, doesn't deviate from the script and still gets a laugh by drawing the audience's attention to the blood-bath he just took offstage.

Taken together, the blood-and-dagger anecdotes register theatre's uneasiness with its own signs of wonder, which ultimately include the actors who manage theatre's tangible properties. Samuel Johnson, with characteristic perspicuity, used the dagger scene to comment upon the audience's ability to separate sham and sign, a question not limited to props, but usefully reified by them:

> The appearance of a player, with whom I have drunk tea, counteracts the imagination that he is the character he represents. Nay, you know nobody imagines he is the character he represents. They say, 'See Garrick! How he looks to-night!' 'See how he'll clutch the dagger!' That is the buz [*sic*] of the theatre.[36]

Johnson's point is that it is Garrick, not 'Macbeth', who clutches the dagger, but in the process he identifies the scene as the place where theatre's illusions are most readily dispelled. Having tea with a player is like finding out that woods don't walk. The joke's on you, however, since you shouldn't have believed it in the first place. Like witches, actors will always deceive us, especially when they seem to be telling the truth.

The journalist who recorded Stone's adventures summons up the importance of theatre's materials in his description of Stone: 'He at once represents Time, Death, and Fate, with all their awful properties.' *Macbeth* is a play of awful properties, not least time, death, and fate, but also air-drawn daggers that can still get under your skin. William Rignold, for instance, who in 1882 suffered the indignity of the interrupting cat, just a few evenings later 'was accidentally stabbed in the chest' by his Macduff, who 'instead of thrusting his sword in the side of his opponent, accidentally thrust it into his chest. A doctor was immediately called, and it was found the wound was rather serious.'[37] The imaginary dagger of the play's early scenes, which marshals Macbeth the way offstage to commit a phony regicide, turns itself upon the actor. As the play proceeds on its relentless way, ruthlessly demystifying itself as it goes, the phony prophecies and air-drawn daggers resolves themselves into the real, resulting in a final lie like truth, which is that phony daggers can draw real blood.

Theatre reviewers often wag their fingers at productions of *Macbeth* for failing to live up to the play's supernatural promise (which, I argue, is part of the play's project). It is fairly clear why. Whether we are seeing the play for the first time or the fortieth, it is always deflating when we learn that the moving wood is simply a military deforestation project and that Macduff was from his mother's womb 'untimely ripped'. Critics often redirect their disappointment in the play at the production. For instance, after complaining that a 1790 production of *Macbeth* at Drury Lane did not stage Banquo's ghost (while others praised it for doing so), a critic suggests, 'It will be proper also to furnish the Soldiers of *Malcolm* with something more than *a few boughs* to conceal them, and to give the idea of *a moving Forest*.'[38] The property man is once more faulted for failing to make tangible what the play tells us is not. Birnam Wood is *not* a moving forest. It is just Macduff's soldiers holding a few branches. But the critic is right. The play contains the 'idea' of a moving forest just as it contains the idea of a dagger that hovers in mid-air. There are some things, perhaps, best left to the imagination, but one could argue that the tawdrier *Macbeth*'s production the sharper the point. The reviewer, like Macbeth, has fallen victim to the riddle of the stage: just because a property's tangible, that does not make it real.

Crude mechanicals

Back before *Macbeth* was cursed, when it was just another play with the usual run of good luck and bad, it was charmed by a series of madcap anecdotes that celebrated the play's sorcery scenes. But while anecdotes rubbed their hands in glee, reviewers clucked their tongues at the play's gimcrack wonders. The on- and offstage shenanigans of Banquo's ghost and the play's witches provided the crossroads at which the rival perspectives split. For instance, a reviewer of Macready's *Macbeth* in the 1870s complained: 'Every enlightened play-goer of the present day, will, I am satisfied, acknowledge the tragedy is, with all its sublime beauties, almost too much interwoven with supernatural mystery and melo-dramatic effect, to justify any effort to increase it by means of such *clap trap* machinery, the rude mechanical movement of which necessarily divides the attention of the audience, at the most awful point of the piece.'[39] The division of the audience's attention between supernatural mystery and rude mechanicals could be alleged – or at least has been through this chapter – to be the 'awful point of the piece'. Still, another reviewer grumped in 1814: 'The multitude are too apt to form their judgement upon these terrific beings [the witches] from the barbarous exhibitions of the stage, where terror is changed by mummery into contempt, and the characters are degraded into a junto of mischievous old women, dancing round a carpenter's kettle, making laughable grimaces, and croaking like frogs in unison.'[40] A full century earlier, a critic had complained that it 'would be better if [the witches] were not made to fly backwards'.[41] Like critics who praise *Hamlet*'s ghost for its realism, this reviewer from 1792 seems to know something we don't about the aerodynamic property of witches. Perhaps one overlooked mystery of *Macbeth*'s history is the tradition of criticism that takes seriously the question of what will fly, and what will not, when it comes to the staging of witchcraft.

But it was with Edwin Booth's 1887 *Macbeth* that a critic most clearly gave voice to what is at stake at such moments, when another non-actor interrupted *Macbeth*. It was not this time a cat but a bat that showed unbelievable timing:

> A bat, attracted by the light, flew into the Opera house last night. The *Witches* were just in the midst of their incantation, and the bat, as it circled about the stage, lent a strange air of reality to the scene. Through the darkened theater it fluttered, and back and forth across the boiling caldron, as if

> the 'double, double, toil and trouble' invocation has summoned it from some hiding place in the rocky background.[42]

It is obviously a weird kind of criticism to say that an *actual* bat lent 'reality' to an occasion on which three grown men dressed up as witches stood upon stage in Pittsburgh and pretended to cast spells. Oddly enough, it is consistently the case that scenes of unreality prompt paroxysms of critical hand wringing over whether or not they are real enough. Perhaps the real curse of *Macbeth* is the spell it casts over the critics, who want to believe in witches.

It might prove a crude maxim for stage history that what critics take seriously actors will send up. Witches, ghosts and supernatural effects make extraordinary demands upon theatrical resources. It takes a lot of elbow grease to make the stage look wonderful, as a critic of *Macbeth* recognized in the late 1700s, 'what between witches, scene-shifters, trap-workers, ghosts under ground, and *spectres* above, we never remember so general a confusion'.[43] All that work above the boards and below the ground explains why supernatural scenes spin off tales of supernumeraries, those theatrical 'extras' and the apparatuses they command that make *Macbeth* so magical. To produce something above and beyond requires a lot of below-decks work, where scene-shifters and trap-workers toil in anonymity. Usually, that is, for anecdotes, like ghosts, always haunt theatre's thresholds, and plays that traffic in the spaces between are always on the verge of revealing the ordinary means of extraordinary ends.

As with Tarleton's head, nothing is surer to get a laugh on stage than a head without a body, whether it peep through the curtains or peer out of the trap. Perhaps when a head perforates the threshold between onstage and off we are reminded of our desire to see what's hidden. The cauldron around which the witches cavort is always stewing some laughs, therefore, since its appearance and disappearance sets up one of theatre's favourite gags, when the head of a super reminds us of the bodies that labour below decks:

> KEAN . . . had many rough but funny scenes in his early Provincial tours. For example, when in the fourth act of *Macbeth* sundry apparitions rise from the witches' cauldron, it happened on one occasion that this article was no bigger than a hat-box, if not the thing itself, and was, therefore, too small to admit of a man's shoulders to pass into it. Consequently, when an armed head was expected at the top, the stage carpenter, who was raised from below, carried upward the cauldron over his face, and his chest and apron, daubed with paint, were visible to the astonished audience.[44]

The elevation of a carpenter playing a head-that-would-be-king serves as a scene of sacral import in the anecdotal history of Shakespeare in performance. Or would if it wasn't so funny. The anecdote demurs just a bit – one wants to amend its 'rough but funny' to 'rough *and* funny' – but it repeats one of the theatre's treasured jokes, in which a supernumerary briefly appears on stage (and sticking his head in a hatbox smuggles in another gag). The carpenter won't be there every night, only when things get tight. Here, the anecdote shows us what the play withholds. It takes a body to stage the disembodied. Like all of the witches' supernatural projections, this one turns out to be disappointingly natural. As for the carpenter, he's not heard from again. It was just a stage he was passing through.

As detailed previously in the chapter on *Hamlet*, George Frederick Cooke may have appeared posthumously as Yorick's skull, and the distribution of his corpse provides ample material for *Hamlet*'s ghoulish history of what remains of an actor. Yorick was Cooke's unintentional final part, but he made his unintentional debut in *Macbeth*.

> During his boyhood . . . he became anxious to see the regular players, and being short of money, he stole into the theatre unperceived, and hid himself in a barrel containing two 24-pound cannon balls, destined for theatrical thunder. The play happened to be 'Macbeth,' and the thunder being

> required, a carpet was tied over the mouth of the barrel, which at the proper moment was rolled down the stage, the screams from within frightening the man who should have stopped it at the wing, and Cooke, bursting off the carpet, found himself in the presence of the audience.[45]

Hell of an entrance. In addition to providing a fitting frame to Cooke's posthumous career, the story continues to tease out a consistent theme in *Macbeth*'s stage chatter. The anecdotes surrounding the play remind us over and over again that the ghost in the machine is a boy with bowling balls. Ghosts, heads, witches, wonder, it's all the product of clap-trap and gim-crack, and usually played for laughs.

George Frederick Cooke may have stolen into the thunder, but one man suspected that his had been nicked. John Dennis went to see *Macbeth* one night, and Theophilus Cibber tells us what happened when he rumbled his handiwork in the play's fake thunder:

> Mr. Dennis happened once to go to the play, when the tragedy [of *Macbeth*] was acted, in which the machinery of thunder was introduced, a new artificial method of producing which he had formerly communicated to the managers. Incensed by this circumstance, he cried out in a transport of resentment, 'That is my thunder by G-d; the villains will play my thunder, but not my plays.'[46]

Mr. Dennis may not have got credit for his thunder, but at least he got an entry in Bartlett's. It is not Macbeth, though, but King Lear who asks 'what is the cause of thunder' (3.4.151). (He never gets an answer, and the point might be that you have to be mad to ask.) But be they thunder sheets or barrels of balls or Dennis's 'new artificial method' the machinery that produces *Macbeth*'s thunder is the same that puzzles Lear. Repeatedly, anecdotes answer a question that Macbeth does not think to ask. The cause of thunder – and all *Macbeth*'s wonder – is just behind the curtain.

Stage frights

George Frederick Cooke's memorable debut is very nearly topped by that of Edmund Kean, who also made an early appearance in *Macbeth*, a story that affirms that the play's most sombre scenes are just a step away from comedy. All it takes is for an actor to put a foot wrong:

> At five years old he again appeared at Drury, when the following accident is said to have befallen him: – In the tragedy of *Macbeth*, John Kemble thought proper to introduce a band of lilliputian goblins, and young Edmund formed one of the corps; unfortunately, his dexterity and ardour did not keep pace, and, by an unlucky step, he tripped up himself and all his brother demons. This of course produced much merriment amongst the auditory, and the *sombre* Kemble, who could but little enjoy a laugh occasioned by the failure of one of his own introductions took the infantine performer severely to task upon the subject, who, it is said, wittily excused himself, by begging the manager 'to consider that he (Kean) had never appeared in *tragedy* before.'[47]

John Phillip Kemble's sober mien made him constant source of ridicule, but the joke here is also a generic one. From the mouth of a babe comes the suggestion that tragedy is not invariably at home to lilliputian goblins.

The anecdote does not report if the older Kemble scared the younger Kean, but even before the curse arose it collected episodes of stage fright when its stars run into its supers. Theatrical debuts form an entire sub-genre of anecdotes, though they cluster thickly around *Macbeth*. The play's supernatural scenes used to demand large numbers of supernumeraries, an opportunity for youngsters to make their stage debuts. At the same time, these debuts often bring extras into contact with the star, and anecdotes take their cues from Macbeth's rough hand with the help, who arrive late in the play in the form of bad news. James Stoddart recalls a confrontation like Kean's, where, as a young man, he displeased an older one whose acting was a fright:

> I made my second appearance . . . in 'Macbeth.' I was cast for one of the apparitions. Macready was playing the great Thane. I had to say: 'Macbeth, Macbeth, Macbeth, beware Macduff! / Beware the Thane of Fife! Dismiss me: enough!' I was nervous, but . . . thought it absolutely necessary for my future well-being that, this time, I should convince Mr Alexander [the manager] of my stability. I stood at the wings watching Macready. He was so particular everybody dreaded him . . . I made my way under the stage and found the step-ladder by which I was to reach the caldron. The witches were stirring something in it with their sticks. I kept repeating my lines, fearful that I should forget them. At last my time came to appear. I popped my head through the caldron and heard my cue. One of the witches says: 'He knows thy thought: Hear his speech, but say thou nought.' I was trembling like a leaf, but I began: 'Muckbeth, Muckbeth.' Mr. Macready instantly interrupted me: 'Oh, no, no, young man; not Muck, not Muck. Go on, sir; try again.' I said once more, 'Muck-beth.' 'Oh, no, no! Mack, Mack, Mack! D—— it, can't you say "Macbeth"?' At this moment Mr Alexander kindly came to my rescue. 'I think, Mr Macready,' he said, 'you will find the boy all right at night. Besides,' he added, '"Macbeth" is a Scotch piece, and a little of the Scotch dialect may not be altogether out of place.' Alexander had a very broad accent himself. I was at last allowed to proceed in my own way, but I do not remember whether I finally said 'Muck' or 'Mack.'[48]

Macready's 'D—— it, can't you say "Macbeth"?' anticipates the twentieth century, which can't bring itself to say 'Macbeth' lest it damn itself. Stoddart's future is in the balance, which is what this scene is at least partly about, but ultimately this witch is excused by recourse to history, which always serves as the witches' excuse. The play is a 'Scotch piece', the manager explains, which provides a broad warrant for all sorts of innovations tricked up as tradition.

The episode erases Stoddart's memory of his debut. What remains is a memorable encounter with a man whom everyone dreaded. As Stoddart suggests, Charles Macready was famously fearsome, which leads to tales that promise, but don't ever quite deliver, the punch line, that if you think Macbeth's scary, just wait until you see Macready. Stoddart survived his initial encounter by falling back on history, but not every young aspirant was so lucky.

> In one small country town Macready was once announced to play Macbeth, and the resources of the company were used to the utmost to fill all the parts. Every variety of doubling was resorted to, but at last one part, that of the messenger who brings the news of the moving wood, was left unfilled. In this emergency the sprite of the establishment undertook the part, and duly rehearsed it with the great actor. 'Now,' said Macready, who always stage-managed a great deal when he acted, 'you must rush in so, and look as frightened as you can when you deliver the message, and I shall interrupt you with the exclamation of "Liar! Fool! Slave!"' The sprite practiced the entrance diligently, Macready praising and encouraging him, and gently making him repeat the entrance till he was perfect. On the night of the performance everything went well. Lady Macbeth walked in her sleep, and Macbeth threw physic to the dogs, all with great effect, till at last the final scene arrived, and the sprite rushed in to deliver his message. But he had only seen Macready at rehearsal, when the great tragedian seldom cared to exert himself; and when Macbeth rushed at him roaring out 'Liar! Fool! Slave!' and grasped him violently by the throat, all his presence of mind forsook him. With a terrified scream of 'Oh, crikey!' he shook off Macready's grasp, and turning a back somersault, disappeared from the scene amidst roars of laughter. It is

> needless to say that the sprite never ventured upon 'responsibility' again, and this his sad fate was long remembered as a warning to the ambitious.[49]

This story emerges out of a labour crisis, an unusual one, since the theatre usually deals in surplus not scarcity. Despite all the doubling, there were no actors left and only a 'sprite' remained. The word refers, of course, to a juvenile boy, who both proverbially and actually haunted old playhouses, who employed them as general factotums. The word also hints that there may not be that much difference between the supernatural and the supernumerary. One way to put the fear back into the play is to scare the sprites off the stage, which turns the tale into a cautionary one that puts the fear of Macbeth into the ambitious. Stage fright is hazing ritual that checks the supers at the door, enforcing a strict division between extras and indispensables.

This sprite was not alone in not being able to take Macready at full volume. Another version of the same anecdote chooses more or less the same moment, but substitutes for 'Oh, crikey!' a more plausible reply. 'Crikey' is a contraction of 'Christ kill me', an expression of astonishment that is also an invocation. The super in the following version invokes not Christ but the management, who also stands as a higher authority:

> When Macready was playing Macbeth in the provinces, the actor cast in the part of the messenger in the last act was absent. So the stage-manager sent a supernumerary on to speak the lines set down for the messenger, vis., 'As I did stand my watch upon the hill, I look'd toward Birnam, and anon methought the wood began to move.' Macbeth: 'Liar and slave!' Super.: 'Pon my soul, Mr Macready, they told me to say it!'[50]

Like Garrick convincing an actor that the blood on his face is real, Macready is even more terrifying when he stays on book. The anecdotes are partly activated by the idea that – call them supers or sprites – the stage's extras are often not conversant enough with the play to distinguish between actor and act. The super here is not fooled about who is addressing him – Mr Macready not Mr Macbeth – but anecdotes put the fear in the play by putting the fear in the extras, who then trip the play into comedy by finding it so convincing. *Macbeth*'s employment of supernumeraries is always potentially a source of laughs, even or especially when Macbeth is at his most terrifying. In a play about the perils of taking things at face value, *Macbeth*'s anecdotes return again and again to credulous encounters between a star actor and extras who cannot tell just what or whom to believe.

Across the ages *Macbeth* stages a host of frightened debuts. The play forms an initiation rite that either makes or mars a young aspirant. Usually, of course, if the anecdote survives it is because the actor did, and can tell the story on himself as an allegory of his success. Colley Cibber, for one, made his debut as a messenger in the play, when 'one night when he was quite a youth he by his terror at giving a message on the stage to the great Betterton disconcerted the latter so much that he desired Downes the prompter to fine him. "Why sir," says Downes "he has no salary." "No!" said Betterton "why them put him down ten shillings a week and fine him five."'[51] In keeping with this tradition, John Philip Samuel Emery began a successful career by failing in *Macbeth*:

> Great was his joy on one occasion, at finding himself cast for the Bleeding Captain in *Macbeth*. He got the words into his head; but from an over anxiety and excitement, when he went on the stage they deserted him: and when he came to the line – 'Like two spent swimmers that do choke their art,' his art was choked, and to use a technical term, 'he stuck dead.'[52]

The technical term to 'stick dead' reveals the morbid theatrical sense that to dry is to die. To die on stage is not to cease to live but to cease to act. Not all recover from a bad case of stage fright, however. John Downes reports in 1709 that Nathaniel Lee '*had the same Fate in Acting* Duncan *in* Macbeth' as Colley Cibber, though it '*ruin'd him for an actor*'.[53] The stage's loss was theatre's gain, since Lee went on to be a successful dramatist, content to script rather than to speak. The point remains that some stage fright is fatal. At least according to anecdote, then, *Macbeth* provides a rite of passage for those bleeding soldiers, those cream-faced loons, those lilliputian goblins who have to face up to a star at full wattage. Some actors are never heard from again.

Along with Coriolanus, Macbeth may be Shakespeare's most antisocial star, one that even grows weary of the sun, whereas lead actors usually crave the light. Macready, again, provides the limit case since it was not only supers that he acted off the stage, but other stars as well. In an account from 1900, Macready turned his wrath on his Lady Macbeth, who dropped her pearls, rather than a line:

> One night, at the Park, 'Macbeth' was the play. Mrs Sloman, an old-fashioned actress, dressed *Lady Macbeth* in the manner which prevailed in her early life – in black velvet, point lace and pearl beads. In the murder scene part of Macready's dress caught on the tassels of her pearl girdle; the string broke, the beads fell on the floor, softly, with a pretty rhythmic sound, distinctly heard through the intense silence of the scene. This so exasperated Mr Macready that he was almost frantic, until, with the final line of the scene, 'Wake, Duncan, with the knocking, oh! Would thou couldst,' he threw Mrs Sloman off the stage, with words which I hope were unheard by the public, and were certainly unfit for publication.[54]

Macready's curse words turn him into a wraith who cannot stand the company of mere mortals. By saying words unfit for publication, his curses turn into the truest anecdotes, since both obscenities and anecdotes are forms whose etymologies insist that they remain behind closed curtains.

Supers get their own back, on occasion, as in a story of another powerful Macbeth. Included in *Blobson's Dire Mishaps* is a story of one 'Mr Bearbull' who got his revenge on a bully Macbeth:

> I will never forget the time I played 'Seyton' to the 'Macbeth' of an old time Barnstormer – Mr Edwin Forrest – whose voice was like thunder, and whose strength was unparalleled. We were at the Griswold Opera House, in Troy, and he was our first star in the opening of the season. He informed me I would have to wear a belt, so that he could seize me quickly and throw me gently from right to left at night after I make my announcements. Well, instead of wearing a strong leather belt, I wore a thin and very flexible rubber belt. The night arrived, and with it my scene and cue. On I came and made my announcement, when in a voice of thunder he rounded upon me to throw me to the left of the stage, when instead of throwing me, he threw himself by the flexibility of the rubber belt, landing some fifteen feet from me.[55]

Bearbull gets some payback for every Macbeth who ever manhandled an extra or scared one out of his lines. But it is not always and only the extras whom the play terrifies. It is reported by 'keen-eared critics that on the first evening of *Macbeth* at the Lyceum Mr Irving's armour could be heard to rattle in the stalls'.[56] And a much circulated anecdote about Sarah Siddons provides the apotheosis to this strain of frightened and frightening actors. One of, if not *the* most famous Lady Macbeths of the English stage, Siddons' appeal to her critics was nearly transcendental. Lord Byron is reported to have said of her Lady Macbeth, 'It is something above nature. It seemed almost as if a being of a superior order had dropped from a higher sphere to awe the world with the majesty of her appearance.' Siddons is, in Byron's terms, literally 'super-natural'.[57] It is therefore fitting her preparation for the part scared her right out of her wits:

A writer in the London *Argosy* says: Late one night Mr. Siddons was sitting by the fire in the modest family parlor, which, in that most unassuming household, served as dining-room or drawing-room, as the case might be. He was smoking calmly his last pipe, and beginning to think about going to bed, whither, as it was not one of his evenings at the theatre, he believed his wife had gone already. The house was sunk in dreamy silence, so was the quiet street outside – silence only broken now and then by the roll of distant wheels. The actor had been drawing a vague picture of a little holiday trip which he and Sarah would take next summer, and had fallen into a half doze, in which he was driving down a country lane all scented with honeysuckle, all draped with eglantine. Suddenly he was roused, with a start, by hurried footsteps, that were flying rather than running down the passage. Who could it be? He asked himself, all in a maze and a wonder as he jumped up and rubbed his sleepy laden eyes. He had hardly had time to let the question go darting through his brain, when the door of the room was flung open quickly, as by a hasty, trembling hand, and a female figure rushed in. Mr. Siddons gazed in speechless astonishment, not unmixed with a touch of fear. There before him stood his wife, her fine hair disheveled, her dress all in disorder, her face all quivering with strong emotion. In bewildered alarm he asked her what was the matter, but her only answer was to throw herself into his arms, and burst into a torrent of tears. He soothed her tenderly, not knowing what to think, and gradually she grew calmer. Then her words made the mystery plain enough. Instead of going to bed, as he had bade her to, she had been sitting up studying her part as Lady Macbeth; and the character had so completely absorbed her in itself, she had so entirely realized the horror of each situation in the play, had seen it all so distinctly before her eyes, as if she had been there in the body, that a wild, unreasoning terror had seized her, and she had rushed away to seek human companionship.[58]

Perhaps, just perhaps, it is possible to locate in this an incipient form of the play's later curse. Rather than fold the anecdote into a foregone history, it is possible to see in this anecdote a domesticated drama called 'At Home with the Macbeths', one the play hints at but withholds. As Macbeth dreams of a honeysuckle weekend his wife sees clearly the horror ahead. The anecdote unapologetically *reads* the play. Macbeth is a dreamer who wakes up too late while his wife has her eyes wide open from the start. It also suggests – for all those actors frightened out of their wits by *Macbeth* – a modicum of comfort, which is that if you realize the horror ahead you should be terrified.

Exeunt, cursing

The air-drawn dagger points Macbeth in the direction he was going anyway and therefore materializes – and demystifies – the witches' prophecies. The witches also point Macbeth in the direction he was already going. They greet him as Thane of Cawdor, for instance, which is old news to the audience, since Duncan made him so in the previous scene. We already know the witches' prophecy has come to pass, and so it's not a prophecy. But then the witches aren't prophets, they're historians. Macbeth is usually the only one in the theatre who confuses the one with the other.

Macbeth repeatedly disappoints and disillusions, just as though it knows how it will end. When the actor William Powell passed from the world, it was 'a sentence from this play which rose to poor Powell's lips at his last moment. Hannah More was watching by his bedside, when the dying man suddenly sat up, and assuming the proper expression and attitude exclaimed, "Is this a dagger which I see before me?" A moment later he was dead.'[59] Powell's famous last words give voice for Mr Harris, the actor killed on stage in 1672, who 'could not bring out the last words of his part'.[60] Of course, 'Is this a dagger . . .' are not the last words of the part, but they are the last word in theatrical scepticism and form a fitting exit line for any expiring actor.

While *Macbeth* may turn out to be disappointingly unmysterious, it is spectacularly theatrical. That is not a paradox. It is a redundancy. The play waits until the last possible moment to spring this trap on Macbeth, so that it might deflate his illusions in a single spectacular blow out. Anecdotes, on the other hand, cannot wait to puncture our illusions and to do so with a thousand cuts. Before the curse, anecdotes were all quick to point out that the blood that quickens our most treasured mysteries is made by the property man. The twentieth century has reinflated the mystery with a lot of hot air about a curse. But you can hardly blame people for believing in it. Everyone makes mystiques.

CODA: ARCHIVES AND ANECDOTES

And then there was the time that Edward Alleyn got such a bad case of stage fright that he promised, if he lived, to build a college. John Aubrey reports in 1719 in the *Natural History and Antiquities of Surrey* under the heading 'Dulwich College' that 'the Tradition concerning the Occasion of the Foundation runs thus':

> That Mr *Alleyne*, being a Tragedian and one of the original actors in many of the celebrated *Shakespear*'s plays, in one of which he play'd a *Demon*, with six others, and was in the midst of the play surpriz'd by an *Apparition* of the *Devil,* which so work'd on his Fancy, that he made a Vow, which he perform'd at this Place.[1]

Edward Alleyn kept his vow and then some. He not only founded the college but English theatre history. For Dulwich's archive contains thousands of Alleyn's papers, his own and those he inherited from his father-in-law, Philip Henslowe, the great theatrical entrepreneur and builder of The Rose and Fortune playhouses. As the Henslowe-Alleyn Digitisation Project categorically puts it, 'As a group, these manuscripts comprise the largest and most important single extant archive of material on the professional theatre and dramatic performance in early modern England, the age of Shakespeare, Marlowe, Jonson, Middleton, Heywood, Dekker, Chettle, and so many of their contemporaries and colleagues.'[2] In sum, we owe the existence of the greatest archive of theatrical activity in the Shakespearean age to stage fright.

Or not. The suggestion that Alleyn founded Dulwich on these terms is just an anecdote. Moreover, the story of the extra devil was already old by the time that Aubrey got to it, and though he tries to attach it to Shakespeare, it failed to stick. It had to settle for *Faustus*, to which it has stuck ever since. One seventeenth-century version of this tale concerns a group of players at Exeter, who

> acting upon the stage the tragical storie of Dr Faustus the Conjurer; as a certain nomber of Devels kept everie one his circle there, and as Faustus was busie in his magicall invocations, on a sudden they were all dasht, every one harkning other in the eare, for they were all perswaded, there was one devell too many amongst them.[3]

This wasn't just the kind of thing that happens in Exeter since the anti-theatrical berserker William Prynne reports in his *Histriomastix* on '[t]he visible apparition of the Devill on the stage at the Belsavage Play-house, in Queen Elizabeths days . . . while they were there prophanely playing the History of Faustus'.[4] The account jibes with Thomas Middleton's memory, who in his *Black Booke* of 1604 describes a demon as having 'hayre like one of my devils in Doctor Faustus, when the theatre crackt and frighted the audience'.[5] Neither is the anecdote entirely English since Rousseau relates in his *Œuvres Diverses* of 1761 that (in a later translation):

> I have in my youth read a tragedy called the 'Slave,' in which the devil was presented by one of the actors. The piece was once performed, as I am informed, when this personage coming on the stage, found himself in company with a second devil, the original, who, as if jealous of the audacity of the counterfeit, appeared in *propria persona*, frighted all the people out of the house, and put an end to the representation.[6]

Theatre history is bedevilled by this anecdote, and its ubiquity mitigates its credibility. In fact, there is nothing more than anecdote to suggest that Alleyn's demonic encounter led to the founding of Dulwich College. J.R. Pigott, the former Keeper of the Archives at Dulwich, does not even mention it in *Dulwich College: A Brief History and Guide to the Building*. Pigott reports that King James signed letters patent on 21 June 1619 to establish the College of God's Gift in Dulwich, Surrey. Not a devil in sight, on the guest list or otherwise. (Perhaps being 'Keeper of the Archives' means keeping them safe from anecdotes.) We cannot conclude then that England's greatest theatrical archive owes its existence to stage fright. It owes its existence to an anecdote, at least according to this anecdote, which uses an old story to invent a tradition about the founding of the archive which would then exclude it. But it is in keeping with anecdotes' outsized claims to take credit for something that isn't true.

While Aubrey tries to marry them, there has historically been – in both senses of the words – a fundamental incompatibility between archives and anecdotes. And while they are conjoined here by a simple conjunction, it remains to ask if there is an historical syntax that can parse both parts of speech. Recently, at least, theatre history has calved off the anecdote and focused instead on affiliations and transactions – architectural, political, economic – ones that left a trace for the archive to index. These traces are usually about something other than the immediacy of performance, however. It sets up a peculiar paradox: it is the fact that these traces are peripheral to performance that makes them so trustworthy. (The other buried paradox here is that the closer archives get to performance the more dubious they become.) We have a record, for instance, that Henslowe paid Rowley and Bird four pounds in 1604 to make some additions to *Faustus*, but no archives will tell us who added the extra devil at the 'Belsavage Play-house, in Queen Elizabeths dayes'. But then, Henslowe's records of his financial transactions are not trying to convey the experience of watching grown men and boys dress up in outrageous costumes and relate a fable about a German necromancer. In fact, the archives gather their authority from their own impertinence, an impertinence at least to the experience of playgoing. They tell us something about theatre because they're not trying to tell us something about theatre.

What the archives *can* do is bring together people, places, and times into a spatio-temporal map of activity and in so doing give us theatre's coordinates. Consider Philip Henslowe's diary as a kind of map. This 'map' allows us to track Henslowe as he moves across space and time and comes into and out of contact with others – some of them, like Edward Alleyn, related to the theatre, but many who are not. Henslowe's non-theatrical business transactions count as theatre history only because we know he owned a theatre. We admit archives onto the map of English theatre history to the extent that they relate to other locations already on the map. The map grows ever more detailed, ever more 'accurate' with the accumulation and arrangement of data made credible by other data. The archive authenticates itself by admitting material on its own terms.

And yet anecdotes are not the opposite of archives. The opposite of the archive is absence; the 'blank' that Viola tells Orsino makes up her sister's history. Perhaps anecdotes have laboured in the service of history long enough. In the diminishing wake of the new historicism – and the time seems past that we need to capitalize it – we might turn to the anecdote as a form of theatrical chatter that has less to say about history and more to tell us about performance. Put another way, John Aubrey may seem engaged in spurious theatre history when he lays the foundation of Dulwich College at the cloven feet of an extra devil. But he is, instead, offering an early version of performance studies, one that understands the life of the live to live in its recollection, even, or especially, when it strains credibility. To come to grips with what happened after the archive gets us to the theatre's front door, we turn to anecdotes – though we shouldn't give them our ticket because they might not actually work there.

'Where memory is, theatre is', Herbert Blau memorably wrote, and since the 1990s performance studies has learned to sing in this elegiac key.[7] Indeed, melancholia sits brood upon performance studies, which understands the disappearing act to be the defining trick of performance. Within the terms of this influential paradigm, archives are the fragments, shored against theatre's ruin. But what of anecdotes? They may seem to abet this process, to remind us of something that happened 'one time' and then was gone again, a theatre historical nova. In these terms, anecdotes play the goonish sidekick to the archive's straight man. Certainly, anecdotes can function in that way. At the same time, anecdotes encode their own iterability and so promise not just a record but a repetition. Aubrey's appropriation of the extra-devil tale is therefore not just a memory of an event that's already gone, it is a kind of promissory note that it will come again, a cultural cell where we can store our memory until we need it again (and indeed the extra devil makes a reappearance across theatre history). Anecdotes are recollections of the past, therefore, but they are also memories of the future. They prophesy a performance future in which a singular event will reoccur – as event turns into eventuality, as this book has argued.

This might seem to leave us back where we started, stuck between archives and anecdotes – or between facts and truth. A crude cartoon of this position would see work on Shakespeare and performance pinioned between things that are too good to be true and things that are too boring to make up. To be fair, if archival traces are 'too boring to make up' (and they aren't) anecdotes are more often just as absurd. If archives are not trying to tell us anything about performance, anecdotes are trying too hard, and so the historiographic utility of the anecdote is attenuated by its own operation. If archives are the raw goods, anecdotes are overcooked. As Hayden White and other scholars of historiography have pointed out, narrative embarrasses history, since narrative commits us to causality; events and consequences; beginnings, middles, and ends – and history is rarely so tidy, though historiography sometimes is. Narrative is not primarily designed to represent reality, however, its purpose is to convey it. As Scott McMillin once put it, 'we do not tell narratives because we believe them, we do so to remember the evidence.'[8] Narrative brings the principle of organization to the chaos of material evidence, though the narrative inevitably misrepresents the relationship of one piece of evidence with another. Or, narrative *is* the relationship of one piece of evidence with the other unless we are entirely content to treat the archive as parataxis, a list of places without coordinates.

An anecdote is a narrative – a 'drama of the short time span' as Fernand Braudel calls it in his important essay 'History and the Social Sciences'. Since the 'short time span is the most capricious and delusional of all',[9] we are left on the one hand with traces of activity that give us locations without experience and with short narratives that we cannot in good conscience trust. If there is a possible rapprochement between the archive and the anecdote it must be a provisional one. It might begin by treating them not as wary opposites but as categorically distinct: the archive as evidence of theatre history, the anecdote an index to theatre's futurity. After all, anecdotes will never stand up to the kind of scrutiny that validates the archival trace. For if, according to Roland Barthes, myth is depoliticized speech, an anecdote is dehistoricized history.[10] Anecdotes curdle at the sight of a date, and thus once a single name, date, or place is assigned to an anecdote – as opposed to multiple ones – it becomes something else. It becomes an archive.

Even calling up the scrapbooks that contained much of this book's primary material rehearsed the challenge that anecdotes make to traditional historiography. The Folger Shakespeare Library's request slips ask for a book's call number, its title, its author, and its publication date. The vast majority of the library's hundreds of scrapbooks possess only one of those attributes: call number, accompanied – nearly but not always – by the name of the theatre, actor, or play the scrapbook most immediately treats. Who, then, is the author? What is the title? When is the book published? Scrapbooks are miscellanies, composed and compiled over time, a collection of clippings and hand annotations. They therefore present cataloguing challenges to protocols that index by time, title and author. If print turns a process into an object – in Jerome McGann's terms – scrapbooks represent acts of aggregation extended over time. They may even challenge McGann's sharp distinction. Objects are processes too, after all, just extremely slow ones.

To be sure, an anecdote could be authenticated by the logic of the archive, could at least notionally become archival. Though the opposite is also true. For if another record emerged of Henslowe paying two men other than Rowley and Bird a sum other than four pounds to make additions to *Faustus*, and then another and then another still, the archival trace might become anecdotal. The accumulative force of incompatible accounts of Henslowe paying to have *Faustus* altered would invalidate all of those accounts. The means by which we verify and discredit archives and anecdotes will always turn the one into the other by the same means that they become themselves. Michel de Certeau suggests a version of this dynamic when he writes that historiography oscillates between 'producing history' and 'telling stories', but cannot be reduced to either one or the other.[11] Archives and anecdotes are not opposites, they are quantum.

Authentication is not the name of the game, then, when it comes to anecdotes, or at least not the kind of authentication history is at home with. Thomas Postlewait has written the most searching analysis of the use of anecdote to theatre history, pointing out that 'suspect anecdotes are pervasive in all historical scholarship. The challenge, then, is not simply to reject them but to analyze anecdotes carefully in order to establish their historical authenticity.'[12] There are more kinds of authenticity than one, however. Even the most positivist historian might agree that while the *event* the anecdote narrates likely did not happen, the anecdote did. For the purposes of this book, that has been enough. Postlewait closes his inquiry with the question, 'What indeed is the nature of a "genuine anecdote"?'[13] The answer to this plaintive question will sound more tautological than I intend: a genuine anecdote is one that has become anecdotal. Archives are authenticated by the presence of other archives, but anecdotes are self-documenting.

What kind of 'history' does this book's subtitle promise, then? In the end, the idea here is that the anecdote is an apparatus of capture. In his essay 'What is an Apparatus?' Giorgio Agamben defines it as 'literally anything that has in some way the capacity to capture, orient, determine, intercept, model, control, or secure the gestures, behaviors, opinions, or discourses of living beings'.[14] Agamben's definition is so broad that it could include everything from the law to a limerick to an etch-a-sketch, but it might be adopted here. Anecdotes capture the theatrical chatter that emerges about the edges of Shakespeare's canonical plays. In doing so, they capture and convey – while they also control – the kinds of things actors and audiences have felt, or might want to feel, about these plays across many, many years. Braudel's description of the anecdote as 'the drama of the short time span' notwithstanding, history, as the saying goes, has both a minute hand and an hour hand. Just as an hour is made of many minutes, the many minute tales that come together in the pages of this book add up to a kind of chronicle history of Shakespearean chatter.

The word 'history' in the book's subtitle has a highly qualified meaning, therefore, since it is a history of what has seemed to be true rather than what in fact happened. But it is modified by 'new', and 'anecdotal' is the first word on the cover, flirting with the new historicism if not outright courting it. The work here differs, however, from the new historical application of the anecdote in that it is primarily interested in those that recur. The durable anecdote might become more dubious with each repetition but what it loses in credibility it gains in predictive force.

The argument of the new historicism, it seems to me, was that history required creative resistance – required the oxymoronic 'new historicism' – because history is preoccupied by the end, and with it for that matter. Our telling of it is, like the work of the actor, finished before it is started. For the new historicism, the anecdote provided a form of history less in love with endings, less certain of its outcomes, though, ultimately, a form of history that foreclosed upon all hopes of resistance, creative or otherwise.

I am, that is, less interested in the inevitable fatality of new historicism than in articulating a renovated historiography of the theatre, one less in love with facts and their outcomes and more alert to a history in which anything might happen, and then do so over and over again. I think that theatre history is, in other words, a place where anecdotes can make a difference – because anecdotes are made *of* difference – and a history with a difference is what this book is about. I have been throughout not interested in theatre anecdotes for their allegorical properties or their synechdochal ones but for the ways they actively forestall the end by speaking an event into the teeth of the eventual.

Ultimately, what distinguishes my treatment of the anecdote here from that of the new historicism is they were interested in anecdotes as a form of disturbance while I'm concerned with anecdotes that endure – of history in the future tense. While anecdotes *can* function as memorials for lost performances, they also work, as Jaqueline Bratton argues, 'as a kind of history that is perceived as a possible continuity in an evanescent tradition'.[15] Stephen Fry did not, on the night of Peter O'Toole's death, tell the 'you should see the Duke of Buckingham' tale because he believed it happened that way, or even because he believed we had not heard it before. He told it to remember Peter O'Toole, lest we forget. And the surest way to guarantee that we don't forget something is to tell us something we already know.

The history of Shakespeare in performance told through anecdotes might add up to a kind of chronicle history, but the teleology that governs here is not chronology, but accumulation. It is the cumulative status of a recurrent anecdote that enters it into the historical record. A correspondent to *The Era* in 1869 wrote into the paper to correct some of the details in its recently published life of Edmund Kean. The anonymous writer makes some minor corrections, and though his contribution is minor, his conclusion is grand: 'I am anxious that *The Era* should ever be the first to set at rest all subjects of Histrionic interest or doubt, especially when the Histrionic becomes from the lapse of years not only *Histrionic but Historic*.'[16] The histrionic, plus time, equals history, at least in this correspondent's addition. As Malina Stefanovska suggests, 'anecdotes follow the logic of accumulation rather than that of narrative progression, [and are] governed by the pleasure principle which allows for repetition, accumulation and exhibition.'[17] Anecdotes are in these terms not singular interventions in history but relatively stable apparatuses across time that register the way plays make meaning even in very different times and places, including those yet to come.

Anecdotes make for fabulous history, in every sense of the word. Don't take my word for it. William Thomas wrote in *Anecdotes and Traditions, Illustrative of Early English History and Literature* in the 1830s: 'The fabulous history of every country is part of its history, and ought not to be omitted by later and more enlightened historians; because it has been believed at one time, and while it was believed it influenced the imagination, and thereby, in some degree, the opinions and character of the people.'[18] Anecdotes tell us what people believed, or were happy to believe, and even if they were unbelieving, will tell us what they wanted or even needed to be true. Getting access to that occult array – the imaginative archive or the archival imaginary – can discover for us the ways that actors and audiences have used but also playfully challenged Shakespeare across the last 400 years.

I have tried in every important respect to write a fabulous history, to do justice to the material. What I have described in this closing section is, though written last, my best-case scenario, an outline for an approach the book has tried to live up to. To be on the safe side, I will close with one final anecdote, about not the best case but the worst, of an ambitious writer who tried to tell English history through the medium of anecdotes. The account shows up in the life and times of Charles Kean, and appeared in the mid-nineteenth century.

> The Italian chronicler, Gregorio Leti, who came to reside in England during the reign of Charles II, soon gave out that he intended to employ himself in collecting materials for an anecdotal history of the reign of the merry monarch. The subject was fertile in incident, but likely to be very objectionable in substance. The King, observing him at one of the levves, asked him how his work went on. 'I understand,' said his Majesty, 'that you intend to deal largely in anecdotes of the English court; take care there be no offence.' 'Sire,' answered the Italian, 'I will do what I can, and will be as careful as possible; but if a man were as wise as Solomon, he could hardly publish historical anecdotes without giving *some* offence.' 'Why, then,' retorted Charles, 'do you copy the wisdom of Solomon; write proverbs, and leave history and anecdotes alone.' [He didn't] . . . and it gave outrageous umbrage in certain high quarters, and raised such a clamour about his ears, that he was ordered to quit the kingdom, which he forthwith did, and betook himself to Amsterdam, where he died in 1701.[19]

John William Cole, the author of this account, does not report on the cause of Leti's demise, but the conclusion is hard to avoid that anecdotes were the death of him. He probably should have listened to the King, resisted the anecdotes and offered proverbs instead, but Leti might, upon reflection, have decided that they are one and the same. Anecdotes, like proverbs, are written in the present tense.

NOTES

Preface: Curtain raiser

1 Jody Enders, *Death by Drama and other Medieval Urban Legends* (Chicago: Chicago University Press, 2002), p. xxii.

2 Folger Shakespeare Library Scrapbook B.130.4 'Theatrical Clippings'.

3 This juxtaposition of non-chronological images occurred at 'MOMO 2000', at which New York City's Museum of Modern Art celebrated the millennium by ignoring time.

4 Greil Marcus, *The History of Rock 'n' Roll in Ten Songs* (New Haven: Yale University Press, 2014), p. 53.

5 William Shakespeare, *Romeo and Juliet*, 5.3.307. All references to Shakespeare's plays are from the *Arden Shakespeare Complete Works*, eds. Richard Proudfoot, Ann Thompson and David Scott Kastan (London: Thomson Learning, 2007).

Introduction: Anecdotal Shakespeare

1 Peter Holland and W.B. Worthen, eds., *Theorizing Practice: Redefining Theatre History* (New York: Palgrave Macmillan, 2003), p. 2.

2 William J. Thomas, ed., *Anecdotes and Traditions, Illustrative of Early English History and Literature* (London: Nicols and Son, 1839), Preface.

3 A.M. Nagler, *A Source Book in Theatrical History: Twenty-five Centuries of Stage History in more than 300 Basic Documents and Other Primary Material* (Dover Publications, 1959), pp. 28–34.

4 See Jody Enders, *Death by Drama and Other Medieval Legends* (Chicago: Chicago University Press), esp. pp. 2–3, and passim.

5 Tiffany Stern, *Documents of Performance in Early Modern England* (Cambridge: Cambridge University Press, 2009), pp. 17–18.

6 Folger Shakespeare Library Scrapbook B.133.2 'Theatrical Miscellany'.

7 Thomas Heywood, *An Apology for Actors, Containing Three Brief Treatises* (London, 1612), G2[R].

8 Nicholas L'Estrange, *Merry Passages and Jests: A Manuscript Jestbook*, ed. H.F. Lippincott (Insistut fur Englische Sprache und Literratur Universitat Salzburg, 1974), p. 71.

9 Thomas Nashe, *Pierce Peniless* (London, 1592).

10 Henry Peacham, *The Compleat Gentleman, The Truth of our Times, and The Art of Living in London* (1638) (Ithaca, NY: Cornell University Press, 1962).

11 'The most intense and productive life of culture takes place on the boundaries' in Mikhail Bakhtin, *Speech Genres and Other Late Essays* (Austin, TX: University of Texas Press, 1986), p. 2.

12 Folger Shakespeare Library Scrapbook B.130.5 'Theatrical Clippings'.

13 Natalie S. Loveless, 'Reading with Knots: On Jane Gallop's Anecdotal Theory', *S: Journal of the Circle for Lacanian Ideology Critique*, 4 (2011).

14 James Wright, *Historia Histrionica: An Historical Account of the English Stage, Shewing the Ancient Use, Improvement, and Perfection, of Dramatick Representations, in this Nation, in a Dialogue of Plays and Players* (London, 1699), p. 32.

15 Aoife Monks, 'Collecting Ghosts: Actors, Anecdotes and Objects at the Theatre', *Contemporary Theatre Review*, 23, no. 2 (2013): 146–52.

16 Folger Shakespeare Library Scrapbook A.7.1 London, 'Drury Lane, 1663–1847 (Beaufoy Coll.)'.

17 Folger Shakespeare Library Scrapbook B.133.7 'Theatrical Miscellany'.

18 *The Theatrical Jester: Or Green-Room Witticisms. Being a Collection of Entertaining and Original Anecdotes, Bon Mots, Repartees, &C. Relating to the Stage* (London: J. Hammond, 1795).

19 William Cooke, *Memoirs of Samuel Foote, Esq., with a Collection of His Genuine Bon-mots, Anecdotes, Opinions, &c. Mostly Original. 3 vols.* (London: Richard Phillips, 1805).

20 Henry Curling, *Recollections of the Mess-Table and the Stage* (London: T. Bosworth, 1855).

21 Joel Fineman, 'The History of the Anecdote: Fiction and Friction' in *The New Historicism*, ed. H. Aram Veeser (New York: Routledge, 1989), p. 61.

22 Folger Shakespeare Library Scrapbook A.11.1 'London Theatres'.

23 Folger Shakespeare Library Scrapbook A.2.4 'London, Covent Garden, 1807–1811'.

24 William Macready, *The Diaries of William Charles Macready 1833–1851*, ed. William Toynbee, (New York: G.P. Putnam's Sons, 1912), vol. 2, p. 420.

25 Folger Shakespeare Library Scrapbook B.130.2 'Theatrical Clippings'.

26 Folger Shakespeare Library Scrapbook A.11.1 'London Theatres'.

27 Peter Bowles, *Behind the Curtain: The Job of Acting* (London: Oberon Books, 2012).

28 *Philip Larkin: The Complete Poems*, ed. Archie Burnett (New York: Farrar, Straus and Giroux, 2012), p. 293.

29 Jeremy Lopez, *Constructing the Canon of Early Modern Drama* (Cambridge: Cambridge University Press, 2014), p. 215.

30 Simon Palfrey, 'Strange Mimesis', *The Hare*, 1, no. 3 (2013): http://thehareonline.com/issue-archive.

31 James Stoddart, *Recollections of a Player* (New York: The Century Company, 1902), pp. 18–21.

32 Folger Shakespeare Library Scrapbook A.7.1 'London, Drury Lane,1663–1847 (Beaufoy Coll.)'.

33 Folger Shakespeare Library Scrapbook A.5.9 'London, Drury Lane & Covent Garden, 1776–77)'.

34 *Stage Gossip and Theatrical Tit-Bits Ancient and Modern* (London: Jennins, 1888).

35 Terry Eagleton, 'Base and Superstructure Revisited', *New Literary History*, 31 (2000): 231–40, esp. 236.

36 John William Cole, *The Life and Theatrical Times of Charles Kean FSA* (London: Richard Bentley, 1859), p. 63.

37 Samuel Schoenbaum, *William Shakespeare: A Compact Documentary Life* (Oxford: Clarendon Press, 1970), p. 205.

38 Robert Sellers, *Hellraisers: The Life and Inebriated Times of Richard Burton, Richard Harris, Peter O'Toole, and Oliver Reed* (New York: St Martin's Press, 2009).

39 Antony Sher, *Year of the King: An Actor's Diary and Sketchbook* (New York: Limelight, 1999).

1 *Hamlet*: Skulls are good to think with

1 Elizabeth Williamson, 'Yorick's Afterlives: Skull Properties in Performance', *Borrowers and Lenders: The Journal of Shakespeare and Appropriation*, 6 (2011): 1.

2 John Raynolds, *Dolarny's Primerose, Or The First Part of the Passionate Hermit* (1606), sig. D4' verso.

3 *The Century Magazine*, n.d., Folger Shakespeare Library Scrapbook B.23.1 'Forbes-Robertson, J.'.

4 *New York Times*, n.d., Folger Shakespeare Library Scrapbook B.63.2 'Hamlet'.

5 Folger Shakespeare Library Scrapbook B.63.2 'Hamlet'.

6 *Harper's Weekly*, 1890, Folger Shakespeare Library Scrapbook B.7.5 'Edwin Booth'.

7 Folger Shakespeare Library Scrapbook B.7.6 'Edwin Booth'.

8 *The Morning News*, Paris, Monday 25 October 1886.

9 Folger Shakespeare Library Scrapbook B.7.6 'Edwin Booth'.

10 Folger Shakespeare Library Scrapbook B.133.13 'Theatrical Miscellany'.

11 *Harper's New Monthly Magazine*, Vol. LXIII., no. 373, Folger Shakespeare Library Scrapbook B.7.6 'Edwin Booth'.

12 Harper's Franklin Square Library no. 392 22 Aug 1884. Another account appears in Percy Fitzgerald's hand-annotated scrapbook of theatrical miscellany as 'The American papers publish the following story: – John R. Reed has been the gasman of the Walnut-street Theatre, Philadelphia, for fifty-four years, and has never missed a performance in all that period. He is somewhat eccentric, and in his will is the following provision: – "My head shall be severed from my body, and my body shall be placed in a vault, but the head shall be brought to the Walnut-street Theatre, there to be used as the skull in *Hamlet*, and I do bequeath my head to the said Walnut-street Theatre for that purpose".'

13 In 'Yorick's Afterlives', Williamson notes that 'Kean, Macready, Kemble, Booth, Forrest, Cushman, Davenport, Murdock, and Brooks' are all legible.

14 Williamson, 'Yorick's Afterlives'.

15 Bradbrook is quoted in Peter Thomson, *Shakespeare's Theatre* (London: Routledge and Kegan Paul, 1983), p. 111.

16 William Dunlap, *Memoirs of the Life of George Frederick Cooke, Esquire: Late of the Theatre Royal Covent Garden*, 2 vols. (New York: D. Longworth, 1813), vol. 1, p. 384.

17 Dutton Cook, 'Stage Properties', *Belgravia, an Illustrated London Magazine*, *Belgravia*, 35, 1878: 291–3.

18 Folger Shakespeare Library Scrapbook B.133.4 'Theatrical Miscellany'.

19 Thomas Marshall, *Lives of the Most Celebrated Actors and Actresses* (London: E. Appleyard, 1847), p. 126.

20 Otis Skinner, *Mad Folk of the Theatre: Ten Studies in Temperament* (Indianapolis: Bobbs-Merrill, 1928).

21 Folger Shakespeare Library Scrapbook A.2.4 'London, Covent Garden, 1812–1815'.

22 *The Philadelphia Press*, Sunday, 26 May 1895.

23 Cook, 'Stage Properties': 291–3.

24 Folger Shakespeare Library Scrapbook A.5.10 'London, Drury Lane & Covent Garden, 1777–78'.

25 Arthur Colby Sprague, *Shakespeare and the Actors: The Stage Business in His Plays, 1660–1905* (London: Russell and Russell, 1944), p. 174.

26 Folger Shakespeare Library Scrapbook B.40.2 'Literary Clippings from the Athenaeum'.

27 Folger Shakespeare Library Scrapbook B.63.2 'Hamlet'.

28 Folger Shakespeare Library Scrapbook B.63.2 'Hamlet'.

29 Ian McKellen, 'On the Test of Time', *The Observer Magazine*, 13 April 1975, p. 17.

30 Folger Shakespeare Library Scrapbook A.12.1 'Theatrical Clippings — Drama'.

31 Folger Shakespeare Library Scrapbook B.130.6 'Theatrical Clippings'.

32 Folger Shakespeare Library Scrapbook B.63.2 'Hamlet'.

33 Folger Shakespeare Library Scrapbook A.4.2. 'London, Covent Garden, 1778–1781'.

34 Folger Shakespeare Library Scrapbook B.133.5 'Theatrical Miscellany'.

35 Folger Shakespeare Library Scrapbook B.63.2 'Hamlet'.

36 Folger Shakespeare Library Scrapbook B.7.1 'Edwin Booth'.

37 Folger Shakespeare Library Scrapbook B.63.2 'Hamlet'.

38 *The Theatrical Jester: Or Green-Room Witticisms. Being a Collection of Entertaining and Original Anecdotes, Bon Mots, Repartees, &C. Relating to the Stage* (London: J. Hammond, 1795).

39 Folger Shakespeare Library Scrapbook B.28.1 'Hackett, James H.'.

40 William Cooke, *Memoirs of Charles Macklin, Comedian* (London: Printed for J. Asperne by T. Maiden, 1804), p. 376.

41 Folger Shakespeare Library Scrapbook 'A.11.1 London Theatres'.

42 Folger Shakespeare Library Scrapbook B.132.6 'Theatrical Clippings from the *Times*'.

43 Folger Shakespeare Library Scrapbook B.133.16 'Theatrical Miscellany'.

44 Joseph Roach, *Cities of the Dead: Circum-Atlantic Performance* (New York: Columbia University Press, 1996), p. 92.

45 Henry Curling, *Recollections of the Mess-Table and the Stage* (London: T. Bosworth, 1855), pp. 30–1.

46 Daniel Rosenthal, 'Not All Right on the Night', *The Independent*, http://www.independent.co.uk/arts-entertainment/theatre-dance/features/not-all-right-on-the-night-8998788.html, accessed 12 December 2013.

47 Darren Franich, 'Daniel Day-Lewis Clarifies that he did not see the Ghost of his Father while Performing "Hamlet"', *Entertainment Weekly*, http://popwatch.ew.com/2012/10/29/daniel-day-lewis-hamlet-ghost/, accessed 13 June 2014.

48 Folger Shakespeare Library Scrapbook B.133.6 'Theatrical Miscellany'.

49 Simon Callow, *Being an Actor* (New York: Picador, 2003), p. 141.

50 Folger Shakespeare Library Scrapbook B.7.9 'Edwin Booth'.

51 Folger Shakespeare Library Scrapbook B.133.10 'Theatrical Miscellany1865 c.'.

2 *Othello*: The smudge

1 Joseph Haslewood, *The Secret History of the Green Rooms: Containing Authentic and Entertaining Memoirs of the Actors and Actresses in the Three Theatres Royal* (London: 1790), vol. 1, p. 266.

2 Ellen Terry, *The Story of My Life* (New York: Doubleday, 1908), p. 204.

3 Folger Shakespeare Library Scrapbook B.104.1 'Othello'.

4 Folger Shakespeare Library Scrapbook A.2.2 'London, Covent Garden, 1757–1794'

5 Folger Shakespeare Library Scrapbook B.26.1 'Garrick, David'.

6 Folger Shakespeare Library Scrapbook A.2.4 'London, Covent Garden, 1812–1815'.

7 Folger Shakespeare Library Scrapbook A.2.4 'London, Covent Garden, 1812–1815'.

8 Bosley Crowther, 'The Screen: Minstrel Show "Othello": Radical Makeup Marks Olivier's Interpretation', *New York Times*, 2 February 1968.

9 Barbara Delatiner, 'For a Polish Outsider, "Othello" Rings True', *New York Times*, http://www.nytimes.com/2002/08/04/nyregion/for-a-polish-outsider-othello-rings-true.html, accessed 9 February 2015.

10 Folger Shakespeare Library Scrapbook A.2.4 'London, Covent Garden, 1812–1815'.

11 Folger Shakespeare Library Scrapbook A.2.3 'London, Covent Garden, 1780–1799'.

12 Folger Shakespeare Library Scrapbook A.2.3 'London, Covent Garden, 1780–1799'.

13 Folger Shakespeare Library Scrapbook A.2.3 'London, Covent Garden, 1780–1799'.

14 Folger Shakespeare Library Scrapbook A.3.1 'London, Covent Garden, 1763–1848 (Beaufoy Coll.)'.

15 Folger Shakespeare Library Scrapbook A.2.4 'London, Covent Garden, 1807–1811'.

16 Folger Shakespeare Library Scrapbook B.7.2 'Edwin Booth'.

17 Folger Shakespeare Library Scrapbook B.83.1 'Othello'.

18 Kate Terry Gielgud, *A Victorian Playgoer*, ed. Muriel St Clare Byrne (London: Heinemann, 1980), p. 108.

19 See Virginia Vaughan, *Othello: A Contextual History* (Cambridge: Cambridge University Press, 1994), where she describes the progressive whitening of Othello in performance in the post-civil war American South: '[D]espite the whitening and orientalizing of the main character,' contends historian Tilton G. Edelstein, 'the fear of one drop of black blood in the men whom white daughters married continued to haunt and fascinate Americans with the tenacity of a morbid compulsion' (p. 160).

20 Folger Shakespeare Library Scrapbook B.121.2 'Sh. Productions'.

21 Philip C. Kolin, 'A Survey of Othello in Criticism, on Stage, and On Screen' in *Othello: New Critical Essays*, ed. Philip C. Kolin (New York: Routledge, 2002), pp. 1–89, esp. p. 35.

22 Catherine Belsey, 'Invocation of the Visual Image: Ekphrasis in "Lucrece" and Beyond', *Shakespeare Quarterly*, 63 (2012): 175–98, esp. 187.

23 Rowe's modern readers often quarrel over this problem.

24 Thomas Dibdin, *The Biography of the British Stage; Being Correct Narratives of the Lives of all the Principal Actors & Actresses . . . Interspersed with Original Anecdotes and Choice and Illustrative Poetry* (London: Sherwood, Jones, & Co., 1824).

25 Jacob Larwood, *Theatrical Anecdotes or Fun and Curiosities of the Play, the Playhouse, and the Players* (London: Chatto and Windus, 1882), p. 176.

26 Other anecdotes remember differently: 'At all events, we hear of a Mrs Colman acting Ianthe in the first part of Davenant's *Siege of Rhodes*, in 1656' (Jacob Larwood, *Theatrical Anecdotes*, pp. 35–6).

27 Folger Shakespeare Library Scrapbook B.104.1 'Othello'.

28 C.M. Ingleby, L. Toulmin Smith, and F.J. Furnivall, *The Shakespeare Allusion-Book: A Collection of Allusions to Shakespeare From 1591–1700*, 2 vols. (London: Oxford University Press, 1932), vol. 1, p. 87: Thomas Jordan, 'A Prologue to introduce the first Woman that came to Act on the Stage in the Tragedy, call'd *The Moor of Venice*'.

29 Folger Shakespeare Library Scrapbook. Percy Fitzgerald's hand annotated scrapbook of theatrical miscellany (Harry Sanders, 1870–80).

30 Folger Shakespeare Library Scrapbook B.34.1 'Irving, Henry; Terry, Ellen'.

31 Folger Shakespeare Library Scrapbook A.16.2 'Theatrical Clippings (Collectanea by Lysons)'.

32 Marvin Rosenberg, *The Masks of Othello* (Newark: University of Delaware Press, 1961), p. 5.

33 Frank Benson, *My Memoirs* (London: Ernest Bunn Limited, 1930), p. 218.

34 Folger Shakespeare Library Scrapbook B.130.10 'Theatrical Clippings'.

35 Jacob Larwood, *Theatrical Anecdotes*, p. 259.

36 L.F. Austin, *The North American Review*, Folger Shakespeare Library Scrapbook B.34.3.

37 Madge Kendal, *Dramatic Opinions* (Boston: Little, Brown, and Company, 1890), p. 29.

38 Folger Shakespeare Library Scrapbook A.16.3 'Theatrical Clippings (Collectanea by Lysons)'.

39 Samuel Pepys, *Diary of Samuel Pepys* (1660), vol. 1, p. 89.

40 Folger Shakespeare Library Scrapbook B.7.3 'Edwin Booth'.

41 Simon Callow, *Being an Actor* (New York: Picador, 2003), p. 184.

42 James Stoddart, *Recollections of a Player* (New York: The Century Company, 1902), p. 95.

43 Edward Pechter, '"Iago's Theory of Mind": A Response to Paul Cefalu', *Shakespeare Quarterly*, 64 (2013): 298.

44 Thomas Marshall, *Lives of the Most Celebrated Actors and Actresses* (London: E. Appleyard, 1847), p. 126.

45 Robert Sellers, *Hellraisers: The Life and Inebriated Times of Richard Burton, Richard Harris, Peter O'Toole, and Oliver Reed* (New York: St Martin's Press, 2009), p. 56.

46 Rosenberg, *The Masks of Othello*, p. 141.

47 *New York Daily Tribune* Folger Shakespeare Library Scrapbook B.33.2 'Irving, Henry'.

48 Folger Shakespeare Library Scrapbook B.130.6 'Theatrical Clippings'.

49 Frank Benson, *My Memoirs* (London: Ernest Bunn Limited, 1930), p. 218.

50 Percy Fitzgerald, *The Book of Theatrical Anecdotes* (London: George Routledge and Sons, 1873), pp. 14–15.

51 Sellers, *Hellraisers*, p. 137.

52 Folger Shakespeare Library Scrapbook B.7.6 'Edwin Booth'.

53 Folger Shakespeare Library Scrapbook A.11.2 'London Theatres'.

54 Folger Shakespeare Library Scrapbook A.11.2 'London Theatres'.

55 Folger Shakespeare Library Scrapbook B.73.1 'King Lear'.

56 Folger Shakespeare Library Scrapbook B.83.1.

57 Folger Shakespeare Library Scrapbook B.21.1 'Forrest, Edwin'.

58 *Stage Gossip or Theatrical Tit-Bits Ancient and Modern* (London: Jennins, 1888).

59 Benson, *My Memoirs*, p. 218.

60 Fitzgerald, *The Book of Theatrical Anecdotes*, p. 26.

3 *Romeo and Juliet*: Central casting

1 David Garrick, *The Plays of David Garrick: Garrick's Adaptations of Shakespeare, 1744–1756*, eds. Harry William Pedicord and Fredrick L. Bergmann (Carbondale: Southern Illinois University Press, 1982), p. 407.

2 John Hill, *The Actor, A Treatise on the Art of Playing* (London: 1751), pp. 134–5.

3 Folger Shakespeare Library Scrapbook A.4.13 'London, Covent Garden, 1814–16'.

4 Folger Shakespeare Library Scrapbook A.15.9 'Theatrical Scrapbooks, Vol. 9 1820–1830'.

5 Folger Shakespeare Library Scrapbook B.121.1 'Sh. Productions'.

6 Folger Shakespeare Library Scrapbook A.3.2 'London, Covent Garden, 1804–1848 (Beaufoy Coll.)'.

7 Dolly Parton's 1993 hit 'Romeo' put a twist on this old saw. She sung that she was 'old enough to be that boy's lover'.

8 Folger Shakespeare Library Scrapbook B.25.1 'Gale-Haynes, M.'.

9 Folger Shakespeare Library Scrapbook B.130.1 'Theatrical Clippings'.

10 Folger Shakespeare Library Scrapbook B.85.1 'Romeo and Juliet'.

11 Dion Boucicault, *London Assurance*, revised by Richard Bean (London: Oberon Books, 2011).

12 Folger Shakespeare Library Scrapbook A.16.3 'Theatrical Clippings (Collectanea by Lysons)'.

13 James Stoddart, *Recollections of a Player* (New York: The Century Company, 1902), p. 21.

14 *Middlesex Journal*, 1786, Folger Shakespeare Library Scrapbook A.16.2 'Theatrical Clippings (Collectanea by Lysons)'.

15 18 May 1919, *New York* Times, Folger Shakespeare Library Scrapbook B.85.2 'Romeo and Juliet'.

16 Folger Shakespeare Library Scrapbook A.2.6 'London, Covent Garden, 1820–1827'.

17 John Gielgud, *Acting Shakespeare* (New York: Applause, 1991).

18 Folger Shakespeare Library Scrapbook B.49.1 'New York, Park Theater'.

19 George Jean Nathan, *The Entertainment of a Nation: Or, Three Sheets in the Wind* (1942; rpt. Cranbury, NJ: Associated University Presses, 1971), pp. 178–9.

20 Folger Shakespeare Library Scrapbook A.15.9 'Theatrical Scrapbooks, Vol. 9 1820–1830'.

21 Folger Shakespeare Library Scrapbook A.4.2 'London, Covent Garden, 1778–1781'.

22 Folger Shakespeare Library Scrapbook A.14.20 'Theatrical Clippings, From the European Magazine'.

23 Folger Shakespeare Library Scrapbook A.7.1 'London, Drury Lane, 1663–1847 (Beaufoy Coll.)'.

24 Folger Shakespeare Library Scrapbook B.85.2 'Romeo and Juliet'.

25 Folger Shakespeare Library Scrapbook A.2.3 'London, Covent Garden, 1780–1799'.

26 Folger Shakespeare Library Scrapbook B.46.1 'Mather, Margaret'.

27 Folger Shakespeare Library Scrapbook B.46.1 'Mather, Margaret'.

28 Folger Shakespeare Library Scrapbook A.1.1 'London, Covent Garden, undated, 1 vol.'.

29 Folger Shakespeare Library Scrapbook B.123.1 'Shakespearean Actresses'.

30 Laurence Olivier, *Confessions of an Actor: An Autobiography* (New York: Simon and Schuster, 1982), p. 97.

31 Folger Shakespeare Library Scrapbook B.85.2 'Romeo and Juliet'.

32 Folger Shakespeare Library Scrapbook B.7.5 'Edwin Booth'.

33 Folger Shakespeare Library Scrapbook B.7.5 'Edwin Booth'.

34 Folger Shakespeare Library Scrapbook B.7.6 'Edwin Booth'.

35 Arthur W. Bloom, *Edwin Booth: A Biography and Performance History* (New York: Macfarland, 2013), p. 97.

36 Folger Shakespeare Library Scrapbook B.1.12 'Actors and Actresses'.

37 Folger Shakespeare Library Scrapbook B.9.1 'Booth Family'.

38 Folger Shakespeare Library Scrapbook B.9.1 'Booth Family'.

39 *The Bostonian, An Illustrated Monthly Magazine of Local Interest.* vol. 1 (1894–95), p. 128.

40 John Marston, *Scourge of Villainy* (1598), *satyre* 10, sig. H3, verso.

41 Frank Benson, *My Memoirs* (London: Ernest Bunn Limited, 1930).

42 Jacob Larwood, *Theatrical Anecdotes or Fun and Curiosities of the Play, the Playhouse, and the Players* (London: Chatto and Windus, 1882), p. 277.

43 Olivier, *Confessions of an Actor: An Autobiography*, p. 97.

44 John Dryden, 'Defence of the Epilogue', *The Conquest of Granada by the Spaniards* (London: 1672).

45 Folger Shakespeare Library Scrapbook B.31.1 'Hanford, Charles; Spenser, Elihu; and O'Brien, Nora'.

46 Folger Shakespeare Library Scrapbook B.25.1 'Gale-Haynes, M.'.

47 John Hill, *The Actor, A Treatise on the Art of Playing* (London: 1751).

48 Folger Shakespeare Library Scrapbook A.11.1 'London Theatres'.

49 Hal Burton, *Great Acting* (New York: Hill and Wang, 1967), pp. 17, 139.

50 Gielgud, *Acting Shakespeare*, p. 41.

51 Percy Fitzgerald, *The Book of Theatrical Anecdotes* (London: George Routledge and Sons, 1873), p. 52.

52 Folger Shakespeare Library Scrapbook B.132.1 'Theatrical Clippings from the Times'.

53 Marjorie Garber, *Sex and Real Estate: Why We Love Houses* (New York: Anchor, 2001).

54 Folger Shakespeare Library Scrapbook B.85.2 'Romeo and Juliet'.

55 Folger Shakespeare Library Scrapbook B.130.9 'Theatrical Clippings'.

56 qtd. in James Loehlin, *Romeo and Juliet: Shakespeare in Production* (Cambridge: Cambridge University Press, 2002).

57 Loehlin, *Romeo and Juliet: Shakespeare in Production.*

58 Larwood, *Theatrical Anecdotes*, p. 253.

59 Anthony Pasquin, *The Eccentricities of John Edwin, Comedian. Collected from his Manuscripts, and Enriched with Several Hundred Original Anecdotes. Arranged and Digested by Anthony Pasquin, Esq.* 2 vols. (London: John Strahan, 1791), vol. 1, p. 207.

60 John Downes, *Downes's Roscius Anglicanus, or an Historical Review of the Stage* (London, 1708), p. 22.

61 The anecdote survives in a twisted modern form: 'I was once assured by the actor Hugh Hastings that while appearing in a play called *I Killed the Count*, he noticed that the 'O' of Count disappeared for some days after a bulb burst, thus transforming the production from a taut detective thriller set in fogbound London to a brutal slice of life on a cattle ranch in the Australian outback.' Michael Simkins, *The Rules of Acting*. (London: Ebury Press, 2013), p. 252.

62 Folger Shakespeare Library Scrapbook B.85.2 'Romeo and Juliet'.

63 Larwood, *Theatrical Anecdotes*, p. 311.

64 Fred Belton, *Random Recollections of an Old Actor* (London: Tinsley Brothers, 1880), pp. 13–14.

65 Folger Shakespeare Library Scrapbook B.85.2 'Romeo and Juliet'.

66 Folger Shakespeare Library Scrapbook B.25.1 'Gale-Haynes, M.'.

4 *Richard III*: Oedipus text

1 Folger Shakespeare Library Scrapbook B.130.9 'Theatrical Clippings'.

2 Chris Williams, ed., *The Richard Burton Diaries*, (New Haven: Yale University Press, 2012), p. 256.

3 Antony Sher, *Year of the King: An Actor's Diary and Sketchbook* (New York: Limelight, 1999), p. 28.

4 Folger Shakespeare Library Scrapbook B.21.2 'Forrest, Edwin'.

5 C.M. Ingleby, L. Toulmin Smith and F.J. Furnivall, eds., *The Shakespere Allusion-Book: A Collection of Allusions to Shakespere From 1591–1700*, 2 vols. (London: Oxford University Press, 1932), p. 64, LL. 45–7.

6 Folger Shakespeare Library Scrapbook B.35.1 'Kean, Charles'.

7 Folger Shakespeare Library Scrapbook A.2.6 'London, Covent Garden, 1820–1827'.

8 Colley Cibber, *The Plays of Colley Cibber*, vol. 1, eds. Timothy J. Viator and William J. Burling (Cranbury, NJ: Associated University Presses, 2001).

9 Folger Shakespeare Library Scrapbook A.2.4 'London, Covent Garden, 1807–1811'.

10 Williams, *The Richard Burton Diaries*, p. 598.

11 Folger Shakespeare Library Scrapbook B.130.9 'Theatrical Clippings'.

12 Otis Skinner, *Mad Folk of the Theatre: Ten Studies in Temperament* (Indianapolis: Bobbs-Merrill, 1928), p. 251.

13 Folger Shakespeare Library Scrapbook B.8.1 'J. B. Booth'.

14 Folger Shakespeare Library Scrapbook B.130.6 'Theatrical Clippings 1879'.

15 *Saunder's Daily Advertiser* Dec. 22, 1860: Folger Shakespeare Library Scrapbook B.35.1 'Kean, Charles'.

16 *The Theatrical Jester: Or Green-Room Witticisms. Being a Collection of Entertaining and Original Anecdotes, Bon Mots, Repartees, &C. Relating to the Stage* (London: J. Hammond, 1795), p. 20.

17 Folger Shakespeare Library Scrapbook A.3.1 'London, Covent Garden, 1763–1848 (Beaufoy Coll.) 1805'.

18 Sher, *Year of the King*, pp. 30–1.

19 Skinner, *Mad Folk of the Theatre*, pp. 237–8.

20 Folger Shakespeare Library Scrapbook A.2.4 'London, Covent Garden, 1812–1815'.

21 Kaite O'Reilly, '"Cripping up is the Twenty First Century Answer to Blacking up." Peeling and The "d" Monologues', http://kaiteoreilly.wordpress.com/2011/11/08/cripping-up-is-the-twenty-first-century-answer-to-blacking-up-peeling-and-the-d-monologues/, accessed 23 July 2014.

22 *The Return From Parnassus; or The Scourge of Simony* (1606) sig. B2, verso.

23 John Hill, *The Actor: A Treatise on the Art of Playing* (London: 1751), pp. 56–7.

24 Sher, *Year of the King*, p. 21.

25 Folger Shakespeare Library Scrapbook B.133.15 'Theatrical Miscellany'.

26 'Kevin Spacey Perfected Richard III Gait to Avoid Thespian Injury' http://blog.wenn.com/all-news/kevin-spacey-perfected-richard-iii-gait-to-avoid-thespian-injury/, WENN, accessed 3 June 2014.

27 Tom Dale Keever (18 December 1995), 'Richard III as Rewritten by Colley Cibber,' *Primary Texts and Secondary Sources On-line*. Richard III Society – American Branch, accessed 23 July 2014.

28 Laurence Olivier, *Confessions of an Actor: An Autobiography* (New York: Simon and Schuster, 1982), p. 158.

29 'Richard III (Laurence Olivier, 1955)', Classic Movie Hub, http://www.classicmoviehub.com/article/32509/, accessed 24 July 2014.

30 William Redfield, *Letters from an Actor* (New York: Limelight, 1967), pp. 238–9.

31 Sher, *Year of the King*, pp. 26–7.

32 Roland Barthes, *Mythologies*, trans. Richard Howard (New York: Hill and Wang, 2013).

33 Simon Callow, *Being an Actor* (New York: Picador, 1984), p. 111.

34 Hal Burton, *Great Acting* (New York: Hill and Wang, 1967), pp. 24–5.

35 'Richard III (1955) Trivia', IMDB, http://www.imdb.com/title/tt0049674/trivia, accessed 24 July 2014.

36 Folger Shakespeare Library Scrapbook B.7.5 'Edwin Booth'.

37 Folger Shakespeare Library Scrapbook B.7.5 'Edwin Booth'.

38 Folger Shakespeare Library Scrapbook B.7.5 'Edwin Booth'.

39 Folger Shakespeare Library Scrapbook B.7.6 'Edwin Booth'.

40 Folger Shakespeare Library Scrapbook B.7.5 'Edwin Booth'.

41 Folger Shakespeare Library Scrapbook B.7.5 'Edwin Booth'.

42 Folger Shakespeare Library Scrapbook B.7.5 'Edwin Booth'.

43 Folger Shakespeare Library Scrapbook B.7.5 'Edwin Booth'.

44 Folger Shakespeare Library Scrapbook B.7.5 'Edwin Booth'.

45 Folger Shakespeare Library Scrapbook B.7.5 'Edwin Booth'.

5 *Macbeth*: An embarrassment of witches

1 Thomas Davies, *Dramatic Miscellanies*, vol. 2, pp. 9, 7.

2 Thomas Isham, *The Journal of Thomas Isham*, trans. Rev. Robert Isham, with an Introduction by Walter Rye (Norwich: Privately printed, 1875), p. 102.

3 Gerard Langbaine, *An Account of the English Dramatick Poets* (London, 1691), p. 46.

4 Folger Shakespeare Library Scrapbook A.4.6 'London, Covent Garden, 1792–1795'.

5 Folger Shakespeare Library Scrapbook A.2.3 'London, Covent Garden, 1780–1799'.

6 Frank Benson, *My Memoirs* (London: Ernest Bunn Limited, 1930), pp. 227–9.

7 Folger Shakespeare Library Scrapbook B.77.1 'Macbeth'.

8 Folger Shakespeare Library Scrapbook B.77.1 'Macbeth'.

9 Folger Shakespeare Library Scrapbook B.29.1 'Hackett, James K.'.

10 Richard Huggett, *The Curse of Macbeth and other Theatrical Superstitions* (London: Picton Publishing, 1981), p. 133.

11 Dennis Bartholomeuz, *Macbeth and the Players* (Cambridge: Cambridge University Press, 1969), p. 245.

12 Marjorie Garber, *Shakespeare's Ghost Writers: Literature as Uncanny Causality* (New York: Methuen, 1987), p. 88.

13 John Wilders, *Macbeth: Shakespeare in Production* (Cambridge: Cambridge University Press, 2004).

14 Kenneth Tynan and Cecil Beaton, *Persona Grata* (London: Wingate, 1953), p. 53.

15 Jody Enders, *Death by Drama and other Medieval Urban Legends* (Chicago: Chicago University Press, 2002), p. 53.

16 Huggett, *The Curse of Macbeth*, p. 153.

17 qtd. in C.M. Ingelby, *Shakespere Allusion-Book, II* (London: Chatto and Windus, 1909), pp. 92–3.

18 William Appleton, *Charles Macklin: An Actor's Life* (Cambridge: Harvard University Press, 1960), p. 171.

19 qtd. in Wilders, *Macbeth: Shakespeare in Production*, p. 42.

20 Folger Shakespeare Library Scrapbook B.33.1 'Irving, Henry'.

21 *The Invention of Tradition,* eds. Eric Hobsbawm and Terence Ranger (Cambridge: Cambridge University Press, 2012), p. 1.

22 Gabriel Egan claims an early allusion to the *Macbeth* superstition in Richard Brome and Thomas Heywood's *The Late Lancashire Witches*, but the allusion is opaque (see http://gabrielegan.com/publications/Egan2002k.htm). See also Lina Perkins Wilder's article 'An Alternate Form of the *Macbeth* Superstition' in *Notes and Queries*, (2010) 57 (3): 393–5.

23 Hobsbawm, *The Invention of Tradition*, p. 1.

24 *Great West End Theatres*, Sky Arts, 10 August 2013.

25 Folger Shakespeare Library Scrapbook B.101.1 'Macbeth'.

26 James Boswell, *Journal of a Tour of the Hebrides* (1785) (New York: Viking Press, 1976).

27 Matt Trueman, 'Curse of Macbeth? Actor taken to hospital after Branagh battle', *The Guardian*, http://www.theguardian.com/stage/2013/jul/15/macbeth-rsc-kenneth-branagh-hospital-battle, accessed 13 August 2014.

28 Brian Dobbs, *Drury Lane: Three Centuries of the Theatre Royal 1663–1971* (West Sussex: Littlehampton Book Services, 1972).

29 'The Curse of the Scottish Play', Stageview, http://www.stageview.co/page.php?tSCID=755&tON=Shakespeare%20in%20the%20Park&tSN=Shakespeare%20in%20the%20Park&tSVID=642, accessed 4 September 2014.

30 Folger Shakespeare Library Scrapbook A.7.1 'London, Drury Lane, 1663–1847 (Beaufoy Coll.)'.

31 Mortimer Shelly, *Blobson's Dire Mishaps in a Barnstorming Company* (New York: 1890), pp. 81–3.

32 Folger Shakespeare Library Scrapbook B.133.2 'Theatrical Miscellany'.

33 Folger Shakespeare Library Scrapbook A.7.1 'London, Drury Lane, 1663–1847 (Beaufoy Coll.)'.

34 Folger Shakespeare Library Scrapbook B.26.3 'Garrick, David'.

35 Timothy West, *A Moment Towards the End of the Play* (London: Nick Hern Books, 2001).

36 Folger Shakespeare Library Scrapbook A.11.1 'London Theatres'.

37 Dobbs, *Drury Lane*, p. xx.

38 Folger Shakespeare Library Scrapbook A.12.1 'Theatrical Clippings — Drama'.

39 Folger Shakespeare Library Scrapbook B.21.2 'Forrest, Edwin'.

40 Folger Shakespeare Library Scrapbook A.14.18 'Theatrical Clippings, From the European Magazine'.

41 Folger Shakespeare Library Scrapbook A.16.3 'Theatrical Clippings (Collectanea by Lysons)'.

42 Folger Shakespeare Library Scrapbook B.7.2 'Edwin Booth'.

43 Folger Shakespeare Library Scrapbook A.5.8 'London, Drury Lane & Covent Garden, 1775–76'.

44 Folger Shakespeare Library Scrapbook B.133.10 'Theatrical Miscellany'.

45 Folger Shakespeare Library Scrapbook B.130.6 'Theatrical Clippings'.

46 Theophilus Cibber, *Lives of the Poets of Great Britain and Ireland* (1753), vol. IV, p. 234.

47 Folger Shakespeare Library Scrapbook B.36.1.

48 James Stoddart, *Recollections of a Player* (New York: The Century Company, 1902) pp. 15–17.

49 Folger Shakespeare Library Scrapbook B.77.1 'Macbeth'.

50 Folger Shakespeare Library Scrapbook B.77.1 'Macbeth'.

51 Percy Fitzgerald's hand annotated scrapbook of theatrical miscellany (Harry Sanders, 1870–80).

52 Folger Shakespeare Library Scrapbook B.20.1 'Emery, John Philip Samuel'.

53 John Downes, *Downes's Roscius Anglicanus, or an Historical Review of the Stage* (London, 1708), p. 34.

54 Owen Fawcett, *Scribner's Magazine*, Vol. XXVI (1899), p. 428.

55 Shelly, *Blobson's Dire Mishaps*, pp. 56–7.

56 Percy Fitzgerald's hand annotated scrapbook of theatrical miscellany (Harry Sanders, 1870–80).

57 Folger Shakespeare Library Scrapbook B.130.6 'Theatrical Clippings'.

58 Folger Shakespeare Library Scrapbook B.130.3 'Theatrical Clippings'.

59 Folger Shakespeare Library Scrapbook B.101.1 'Macbeth'.

60 Isham, *The Journal of Thomas Isham*, p. 102.

Coda: Archives and anecdotes

1 John Aubrey, *The Natural History and Antiquities of Surrey. Begun in the year 1673*, 5 vols. (London, 1719), vol. 1, p. 190.

2 Henslowe-Alleyn Digitisation Project, http://www.henslowe-alleyn.org.uk/index.html.

3 E.K. Chambers, *The Elizabeth Stage*, 4 vols. (Oxford: The Clarendon Press, 1866–1954), vol. 3, p. 424.

4 William Prynne, *Histriomastix: The Players Scourge* (London, 1633), f. 556.

5 Thomas Middleton, *The Black Booke* (London, 1604), p. 13.

6 The translation appears in *The Polyanthos* (Boston: J.T. Buckingham, 1812), vol. 1, p. 318.

7 The quote appears in Herbert Blau, *The Audience* (Baltimore: Johns Hopkins University Press, 1990), p. 382. For representative works in the 'elegiac key', see, in particular, Peggy Phelan, 'The Ontology of Performance: Representation Without Reproduction', in *Unmarked: The Politics of Performance* (London: Routledge, 1993); and her introduction to *The Ends of Performance*, edited by Phelan and Jill Lane (New York: New York University Press, 1998); and Peggy Phelan, *Mourning Sex: Performing Public Memories* (London: Routledge, 1997). See also Joseph Roach, *Cities of the Dead: Circum-Atlantic Performance* (New York: Columbia University Press, 1996); Marvin Carlson, *The Haunted Stage: The Theatre as Memory Machine* (Ann Arbor: University of Michigan Press, 2001); and Alice Rayner, *Ghosts: Death's Double and the Phenomena of Theater* (Minneapolis: University of Minnesota Press, 2006).

8 Scott McMillin, 'The Sharer and His Boy: Rehearsing Shakespeare's Women' in eds. Peter Holland and Stephen Orgel, *From Script to Stage in Early Modern England* (Basingstoke: Palgrave, 2004), p. 242.

9 Fernand Braudel, 'History and the Social Sciences', *American Behavioral Scientist*, 3, no. 6 (1960): 3–13.

10 Roland Barthes, *Mythologies*, trans. Richard Howard (New York: Hill and Wang, 2013).

11 Michel de Certeau, *The Writing of History* (New York: Columbia University Press, 1988), p. 102.

12 Thomas Postlewait, 'The Criteria for Evidence: Anecdotes in Shakespearean Biography, 1709–2000' in *Theorizing Practice: Redefining Theatre History*, eds. W.B. Worthen and Peter Holland (Basingstoke: Palgrave Macmillan, 2003), pp. 47–70, esp. p. 70.

13 Postlewait, 'The Criteria for Evidence', p. 66.

14 Giorgio Agamben, *What Is An Apparatus? And Other Essays* (Palo Alto: Stanford University Press, 2009), p. 11.

15 Jaqueline S. Bratton, *New Readings in Theatre History* (Cambridge: Cambridge University Press, 2003), p. 106.

16 Folger Shakespeare Library Scrapbook B.133.11 'Theatrical Miscellany'.

17 Malina Sefanovska, 'Exemplarity or Singularity? The Anecdote in Historical Narrative', *Substance*, 38 (2009): 16–30.

18 *Anecdotes and Traditions, Illustrative of Early English History and Literature*, ed. William J. Thomas (London: Nicols and Son, 1839), pp. vi–vii.

19 John William Cole, *The Life and Theatrical Times of Charles Kean, F.S.A., Including a Summary of the English Stage for the Last Fifty years* (London: 1859), pp. 169–70.

INDEX